Collective Skill Formation in Liberal Market Economies?

studies in vocational and continuing education

vol. 16

edited by
philipp gonon & anja heikkinen

peter lang
Bern · Berlin · Bruxelles · New York · Oxford · Warszawa · Wien

Janis Vossiek

Collective Skill Formation in Liberal Market Economies?

The Politics of Training Reforms in Australia, Ireland and the United Kingdom

peter lang
Bern · Berlin · Bruxelles · New York · Oxford · Warszawa · Wien

Bibliographic information published by Die Deutsche Bibliothek
Die Deutsche Nationalbibliothek lists this publication in the Deutsche Nationalbibliografie; detailed bibliographic data is available on the Internet at <http://dnb.d-nb.de>.

Library of Congress Cataloging-in-Publication Data
A CIP catalog record for this book has been applied for at the Library of Congress.

ISSN 2235-7319 pb.
ISSN 2235-7327 eBook
ISBN 978-3-0343-2969-9 pb.
ISBN 978-3-0343-2970-5 eBook
ISBN 978-3-0343-2972-9 MOBI
ISBN 978-3-0343-2971-2 EPUB
DOI 10.3726/b11227

This publication has been peer reviewed.

Wabernstrasse 40, CH-3007 Bern, Switzerland
bern@peterlang.com, www.peterlang.com

Contents

Preface and acknowledgements

This book and its author have come a long way. Thus, I would like to thank the many individuals without whose generous support this book would not have been possible. It is fair to say that the long road to the publication of this monograph, which is based on the dissertation that I wrote in Konstanz from 2011 to 2015, started early on in my undergraduate studies at the University of Bremen. In 2004 I met Herbert Obinger, who spurred my interest in comparative welfare state research and gave me the opportunity to work as his research assistant until 2009. Just when I had almost given up hope to find my place in the academic market for doctoral positions, his extremely generous letter of recommendation supported the invitation for a job interview with Marius Busemeyer in 2010, who then hired me as a doctoral researcher for his new research group on the 'The Politics of Education and Training Reforms in Western Welfare States'. I gratefully acknowledge the German Research Foundation's funding for that project (Grant BU 1852/4-1), without which this book probably had never seen the light of day. Words cannot express how lucky I feel to have worked with Marius, whose intellectual rigour, prudence and kind-heartedness still strike me as a scarce combination in academia.

When I started my position at the University of Konstanz in 2011, I was very happy to find a stimulating and intellectually challenging work environment at the Fachbereich Politik- und Verwaltungswissenschaft, and I wish to thank its whole administration, but especially Michael Schumacher, Werner Palz and Ulrike Haas-Spohn, for supporting us busy researchers with whatever queries we brought forward to them. In my six years at the University of Konstanz, I had the pleasure of working and conversing with my colleagues at the chair of Marius and I profited from the intellectual input and support of Julian L. Garritzmann, Raphaela Schlicht-Schmaelzle, Michael Dobbins, Susanne Münn, Erik Neimanns, Aurélien Abrassart, Roula Nezi, Ulrich Glassmann, Susanne Haastert, Dominik Lober, Nona Bledow, Philip Rathgeb, Margot Beier, Yvonne Aymar and our 'adjunct chair member', Sophia Timmermann.

Moreover, I gratefully acknowledge the work of Anne-Sophie Fendrich, Lina Seitzl, Dana Behrens, Marie-Louise Zeller, Friederike Strub, Tobias Tober, Maximilian Gahntz, Teuta Kallco and Charlotte Kurz who worked with me as student assistants and who superbly carried out the tasks, both complicated and menial, that I gave them. I am also indebted to the brilliant Silja Häusermann for agreeing to become my second supervisor and to Sven Jochem, who chaired my dissertation committee on 12 May 2015.

Of course the preface to a book such as this one would be incomplete if it did not mention all the wonderful people, who supported me in my fieldwork in England, Ireland and Australia. Paul Ryan from King's College Cambridge kindly hosted my stay in England from September to December 2012 and I benefited massively from his insightfulness and deep understanding of the intricacies of British post-war vocational education and training development. Len O'Conner gave me a second home in Ireland in October 2012 and supported me in manifold ways and I wish him all the best for the future. Finally, the management of the National Centre for Vocational Education Research, but especially Josie Misko and her partner Michael, made Adelaide a splendid experience for me, and Craig Robertson and Phillip Toner made getting in touch with Australian VET experts much easier than I had expected. I feel deeply indebted to all of them. Finally, I wish to thank all my interviewees for sharing their invaluable insights, which made my research possible in the first place.

I am also grateful for the opportunity to present my work on various workshops and conferences in Paris, Bern, Konstanz, Zurich, Milan, Bremen, Cambridge (MA), Berkeley (CA), Berlin, Rotterdam and Dublin and for the insightful feedback, encouragement and – sometimes harsh – criticism from which this book has profited enormously. For supporting me in my intellectual ventures, I want to thank Ben Ansell, Fabienne-Agnes Baumann, Chiara Benassi, Robert J. Bennett, Lorenzo Bonoli, Christian Breunig, Tracy Burns, Remi Castioni, Ute Clement, Pepper D. Culpepper, Thomas Deissinger, Camilla Devitt, Philipp Eigenmann, Patrick Emmenegger, Dietmar Frommberger, Leonard Geyer, Howard Gospel, Lukas Graf, Anton Hemerijck, Jens Jungblut, Florian G. Kern, Dirk Leuffen, Guilherme Magalhães, Jörg Markowitsch, David Marsden, Cathie Jo Martin, Rita Nikolai, Barry

Nyhan, Kerstin Rothe, David Rueda, Lisa Rustico, Detlef Sack, Erica Smith, Christine Trampusch and Tim Vlandas. Of course, the usual disclaimer applies: all those named in this preface bear no responsibility for any remaining errors and this book might be more lucid had I heeded all their advice. I would also like to thank Anja Heikkinen and Philipp Gonon for generously accepting my work into their series, and especially Johanna Lüder of Peter Lang, whose patience I have stretched more than I wished. Thanks are also due to David Michael for improving the style of the manuscript from its original Teutonic English into the current version.

Last, but most important, this book would not have been imaginable without the unwavering support of my friends and family. Niels Borgmann comes closest to being the brother that I will never have, and Jan Neugebauer was a congenial company during my stay in Australia. Günter Vossiek will always inspire me to be creative. My aunts and uncles, Doro, Irmi, Ronny, Julia, Anna, Dagmar, Wigbert, Stefan and Georg, always had kind words for me. I am always happy to enjoy the company and kindness of my grandfather Henry and his partner Helene, and, and I cannot express the gratitude to my mother Ulla enough – I am truly proud to be the son of such a wonderful, warm-hearted person.

Finally, I dedicate this book to my father, Heri, who passed away far before his time and to my grandmother, Irmgard Roecken, who passed away at the point of writing. Having lived through the Second World War and its aftermath, she managed to raise ten fine children and I am certain that thinking of her will always keep me humble and remind me how privileged I am to be an academic.

On a final personal note, I hope that this book will be heavily criticised if this leads to more intellectual exchange between political economists and vocational training scholars as both would profit from a more careful reading of each other's work. I attempted to make this book accessible to both 'camps' to the best of my abilities.

Janis Vossiek
Cologne

1. Introduction

In the last two decades, debates on skill formation have gained the attention of politicians and political economist alike. Elaborate typologies of different skill-formation regimes have been established but there remains a large and unresolved debate on how far different models of producing skills are transferable from one institutional context to another. There is a closely related question: under which domestic politico-economic conditions will *vocational education and training* (VET) regimes converge on a common model of training (Busemeyer & Vossiek 2016). This pertains to the institutions underpinning different systems of skill formation, but especially to the *political conditions* under which such transformations might occur. The present book contributes to this debate by analysing the trajectory of dual apprenticeships in three countries, which are commonly assumed to offer little institutional support for this type of training: Ireland, Australia and the United Kingdom.

Dual apprenticeships are the prevalent form of VET in *collective skill-formation regimes* (Busemeyer & Trampusch 2012a), which are based on intensive cooperation between multiple actors in the design of VET policies and the politics of VET reform. The two main characteristics of collective skill formation are that responsibilities for training provision and governance are shared between employers, trade unions and governments *and* that firms are strongly involved in the financing of training, which offers young workers certified and portable skills (*ibid*). Initial VET in the form of dual apprenticeships can provide young workers and companies with skills that are viable for a large number of occupations and thus contribute to the overall skill stock of an economy. Today, among policy circles and political scientists, it is conventional wisdom that dual apprenticeships are important for economic competitiveness in *coordinated market economies* (CMEs), whereas they have languished in *liberal market economies* (LMEs), which instead relied on higher education as the principal mode of post-secondary education. One crucial, potentially pivotal, difference between these countries is the role of *strategic coordination* between firms, their associations and unions, which can be supported by governments in various ways not only in direct VET-provision, but also in the institutions of industrial relations that embed skill-formation systems (Hall & Soskice 2001a). Whereas CMEs are replete with institutions that facilitate multiple-actor cooperation in VET, these institutions are usually deemed to be absent in LMEs (Bosch & Charest 2008, Finegold & Soskice 1988), which are characterized by liberal labour market institutions and 'voluntarist principles' of training provision and regulation (King 1997).

Nevertheless, historically, apprenticeships were a viable way of skill formation cutting across different configurations of Western European industrial democracies and only started to diverge heavily in their development in the post-war period (Ansell 2010, Busemeyer 2015: 3). Conventional wisdom holds that apprenticeships faced a strong decline across all LMEs (Bosch & Charest 2008), as these countries failed to establish institutions that could have underpinned collective approaches to VET. In their absence, firms are bereft of incentives to invest in the skills of their employees due to coordination and poaching problems (Estévez-Abe et al. 2001, Finegold & Soskice 1988, Hall & Soskice 2001a).

Partly challenging this conventional wisdom, I will show that differences in VET and the *politics of apprenticeship reform* can be found even among LMEs by way of three qualitative case studies of training reform in the United Kingdom (UK), Ireland and Australia for the post-war period to 2008. While all countries under study have tried to reform their apprenticeship system towards more coordinated approaches in the post-war period, the outcomes differed substantively. The UK failed to shore up collective institutions underpinning apprenticeships, but Ireland and Australia moved towards more cooperation, which raises the question of the political determinants of these different trajectories.

1.1 Studying skill formation regimes

For political economists, the analysis of politico-economic reform processes and policy outcomes is central for understanding the evolution of capitalism in rich democratic economies. How do states and economic actors cooperate in response to new socio-economic challenges such as shifts in world markets, the unparalleled growth of consumer-related services or the emergence of new technologies? How do states react towards increased competition by other countries and which strategies do they pursue in order to remain competitive? What shapes political reactions to adapt and reform politico-economic institutions when necessitated by macro-economic problems such as unemployment, inflation, budgetary imbalances of mounting debt that require fiscal austerity? Questions as these are not ephemeral but are at the heart of political economy and have gained renewed interest among scholars and policy-makers alike. Yet, for the question of training reforms in LMEs there is comparatively little evidence that could be used to speak to these important topics.

Answers have always been warranted, but their salience has increased under conditions of open world markets that have put mature nation states under fiscal strain and exposed their firms and workers alike to increased international competition. Moreover, the current financial crisis has prompted discussions about the viability of politico-economic institutions, not only in southern Europe but also in those economies that have relied heavily on financial services to the detriment of their manufacturing sector. In contrast, collective skill formation systems such as Germany and Switzerland relied more heavily on manufacturing and dual systems of initial VET and have weathered the crisis rather well, displaying comparatively low rates of youth unemployment, which has been a pressing problem among many other OECD democracies many years after the crisis.

In turn, current discussions on VET reform and the transfer of training models from one context to another often evolve around the option to move towards a model of collective skill formation in which responsibilities for training are shared between employers, unions, and the state. The four central characteristics of this training regime are: a strong involvement of employers in the administration and financing of initial vocational training, an important role for intermediary associations in training administration and reform, a dual model of training that combines regulated in-firm training with off-the-job education in schools, and, finally the provision of certified and portable occupational skills.

Empirically and theoretically, the varieties of capitalism (VoC) school (Hall & Soskice 2001a) and comparative welfare state research (Esping-Andersen 1990, Huber & Stephens 2001, Korpi 1983) are valuable approaches to the study of skill formation reforms. The former emphasized the role of economic coordination and skill formation for economic competitiveness; the latter focused on the political coalitions behind politico-economic reforms. In this book, I propose an integration of both strands for studying Ireland, Australia, and the United Kingdom as examples of how mature welfare states adapted their skill-formation systems since the mid-1970s in order to remain competitive and to upgrade the skills of their workforce, with high skills being a centrepiece in national competition policies.

Concretely, I study the evolution of VET reforms, but approach this topic as a policy to increase competitiveness *as well as* an 'investive social policy' that is intended to equip individuals with the skills necessary for active labour market participation. I analyse the politics of VET reforms in LMEs, exactly because conventional wisdom holds that they should be unsuited to the development of cooperation between employers, union and the state in the development of dual apprenticeships (Bosch & Charest 2008, Finegold & Soskice 1988, Hall & Soskice 2001a, Ryan 2005). Put differently, from the comparative perspective of the mainstream literature on skill formation, all three countries are 'least-likely cases' (Gerring 2007) for the emergence of collective skill formation. Moreover, the countries have been found to have low propensities for strategic coordination in industrial relations (Crouch 1993, Hall & Soskice 2001a) with a strong role for the market – not only in economic coordination but also in education and social protection.

Despite similar policy legacies in apprenticeships, which were traditionally much contested between craft unions and employers, the three countries started to heavily diverge in their VET policies after the 1980s, which is essentially the puzzle that the present study tries to explain. At that point, Australia, Ireland and the United Kingdom had similar pressing economic problems of dwindling economic competitiveness with a manufacturing-skills base that lagged behind competitors and adversarial industrial relations that made concerted approaches of governments, union and employers to reform economic institutions difficult. Despite these common starting points, I argue that at critical junctures different coalitions between governments, unions and employers shaped VET reforms in different directions. In Ireland and Australia until the mid-1990s, these coalitions approached reforms via policy concertation and modernized their VET-system towards more collective approaches of skill formation and coordination in industrial relations. In contrast, the United Kingdom followed a unilateral government approach under the Thatcher government, which introduced a market for vocational training and heavily liberalized industrial relations.

In the aftermath of these critical junctures, policy concertation was only continued in Ireland where the collective approach to VET survived despite changes in partisan governments. In Australia, the concerted approach to industrial relations and training reforms broke down after a change of government in the late 1990 but collective approaches to skill formation have survived to a certain degree along with a stronger marketization of training provision and decentralization of industrial relations. Finally, the United Kingdom did not succeed in reforming its VET system towards more collective approaches, despite frequent policy changes since the 1990s.

Because of these divergences, which are underappreciated in the comparative mainstream literature, the following questions arise:

1. What are the different aspects of collective skill formation that can be found in the three countries? Why have some of the reforms been successful in the sense that policy change led to sustainable institutional change, which set the countries on different development paths towards or away from a collective model of skill formation?

2. How can we explain reforms towards collective skill formation despite similar policy legacies in the three cases? What were the main driving forces of policy reforms towards a collective model of apprenticeship and which politico-economic coalitions were formed in favour of or against such reforms?

3. What are the implications for the study of (a) skill formation regimes and (b) studies of institutional change?

This book addresses these three questions by employing three time-sensitive case studies of VET reforms in Australia, Ireland and the United Kingdom with the main emphasis on the period between the late 1970s and 2008. By complementing the VoC perspective with an actor-centred historical institutionalist framework, the main emphasis is placed on the analysis of the strategic interactions between governments of different partisan compositions, unions and employers in the course of VET reforms. The theoretical framework that this study builds upon is succinctly outlined in the next section.

1.2 Variations of skill formation politics in LMEs

> Twenty-five years ago, the number of political scientists interested in vocational education and training – an unglamorous topic if ever there was one – could almost certainly have been counted on one hand. [...] In the meantime, however, skills and training have moved to the center of debates among political economists and political scientists who are concerned to understand the pasts, presents, and possible futures of distinctive 'varieties of capitalism'. (Thelen 2012: v)

This quotation illustrates the upsurge of interest that skill formation has gained in contemporary political economy research. This development can partly be accredited to Hall and Soskice (2001a), who present skill formation as one of five domains central to economic performance of rich OECD economies. In contrast to neoliberal assumptions that portray the removal of market imperfections as central to economic competitiveness, scholars of the VoC approach recognize (at least) two distinct varieties of modern capitalist economies that are economically equally viable for competition in open and globalized world markets. The central difference between the two ideal types, LMEs and CMEs, is the institutional logic of coordination in different economic spheres between employers, unions and the state, which is either based on markets and market relationships in LMEs or strategic, non-market coordination in CMEs. Moreover, the comparative advantage of each mode of capitalism is argued to spring from institutional complementarities between economic spheres, which especially effect advantages in product innovation and the generation of specific or general skill profiles among workers.

For the latter, social protection policies are seen to be one main institutional complement (Estévez-Abe et al. 2001). In the absence of social protection for specific skill investments that are only useful for one firm or industry, we can detect the emergence of general skills profiles, which are mainly delivered by secondary and higher education. The split between general (LME) versus specific (CME) skill profiles to a large degree parallels distinct 'worlds of welfare capitalism' (Esping-Andersen 1990). Conservative and social democratic welfare states provide welfare policies that underpin the formation of specific skills in vocational schools or via dual apprenticeship programs but these policies are comparatively underdeveloped in liberal welfare states, which rely heavily on general and academic skills that are provided mainly by higher education or technical colleges.

Despite its merits, the VoC approach has attracted manifold criticisms of which two are centrally important for the present study: the *under-specification of skill-formation regimes* and a *functionalist approach to institutional change.*

The concept of skill specificity used by Hall and Soskice (2001), distinguishes between specific skills with low portability in the labour market and prevalent in CMEs and general skills, with high portability, typically found in LMEs, but fails to grasp the complexity behind skill-formation regimes, as the degree of skill specificity is just one of their aspects. Busemeyer (2009a) and Busemeyer and Trampusch (2012a) identify two dimensions, which are central to VET: Busemeyer and Trampusch show that *firm involvement* and *public support* are crucial determinants for the institutional setup of skill formation among post-industrial economies. Taken together, they argue that firm involvement in collective skill formation systems usually produces skills that are not only firm specific but general in substance and transferable to other occupations because of strong systems of authoritative skill certification. Hence, if firm involvement contributes to the formation of general skills in some regimes, it is a central question for policymakers how to get employers involved in skill formation.

Moreover, although LMEs are regularly classified as a relatively homogenous country group in various typologies of comparative political science (Castles 1993, Esping-Andersen 1990, Hall & Soskice 2001), a closer inspection reveals that differences in their VET systems are more pronounced than usually assumed, especially regarding firm involvement and public support for VET. For example, scholars have shown that apprenticeship, as a main way of initial skill formation, faced an early decline in the United States at the beginning of the last century, whereas its institutions remained more stable in the United Kingdom (Gospel 1994, Thelen 2004). Regarding the often-noted poor performance of the British apprenticeship system, other research points to the superior 'performance' of VET in Australia (Gospel 1994, Smith 2010, Toner 2008) and Ireland (Nyhan 2010, O'Connor & Harvey 2001, Ryan 2000) despite inheriting their VET system from Britain before each country's independence. Notwithstanding the ingenuity of the studies mentioned above, unfortunately they fall short of a common research framework that can explain the observed differences.

A second criticism of the VoC school is its functionalist approach to comparative institutional advantage: The focus on economic competitiveness as the central 'reference frame' (Becker 2007) leaves the questions of institutional origin, genesis and change unresolved and is too insensitive towards actors' motivations for engaging in institutional change (Coates 2005, Deeg & Jackson 2007, Hall & Thelen 2009). The VoC approach explains the persistence of two ideal-typical capitalisms with reference to institutional equilibria, which result from the interplay of 'institutional complementarities' in the political economy of each type, and holds that institutional reforms flow from shifts in coordinating mechanisms. Hall and Thelen (2009) advise the incorporation of actor constellations into the VoC-framework, as their continuous support is needed for the sustainment and reform of institutional equilibria. Regarding institutional change more generally, there has been a threefold move away from 'punctuated-equilibrium models' (Baumgartner et al. 2007, Baumgartner et al. 2009) and towards approaches that are more sensitive to influences of timing and sequencing on policy change (Hall 2003, Pierson 2004), processes of incremental institutional change (Mahoney & Thelen 2010, Streeck & Thelen 2005, Thelen 2009) and diverse actor-constellations between firms, workers, their intermediary organizations and governments (Culpepper & Thelen 2008, Thelen 2004, Thelen & Busemeyer 2012, Trampusch 2010). Apart from

Thelens' (2004) study of intermediate skill formation in the United States and the United Kingdom, however, these innovations in the theories on institutional change have been rarely applied to comparisons of skill formation among LMEs, where the political driving forces of apprenticeship reforms remain somewhat opaque.

I will therefore discuss how political parties and their interactions with different segments of capital and labour can shape institutional change.

1.3. How political parties and organized interests shape skill formation over time

> Distributive conflict is a common feature of capitalist political economies, but the distribution of power is source of variation among them [...] [and] over time. Power relations among collective actors are embedded in institutions and clearly do not change overnight. Yet, power relations among collective actors are fundamentally dynamic. (Pontusson 2005: 185)

The central tenets of the VoC approach focus quite strongly on the effects that different institutional configurations in LMEs and CMEs have on their economic competitiveness. However, in the process of reforming VET systems, employers, unions and governments might not overwhelmingly be motivated by concerns of economic efficiency but also by the distributional consequences these have on their political power and role within the politics of vocational training. Thus, the analysis of the political driving forces of VET reform and the interactions between governing parties, employers and unions will be the central analytical focus in showing which trajectories Australia, Ireland and the United Kingdom followed in their apprenticeship reforms. As a central take away from classical approaches of partisan and power-resource theories (PRT) (Esping-Andersen 1990, Hibbs 1977, Korpi 1983, Schmidt 1982, Stephens 1979, van Kersbergen 1995), we can expect that left and Christian democratic parties favour apprenticeship and industrial relations systems that distribute costs and responsibilities among the major stakeholders (employers, apprentices/unions and the state), whereas conservative-secular and liberal parties favour employer-led, free-market approaches.

In line with recent research by Busemeyer (2011, 2012, 2015), I posit that we cannot fully understand the reforms of apprenticeships and industrial relations without looking at the relationship between governments and employers. As massively grown exit options for capital limit the scope of left and Christian democratic parties with regard to the costs that can be placed on employers in the course of politico-economic reforms, I argue that reforms of apprenticeship systems that equally incorporate the interests of unions *and* employers can serve as instruments to build up cooperative industrial relations, which can no longer be unilaterally imposed on the social partners as was still possible under the conditions of 'embedded liberalism' (Ruggie 1982, Scharpf 2000a, 2000b). Hence, I complement earlier studies and the VoC approach, which focus on cooperative industrial relations as the central prerequisites for *collective approaches* towards skill formation, by exploring the possibility that governments of different partisan compositions use vocational training reforms to influence industrial relations towards their preferred solutions in terms of policy making *and* policy outcomes.

However, for non-right governments this might also necessitate a changed approach towards craft unions, which used their involvement in apprenticeships as a power resource with which non-right governments in the three countries traditionally refrained from interfering. Historically, in LMEs craft unions used their involvement in apprenticeships to shore up union bargaining power to limit the number of skilled tradespersons in their respective sector (Crouch 1993, Lee 1979, Stephens 1979, Thelen 2004), which led to employers becoming reluctant to take on apprentices and made them search for ways to substitute 'expensive' skilled labour with automatized production (Thelen 2004). Such craft union training politics heavily distort market mechanisms in the supply and demand of skilled labour, so market-embracing secular conservative and/or liberal governments might use apprenticeship reforms to contain unions' power in skill formation in order to free up labour markets and the scope of action for individual employers.

Alternatively, for governments wishing to reform adversarial and contested industrial relations towards more cooperation between employers and unions, skill-formation politics can entice employers to cooperate in a field where joint gains in terms of an increased national stock of skills and a higher productivity are more readily available, than in macro-issues such as wage bargaining or social policy. Whether and how social democratic and Christian democratic parties have used VET policies to manufacture a cooperative climate within industrial relations will also be analysed.

I also analyse what explains the political sustainability or fragility of reforms towards a collective apprenticeship system. *Political sustainability*, as understood in this context, means that policy change leads to institutional change in a double sense. On the one hand, it can be understood as policies that effectively reform the apprenticeship system, so that characteristics of collective skill formation – such as cost sharing, firm involvement, effective certification, and cooperation between various actors in designing training profiles, and so forth – are put in place. On the other hand, and more important for sustainability, is, that the central stakeholders come to follow the newly instituted rules and come to recognize the merits of the institutional reforms. In this regard, the second central hypothesis is that the development of cross-class coalitions is a necessary condition for a sustainable institutional development towards collective apprenticeship systems. In the absence of such cross-class compromises, collective apprenticeship systems are bound to be fragile, continuously contested and prone to problems of collective action, credible commitment and market failure and – in effect – ultimately subject to (endlessly recurring) new reforms.

Finally, the timing and sequencing of apprenticeship reforms can matter crucially for their institutional trajectory. Historical institutionalism has discussed the role of 'critical junctures' (Capoccia & Kelemen 2007, Hall 2010, Pierson 2000b, 2004, Thelen 2009), which set countries on differential development paths and are hard to reverse due to institutional stickiness and/or increasing returns (Pierson 2000a, 2004). The main take away for the present study is that governments are heavily constrained in the institutional choices pointed out above. It is conceivable that social democratic or Christian democratic governments cannot use training policies to manufacture cooperative industrial relations once that training is being delivered on a market basis. Conversely, liberal or secular-conservative governments might face stronger opposition towards marketization if the industrial partners are included in skill-formation politics and profit from collective benefits of cooperation in VET.

1.4 Methodology, case selection and empirical approach

In this book, I approach the case studies from the perspective of actor-centred historical institutionalism (Hall & Taylor 1996, Mahoney & Rueschemeyer 2003, Steinmo et al. 1992) is based on an ontology that is sensitive to the timing and sequencing of political processes and how they feed back into the political processes that occur subsequently (Hall 2003, 2010, Pierson 1993, 2004).

The main approach used in the analysis of the single-country case studies is the careful study of how apprenticeship politics developed over time, by tracing the process of reform sequences (Hall 2003), because it is sensible to assume that the politics of apprenticeship reforms not only involved strategic interaction between multiple actors but was also dependent on past political decisions. This method seems adequate being in line with the finding that the behaviour of key actors at critical junctures sets countries on different paths of development (Busemeyer 2015, Hall & Thelen 2009, Pierson 2004, Thelen 2004). In applying this framework the study aims to refine the analysis of how actors shape and sustain institutions (Deeg & Jackson 2007, Hall & Thelen 2009) by exploring diversity within VET in LMEs.

The expectations of actors and reform developments that I present in Chapter 2 serve as the baseline for the analytical narrative along which the case trajectories are presented. Also, they serve as the background for two types of comparison. First, the cases are analysed *comparatively* vis-à-vis each other to identify commonalities and differences in the dependent variable (trajectory of training reforms) and the independent variables (political partisanship, position of unions and employers, control variables). Here, the central goal is to evaluate carefully the evidence that we can find for and against the propositions of Chapter 2. Second, the case studies also provide *within-case* analyses. Here, the central goal is to identify if mechanisms found within reform politics remain stable independent of the passage of time or if they are influenced by past reform processes as hypothesized above, thus pointing to path dependence.

The following aspects are critical for tracing the causal process in each case: critical junctures, the relevant positions of governments, employers and unions prior to the reforms, and, the relative success of actors in achieving their preferred reform outcome. As each cannot be imputed externally, I follow the advice of Paul Pierson to 'go back and look' (2000: 264) in order to avoid 'work[ing] *backwards* from extant institutional arrangements [and| to develop an account of how these institutions were (or might have been) rationally chosen' (Pierson 2004: 104).

To do this, the study uses a broad array of empirical material. Critical junctures were identified with reference to academic studies and corroborated by expert interviews with 69 country and subject expert researchers, trade union and employer association officials and senior civil servants. These semi-structured interviews were conducted in the United Kingdom, Ireland and Australia between October 2012 and March 2013 and a list of interviewees is given in Appendix A. The main goal behind the interviews was to identify in greater depth the policy positions of actors central to the political reform processes of VET. The collected insights were then used for a second round of analysing policy position papers, internal documents and further primary sources such as parliamentary debates and newspaper reports, which were used as background material to explore the validity of the interviewees' statements. In organizing the fieldwork, I tried to gather general recommendations from senior colleagues and collaborators in each of the three cases under study. Some aspects that I found helpful in organizing fieldwork also can be found in Kern & Vossiek (2014).

The case selection follows the 'method of concomitant variation' (Mill 1973), as the principal cases (United Kingdom, Ireland, Australia) not only differed on the dependent variable VET system but also on the extensiveness of cooperation between political parties and organized interests across time. Moreover, the three countries are usually treated as belonging to the same country clusters – besides the LME ideal-type – such as *liberal welfare states* (Castles 2010, Esping-Andersen 1990, 1999) or the Anglo-Saxon *family of nations* (Castles 1993). Moreover these countries share a common history in the early development and institutional design of their VET systems (Gospel 1994, O'Connor 2006) and all had serious experiences with high unemployment during the research period.

Apart from the experiences with unemployment, the United States, Canada and New Zealand would also be potential cases for this study. Their underdeveloped apprenticeship systems are the main reason why I exclude these countries. These have never been as extensive as in the post-war United Kingdom, Australia or, nowadays, Ireland (Bosch & Charest 2008). For example, in the United States, which lacked any institutional mechanism for the development of a joint VET-system, employers tried to adapt their production strategies to minimize the reliance on skilled labour (Gospel 1994, Thelen 2004). In addition, American employers could make use of skilled immigrant labour from European countries with strong apprenticeship systems; the mass production systems of large companies, for the most part, did not require high-level craft skills but could be operated by semi-skilled and unskilled workers; unions were much weaker than in Europe and could not enforce apprenticeship rules and coordination between employers was weak and mostly based on direct competition (Gospel 1994: 510–512).

The research period covers developments from the 1960s onwards, but the main focus of the cases studies is the period from the late 1970s to developments in 2008. While, at the beginning of the research period, most of the Western welfare states were already hit by the macroeconomic shock of the first oil crisis, the pressing issue of 'stagflation' and high rates of unemployment hit all major western economies during the 1980s (Scharpf 2000a). Simultaneously, the foundations of the international economy experienced a huge change, from a system of 'embedded liberalism' (Ruggie 1982), which still provided nation-states with domestic fiscal authority and options of Keynesianist economic policies, to a system of an 'open economy' (Scharpf 2000b) with highly mobile capital, intensified product market competition and budgetary cost-containment pressures.

As a final note, a central problem in studying VET in LMEs is that there are frequent changes in the definitions to what constitutes an apprenticeship (Ryan 2000). This difficulty extends to data on comparative apprenticeship numbers, which complicates quantitative comparisons of national trajectories. I therefore use, as a research template, the definition of Busemeyer and Trampusch (2012a: 23–24): systems of *collective skill formation*. Consequently, in the case studies of Chapters 3, 4, and 5, I focus especially on four aspects that underpin collective skill formation:

- *High firm involvement* in the provision and administration of vocational training.
- *Intermediary associations,* such as employers' associations and trade unions, have an important role in the administration and reform of training systems.
- Provision of *portable, certified occupational skills* that are standardized and fully recognized on national labour markets.
- Vocational education and training provision takes place in schools *and* in companies, usually in the form of *dual training* or *apprenticeship* schemes.

1.5 Contribution and outline of the book

This book contributes to three lines of discussion within contemporary political economy research.

First, it provides a more accessible route into the research on the variety of skill formation and skill-formation politics in LMEs by providing an account of skill-formation reforms in the three countries and using the characteristics of collective skill-formation regimes (see above) as an analytical lens for reform description. The main contributions to the study of skill formation (Busemeyer 2009a, Busemeyer & Trampusch 2012a, Estévez-Abe et al. 2001) do not analyse differences in skill formation among LMEs, although they discuss differences in skill formation in CMEs elaborately. Moreover, although there are some notable exceptions (Crouch et al. 2004 [1999], Gospel 1994, Thelen 2004, Toner 2008), studies that analyse the reform trajectories of apprenticeships in LMEs usually lack a comparative perspective between LMEs. Instead, most studies about reform politics are single case studies that only allow for within-case comparisons (for the United

Kingdom: Evans 1992, Perry 1976, Senker 1992; for Ireland: Boyle 2005, McCarthy 1977; and, for Australia: Ewer et al. 1991, Goozee 2001, Ryan 2002). In focusing on cross-national comparisons between the three countries over a longer period of time, the study intends to more clearly define the conditions under which we witness developments towards collective skill formation in LMEs. In general, this intention builds on the insights of critics of the VoC approach who have rightly pointed out the approach's insensitivity towards varieties within the ideal types CMEs and LMEs (Amable 2003, Busemeyer 2009a, Crouch 2009, Crouch et al. 2009, Lane &Wood 2009) and tries to offer an insight into the analysis of politics that take place in LMEs.

Second, it contributes to a broadening of PRT approaches, as it focuses especially on the incorporation of producer interests (labour *and* capital) by political parties within the politics of industrial relations and skill formation, which is often absent in classical analyses of the welfare state (Esping-Andersen 1990, Korpi 1983).

Third, it adds to the perspective on institutional change presented in the original VoC framework as it focuses on actor constellations as driving forces of institutional change in modern capitalist economies and thus adds a genuinely political perspective. How can governments use training policies to restructure industrial relations? Which political actor constellations were influential, how were cross-class coalitions built and which effect had their emergence or absence on the institutional stability of collective skill formation in LMEs? How does this affect institutional stability and the possibility of further institutional change?

The book is structured as follows. The second chapter briefly describes recent research in the study of comparative political economy and vocational training. As there there are large differences in VET in LMEs, but there are not yet scientific explanations for underlying factors, this part introduces theoretical concepts that guide my empirical analysis. The main research questions, theoretical arguments and working hypotheses are then presented. The last part of the second chapter deals with methodological considerations relating to qualitative research and discusses the case selection.

The next three chapters are devoted to in depth-case studies of the politics and trajectories of apprenticeship reforms in the United Kingdom (Chapter 3), Ireland (Chapter 4) and Australia (Chapter 5). For reasons of comparability, each of the case studies is presented in the following, similar fashion. After a brief introduction of the case-specific historical background, the main parts of the case studies analyse critical junctures that were decisive in shaping the vocational education and training trajectories in each case. Here, a special focus is placed on the interests of, and actor constellations between, partisan governments, employer associations and trade unions as the main organized stakeholders of the training system. Whose interests prevailed in the final reforms? This is followed by an analysis of the politics after the critical juncture in terms of the changed environment that the reforms brought about and how this impacted actor constellations and shaped the menu of reform options for subsequent governments. Each case study ends with a conclusion about its comparative findings and singles out the main dimensions of the politics of apprenticeship reforms. Finally, the concluding part summarizes and discusses the main findings, points to their implications for institutional change and training politics in LMEs and presents open questions for future research.

2. Collective skill formation in liberal market economies? The role of political parties, industrial relations and path dependence

In what follows, I describe the VoC approach (Hall & Soskice 2001a, b) focusing on skill formation within politico-economic institutions of economically advanced OECD democracies. I next examine criticisms and extensions of the VoC approach and point out that it does not capture the full variation of skill formation regimes in CMEs. Then, I discuss historical institutionalist studies on the emergence of skill formation regimes and highlight the importance of partisan politics and power resources for explaining VET reforms. The chapter ends with a discussion of institutional change in VET and the basic expectations that guide my study's analysis of VET reforms in LMEs.

2.1 Varieties of capitalism and skill formation – approaches, criticism and extensions

Earlier studies on the politico-economic institutions across capitalist economies mainly focused on government partisanship and trade unions as central driving forces of institutional variation (Esping-Andersen 1990, Korpi 1983, Schmidt 1982, Stephens 1979). In contrast, the VoC approach centres on employers and the constraints and options that economic institutions confer, for their strategies of production and competition, on global product markets (Hall & Soskice 2001a: 5–21): Institutions surrounding the productive and economic activities of firms offer distinct solutions to coordination problems that firms face in their endeavours, and condition their strategic interactions among each other and with other actors such as governments, trade unions and firms' employees. Hall and Soskice distinguish between two principal solutions to these coordination problems: market and *strategic coordination,* which denotes

> more extensive relational or incomplete contracting, network monitoring based on the exchange of private information inside networks, and more reliance on collaborative, as opposed to competitive, relationships to build the competencies of the firm. (Hall and Soskice 2001a: 8)

Based on the dominant configuration of market or strategic coordination in five institutional spheres that influence firm activities and are central to the foundation of political economies (relationships between trade unions and employers and their associations, relationships between firms and their workers, corporate governance and corporate finance systems, cooperation between individual firms and the *institutional components of education and training systems*), the VoC theory suggest the existence of two 'institutional equilibria' that give rise to two distinct kinds of capitalist organization: the ideal types of LMEs and CMEs.[1] In LMEs, firms typically rely on market mechanisms to solve their coordination problems, while firms and other actors in CMEs primarily rely on strategic coordination. The logic behind the existence and stability of these two ideal types of capitalist organization is based on the concept of 'institutional complementarities' (Hall & Soskice 2001a: 17) between the five spheres named above. Thus, two institutions based on market (or alternatively strategic) coordination can be said to be complementary, 'if the presence (or efficiency) of one increases the returns from (or efficiency of) the other' (Hall & Soskice 2001a: 17). As the theory posits, institutional configurations of the two ideal types should be stable, as they lead to distinct comparative institutional advantages (Hall & Soskice 2001a: 37–44) in firms' innovation strategies, which should exert strong positive feedback effects in each ideal-type of capitalism. Below, I will succinctly discuss which types of innovation by firms are encouraged in both ideal-types, how they are connected to skills and how much firms are willing to invest in their workers skills.

1 Grouping large OECD-countries to these two ideal types, Hall and Soskice (2001a: 19–21) classify the United States, Britain, Australia, Canada, New Zealand and Ireland as LMEs, and Germany, Japan, Switzerland, the Netherlands, Belgium, Sweden, Norway, Denmark, Austria and Finland as CMEs.

The notion of 'positive feedback', also regularly referred to as 'path dependence' (Pierson 2000a, 2004), will be discussed in more detail in the next section.

Following Hall and Soskice (2001a: 36–44), firms in LMEs enjoy a comparative institutional advantage in *radical innovation*, 'which entails substantial shifts in product lines, the development of entirely new goods, or major changes to the production process' (Hall & Soskice 2001a: 38) and confers comparative advantages in rapidly developing technology and research-intensive sectors such as biotechnology, information technologies or software. This advantage, as Hall and Soskice argue, is mainly due to institutions that set an incentive for investments in switchable assets that can easily be diverted to other purposes (Hall & Soskice 2001a: 17). To give some examples for institutions underpinning this institutional advantage of LMEs, flexible and deregulated labour markets allow firms to adapt their workforces quickly, while capital availability is strongly based on stock markets, which make venture capital available for new innovations and sectors. Moreover, relationships between employers and their workers are based on managerial prerogative and are generally more antagonistic than in cooperative production systems, not only at the firm level, but also between employers' associations and unions.

In terms of *skill formation,* authors in the VoC tradition (Estévez-Abe et al. 2001, Hall & Soskice 2001a) argue that the availability of *general skills*, representing switchable assets (Iversen & Soskice 2001), reinforces the advantage for radical innovation. According to this view, reliance on general skills underpins the production strategies of firms as well as incentives for households and individuals faced with the decision of investment in different types of skill.

Drawing on the classical distinction between general and specific skills given by Becker (1993), Iversen and Soskice (2001: 876) argue that 'specific skills are valuable only to a single firm or a group of firms (whether an industry or a sector), whereas general skills are portable across all firms.' In the absence of strategic cooperation between firms, there are few institutional safeguards to prevent employers from poaching skilled employees from their competitors by offering higher wages and/or better working conditions. Thus, firms that want to equip their workers with higher skills face the problem stated by Becker (1993): Without institutional safeguards that prevent poaching between employers, it is not rational for an employer to invest in the formation of general skills of its employees. Competitor firms could simply avoid the training costs by poaching the employee and the firm that invested in training would forfeit the training investments. Thus, only an investment in skills specific to the company's production needs in order to increase workers' productivity might be a viable strategy for a rational employer.

However, in contrast to Becker's conception of pure economic skill, real-world skills are hardly ever so firm specific that they are not portable to other firms at all (Busemeyer 2009a, Stevens 1999, Streeck 1989, Streeck 2012). The logical consequence of the incentives firms face in terms of skill formation is that many firms will refrain from training (see Finegold and Soskice 1988 for the United Kingdom) or try to replace skilled employees via production machinery that can be operated by semi- or unskilled employees. In each case this results in an underinvestment of employers in training.

When the investment of employers in skill formation is low, a large proportion of the training costs has to be borne by individual workers. Combined with the absence of institutional safeguards such as high employment protection and/or a generous unemployment insurance that make an investment in specific skills a viable option, a worker or young person faced with decisions about skill investments will rationally opt for an investment in general, portable skills (Estévez-Abe et al. 2001).[2] In the words of Estévez-Abe et al. (2001: 150) under these conditions the investment in:

> [h]ighly portable skills [...] [is] less risky than highly specific skills because in the former case the market value of the skill is not tied to a particular firm or industry. Faced with future job insecurity, a rational worker will not invest his or her time and money in skills that have no remunerative value outside the firm or industry. In other words, in the absence of institutional interventions into workers' payoff structures, general rather than asset-specific [i.e. firm-specific or industry-specific] skill acquisition represents the utility-maximising strategy.

---

2 According to the theoretical claims posited by Estévez-Abe et al. (2001: 149–150), a young person faced with a decision between investing in specific or general skills will calculate three aspects: the cost of investment (time needed for qualification and lower wages during training/education), the future wage premium of the skill investment, and the risk of losing the current (or aspired) job and the wage premium related to it.

The incentives for individuals consequently lead to a preference for general – academic higher – education. But, in contrast to the ideal-typical choice for and prevalence of general skills in LMEs, employers have more incentives to invest in skills in CMEs. They should make more use of specific and co-specific assets, 'that cannot readily be turned to another purpose and [...] whose returns depend heavily on the active cooperation of others' (Hall & Soskice 2001a: 17). According to the initial VoC propositions, CMEs offer comparative institutional advantages for firms engaging in *incremental innovation*, characterized by improving existing product lines and production processes in small steps. This type of innovation is one of the central cornerstones of competition in 'diversified quality production' (Streeck 1991) in the area of high-quality manufacturing, i.e. in cars, factory machines or consumer durables. Coordinated market economies should be particularly well equipped for this kind of innovation as it requires a strong involvement of the workforce in production processes in order to identify potential for innovation, the availability of patient capital independent from the current stock market value of the respective firm and stronger cooperation between firms in research and product development. These are all characteristic of the 'strategic coordination' prevalent in CMEs.

Moreover, incremental innovation requires not only a workforce with general theoretical skills, but also with firm- and industry-specific skills suited to the production processes and products that are to be optimized in order to gain or retain competitive advantage. In contrast to market-based coordination in LMEs, which offers few institutional safeguards against skilled worker poaching, the prevalence of strategic coordination in the institutional spheres of CMEs constrains the freedom of individual employers, but simultaneously offers solutions to the collective action problem between firms regarding skill investments. These institutions constitute 'beneficial constraints' (Streeck 1989: 94, Streeck 1998) and counteract the tendency of firms to underinvest in skills due to the problem of skilled-worker poaching. Thus they might prevent situations, in which employer investment in skills languishes and counteract 'that voluntary investment in training [...| will produce high skills only in exceptional cases, and even in these the result will likely be suboptimal' (Streeck 1989: 94).

An example of a beneficial constraint typically found in CMEs is collective wage bargaining between employer associations and unions. Collective wage bargaining usually equalizes wages within a sector (and to a certain degree also between sectors), which makes poaching a more costly endeavour for non-training firms that cannot offer substantially higher wages (Acemoglu & Pischke 1998, 1999; also Soskice 1994: 46). Wage compression across firms and industries brought about by collective wage bargaining reduces the risk that non-training firms appropriate the skill investments of competitors by poaching their trainees, thus offering a buffer to foregone training investments. Wage compression also acts as an incentive for firms to up-skill their workforce and raise productivity, as low-skilled workers are comparatively expensive when the skilled wage premiums between skilled and unskilled workers are lowered.

Another aspect beneficial to skill formation in CMEs is strong cooperative relationships between trade unions and employer associations, which facilitate joint investments in, and the joint regulation of, training. Collective bargaining in CMEs usually covers specific regulations for apprenticeship wages and trade unions frequently accept lower apprenticeship wages if employers can guarantee a sufficient amount of firm commitment towards training. As a result, when apprenticeship wages are kept low under collective bargaining, firms can recoup costly training investments as the productivity of apprentices closely matches that of senior workers at the end of apprenticeships (Soskice 1994). Skill certification, which enables workers to access occupational labour markets, is another example of strategic coordination in training that can benefit both employers and apprentices. For both it reduces the risk of wasted training investments as it offers trained workers the entry into occupational labour markets, which makes anticipated wage premiums higher and attrition rates of apprenticeships lower (Soskice 1994).

These aspects might make it rational for employers to invest in specific skills of their workforce but they also mean that it is less risky to invest in 'skills as a *generalized, polyvalent resource* that can be put to many different and, most importantly, *as yet unknown* future uses' (Streeck 1989: 97). Moreover, stronger cooperation between individual firms might also reduce their competition for skilled workers and in some cases even enable joint investments in training facilities, for example by small and medium enterprises that can share training equipment each firm could not afford individually (Culpepper 1999a, 2003). In turn, as skill formation under these conditions is substantially broader than necessitated by the current production strategies of firms in CMEs, the result might often be a certain overinvestment in skills that benefits employers in the long run as it yields a larger pool of skilled workers compared to conditions where firm involvement is stifled by poaching problems and narrow forms of specific skill formation (Streeck 1989).

Firm involvement and beneficial constraints have sustained a high level of vocational training in CMEs when compared to LMEs (Busemeyer 2015) and have suppressed university expansion as the primary route to skill formation to a certain degree. The availability of VET means that pupils with academic credentials that are insufficient for entry into tertiary education enjoy the alternative of skill formation and entry into occupational labour markets at the post-secondary level of education. Relatively high levels of employment protection and reasonably generous systems of unemployment insurance in CMEs make the decision for this type of education, which entails training in firm- and industry-specific skills, more attractive than in LMEs. Although firms in CMEs might incur high training costs in the short term, firm involvement creates significant payoffs in the long term. High training rates contribute to a comparatively large pool of skilled labour and investment in polyvalent skills (Streeck 1989), which in turn enable employers to redeploy their workers if made necessary by technological change or new customer demands.

To sum up, the investment in general skills and the dominance of academic, higher education in LMEs and the investment in specific skills in CMEs via VET are seen as complements to the configuration of politico-economic institutions in each ideal-type of capitalism, and central to the comparative institutional advantage for radical innovation in LMEs and incremental innovation in CMEs (Hall & Soskice 2001a, Estévez-Abe et al. 2001).

However, with regard to institutional change in systems of skill formation, we might ask how stable these ideal types are when confronted with new socio-economic challenges. The answer given by Hall and Soskice (2001a: 57–60) is relatively straightforward. The institutional configurations in LMEs and CMEs equip firms with distinct comparative advantages in radical (LMEs) and incremental (CMEs) innovation, which are strengthened by the institutional complementarities between the main spheres within political economies based on market coordination in LMEs and strategic coordination in CMEs. These institutional configurations are (at least in the short term) a given for firms, which have incentives to adapt their competitive strategies to gear them towards the distinct comparative advantage provided in each ideal-type, i.e. that firm's 'strategy follows structure' (Hall & Soskice 2001a: 15).

Seen from this perspective, firms in CMEs should be strong advocates of VET with high firm involvement, while firms in LMEs should not be interested in specific skill formation and should support general education. Moreover, following from the initial formulation of the VoC-paradigm, governments, unions and individuals should have an equal interest in the preservation and the possible strengthening of the 'institutional comparative advantages' found in CMEs and LMEs, as they are important sources of economic and employment growth as well as stability. Thus, we should expect continued diversity between different models of capitalism in the form of a dual convergence – or two distinct institutional equilibria – in which

> business interests in LMEs are likely to pressure governments for deregulation, since firms that coordinate their endeavors primarily through the market can improve their competencies by sharpening its edges. The government is likely to be sympathetic because the comparative advantage of the economy as a whole rests on the effectiveness of market mechanisms. [...] In [CMEs], however, the political dynamic inspired by globalization should be quite different. Here, governments should be less sympathetic to deregulation [...] [T]he business community is likely to provide less support for [deregulation], because many firms draw competitive advantages from systems of relational contracting that depend on the presence of supportive regulatory regimes. In these economies, firms and workers have common interests to defend because they have invested in many co-specific assets, such as industry-specific skills. (Hall & Soskice 2001a: 57–58).

In this reading, the VoC-approach makes a powerful approach for the stability of two different institutional equilibria and, concomitantly, the stability of two different approaches to skill formation: the LME approach of investment in general education with little firm involvement, and the CME approach that excels in the formation of specific skills underpinned by strong firm involvement and safeguarded by beneficial constraints and the protection of skill investments via social policies.

However, as I will show in the following sections, the VoC approach has to be extended in several ways to account for the analysis of skill-formation reforms. After a short introduction to the relative merits of the VoC approach and criticisms of it, the next section shows that the VoC-approach cannot fully account for the variation in skill formation in developed OECD democracies. Based on newer research contributions, I show that its distinction between general and specific skills as switchable and specific assets fails to capture important aspects that should be included in an analysis of VET reforms in economically developed democracies.

Following Busemeyer and Trampusch (2012a), distinguishing between four skill formation regimes captures the variety of skill formation among post-industrial democracies more adequately. The two dimensions that separate these regimes are the *degree of firm involvement* and the *degree of public support* by the state (and sometimes by trade unions) (Busemeyer & Trampusch 2012a), which in turn affect how specific or general the skills are that they produce. Building on this typology, I show later in this chapter how the perspectives of partisan politics and historical institutionalism can be meaningfully used to study institutional change in VET within the LMEs under study.

Varieties of capitalism and skill formation regimes – criticism and extensions

In the 2000s, the VoC approach was among the most influential paradigms within political economic research and there is now proof of Blyth's early suspicion that it would become 'canonical' in the way we think 'about growth, employment and the critical issues of convergence and divergence in a globalized economy' (Blyth 2003: 215). This might be partly explained by the stronger focus of VoC on employers and their role in the development of politico-economic institutions than stipulated in classical approaches of welfare state theories, such as the seminal works of Esping-Andersen (1990, 1999), Korpi (1983) and Stephens (1979), which focused on the power resources of the working class as a central factor in the emergence and development of politico-economic (welfare-state) regimes.[3]

3 See Hacker and Pierson (2002), Martin (1999) and Swenson (1991, 2002).

However, perhaps the most intriguing aspect of the theory is its assumption about the continued viability of non-market-based institutions for economic competitiveness in the age of a globalized economy, which is diametrically opposed to the neoliberal assumptions that dominated much of the political discourse from, at the latest, the 1990s onwards (European Commission 1993, OECD 1994a, 1994b, Sinn 2002, Tanzi 2002).[4] Yet, the VoC approach has been criticised on a large number of fronts. I will succinctly point to some general examples of VoC criticisms before I discuss specific criticisms of the theory that this book addresses.

For example, some authors question the parsimonious distinction between LMEs and CMEs. While Amable (2003) and Hay (2005) discuss the possibility of more than two ideal-types of capitalism, which could possibly extend to 'Mediterranean', 'Nordic' and 'Asian' types of capitalism, Blyth (2003) and Crouch (2009) discuss the relation of real-types to ideal-types and the possibility that VoC runs the danger of being overly constructed from a perspective of Germany and the United States as a basis for the respective ideal-types of CMEs and LMEs. In a related criticism, some authors (Campbell & Pedersen 2007, Kenworthy 2006) question whether the performance of 'pure-types' of capitalism, i.e. countries that more closely match economic coordination via market *or* non-market mechanism, is superior to an institutional mix of CME and LME characteristics. Seen from this angle, there might be different logics of institutional complementarities, which allow for a substantial variation within each ideal-type of capitalism (Allen 2004, Crouch et al. 2009, Deeg 2007, Lane & Wood 2009). Finally, in contrast to the VoC claims about the resilience of coordinating non-market institutions in CMEs, there is a growing debate about liberalization as a general phenomenon that extends across all modern OECD democracies (Streeck 2009, 2010, Baccaro & Howell 2011, Thelen 2014).

In this study, I explore the viability of these criticisms for VET reforms in LMEs and suspect that there might be different logics among institutional complementarities and, in fact, variations within the liberal ideal-type of capitalism. Moreover, inspired by the arguments on general trend of liberalization taking place even in CMEs, I explore the opposite

4 See Garrett (1998) and Swank (2002, 2005) on the viability of developed social protection systems under the conditions of a globalized economy.

possibility that LMEs can attempt more economic-coordination and cooperation between the state, unions and employers. But this necessitates a more fine-grained understanding of skill-formation regimes and processes of institutional change, which is reasonable in order to get a more nuanced view of the options and processes real-world actors face when trying to reform VET systems.

As pointed out above, the initial VoC theory strongly hinges on the incentives that LMEs and CMEs offer to firms and individuals for investments in *general* or *specific* assets, implying a strong distinction between general and specific skills (Hall & Soskice 2001a, Iversen & Soskice 2001). However, recent contributions (Busemeyer 2009a, Busemeyer & Trampusch 2012a, Streeck 2012) have questioned the definition of skill specificity underlying this theory. They argue that skill specificity is just one among many dimensions that characterize skill-formation regimes, which I – following Busemeyer and Vossiek (2016) – define as the *institutional setup of the provision of skill formation and its connection to labour market institutions*.[5]

Although Estévez-Abe et al. (2001) broadened the concept of skill specificity by differentiating between CMEs more strongly focused on firm specific-skills (as Japan) and occupational skills (as Denmark), it did not address the full variety of skill formation regimes. Thus, Busemeyer (2009a: 380) correctly asserts that the 'VoC literature defines skill specificity by looking at the portability of skills, [where] lower portability implies higher specificity of skills'. But by equating the *content of skill formation* with *skill portability*, the theory risks making false assumptions about firm involvement in training, which necessitates actual content of skill formation and portability of skills must be analysed separately (Busemeyer 2009a: 381). Busemeyer (2009a) then proceeds to an analysis of the two separate dimensions of *authoritative skill certification* and *firm involvement* and finds three different skill-formation models among the CMEs: A *segmentalist* skill system,

5 Essentially, this definition follows Busemeyer (2009a: 387): 'The concept of a skill *regime* [...] [is] conceptualized as an interconnected set of institutions in vocational education and training, industrial relations and labour market and welfare state policies that shapes the incentives of workers and firms to invest in different kinds of skill formation and thus impacts on the overall skill profile of a given economy.'

exemplified by Japan, where employer involvement is high and portability of skills low due to a lack of certification and low labour mobility, an *integrationist* skill system, found in Sweden, with low employer involvement and high skill portability provided by vocational schools, and a *differentiated* skill regime characterized by strong employer involvement in skill formation and high portability produced by dual apprenticeships, as exemplified by Germany. Using these examples, he shows that skill formation regimes are strongly conditioned by the decisions of firms to invest in skills, which in turn depend on beneficial constraints that reduce the risk of poaching.

Streeck (2012) shares this criticism and suggests distinguishing between a substantive definition of skill content, an economic definition of skill portability and an analytical distinction between high and low skills. This presents a powerful challenge to the argument about skill specificity and social protection by Estévez-Abe et al. (2001). General skills with low content might in principle be marketable among many employers, but do not represent a viable option for individuals when low-skilled and unskilled jobs vanish in modern economies or yield only subsistence wages. This points to the importance of institutions for skill formation besides 'high, general skills' tertiary education for those citizens who fail to enter university.

Yet, VET systems with strong firm involvement not only offer access to institutionalized training below higher university education, but also produce specific and general skills that are, in principle, viable for many employers. Thus, Germany has figured prominently in studies of VET, which regarded its system of dual apprenticeships as a role model for the formation of intermediate skills (Crouch et al. 2004 [1999], Culpepper 1999b, Finegold & Soskice 1988, Green 2001, Soskice 1994). These studies pointed out that the institutional infrastructure of the joint, multi-layered regulation of dual apprenticeships by social partners and governments is favourable to a high-quality training system. As it is useful to go beyond the distinction between general, academic skill formation in LMEs and specific, vocational skill formation in CMEs, the theoretical approach of this book follows a typology, which captures the fact that skill formation is not only dependent on employers' and individuals' decisions to invest in a particular type of skill but also on the role that public institutions surrounding skill formation exert.

Busemeyer and Trampusch (2012a: 8–9), build upon 'previous typologies of skill formation, recognizing that the real guises of training systems' – the dominant venue of training (school versus firm), aspects of skill certification, occupational regulations of VET, etc. – and 'the linkages between skill formation and other socio-economic institutions such as the production system, industrial relations, and the welfare state' are likely to appear in varying degrees within national skill formation systems.[6] With this caveat in mind, they identify the two dimensions of *firm involvement* and *public commitment to vocational training* as the two crucial dimensions that separate different skill formation regimes.

Firm involvement connotes the 'willingness of firms to invest in skill formation, in particular initial vocational training [...] [and in] skills that are polyvalent and thus potentially transferable' (Busemeyer & Trampusch 2012a: 12) to other employers, occupations or production processes. The degree of public commitment to vocational training (also referred to as 'state involvement') is not defined as straightforward as is firm involvement and captures the interplay between state and intermediary organizations (employer associations, unions and chambers of commerce) in the institutional setup of vocational training. This dimension includes subsidies that states contribute to VET, the role of public organizations in monitoring training, setting training standards and developing occupational profiles, and the general availability of VET in the general education system as a viable alternative to higher education. In each of the ideal-typical systems introduced below, the main actors involved in the genesis and reform of skill formation systems were and are faced with the challenge of resolving

> four neuralgic points [of conflict] [...]: the relationship between firm autonomy and (semi-) public monitoring (who controls skill formation?), the relationship between firm-based and school-based vocational education and training (who provides skill formation?), the financing of skill formation (who pays for skill formation?), and the relationship between vocational education and training and the general education system (*ibid.*: 16).

6 Older contributions that Busemeyer and Trampusch built upon are Blossfeld (1992), Crouch et al. (2004 [1999]), Finegold & Soskice (1988), Greinert (1993) and Lynch (1994).

Based on these two dimensions, four ideal-typical skill-formation regimes can be identified (see Table 2. 1). Below, I describe the configurations of each regime based on Busemeyer (2009a), Busemeyer and Trampusch (2012a), Crouch (1992), Crouch et al. (2004 [1999]), Estévez-Abe et al. (2001), Ryan (2000) and Sako (1991). Here, I describe the liberal skill-formation regime according to its dominant description, and only challenge this description by the in-depth analysis of the variation in VET institutions and politics among LMEs at a later stage.

Table 2. 1: Four skill regimes in post-industrial democracies

Public commitment to VET	**High**	*Statist* skill formation [Statist model] (SWE, F)	*Collective* skill formation [Corporatist model] (GER, CH, AUT, DK, NL)
	Low	*Liberal* skill formation [Short-term adaptability model] (US, CAN, UK, IRE, AUS, NZL)	Segmentalist skill formation [Big-company model] (JAP)
		Low	**High**
		Firm involvement in initial VET	

Source: own depiction following Busemeyer and Trampusch (2012a: 12). Note: Alternative labels for regimes following Crouch (1992) and in squared brackets. Typical country examples belonging to each skill regime are given in abbreviation in brackets (SWE = Sweden, F = France, GER = Germany, AUT = Austria, DK = Denmark, NL = Netherlands, US = United States, CAN = Canada, UK = United Kingdom, IRE = Ireland, AUS = Australia, NZL = New Zealand, JAP = Japan).

The *liberal skill-formation regime* is characterized by low firm involvement in initial VET and a low degree of public commitment to vocational training. Typical real-world examples are the United States and the United Kingdom, although I will show in Chapter 3 that the latter fits this ideal-typical assignment better nowadays than it did for most of its post-World War II history. In this regime, the education system is heavily geared towards general education. Post-secondary education has a strong focus on academic skills and mostly takes place at universities and colleges, which are to a large extent privately financed by tuition fees. The minor role that VET plays is also underpinned by a lack of certification of those skills, which are produced in vocational tracks within schools or colleges. Typically, if dual training programmes exist that combine workplace and institutional training, these are only lightly regulated by the state and between employers and unions where they are involved. As regards labour-market institutions, the regime is underpinned by low employment regulation, modest unemployment insurance as a basic safety net and decentralized wage bargaining. Thus, in the absence of beneficial constraints, which could increase the willingness of firms (by reducing the poaching problem) and individuals to invest in vocational skills, VET only plays a secondary role in skill formation compared to higher, academic education. Where firms are involved, they are likely to provide short-term and firm-specific on–the-job training courses, which are used to complement the skills delivered by the general education system. Finally, where the state is involved in training provision, this often takes the form of short-term training courses, which are often delivered in the form of employment policies. With reference to the example of the United Kingdom, Crouch (1992: 41) has used the term 'short-term adaptability model'. The term captures the idea that firms in LMEs have little incentive to use skill formation as a long-term competitive strategy and rather use their ability to adapt their workforces by relying on fluid, deregulated labour markets.

The *segmentalist skill regime*, of which Japan is probably the most referenced example in the literature (Busemeyer 2009a, Thelen 2004), shares the focus on general academic education within the public school system with the liberal regime, which is also due to the influence of the US occupation after the World War II. But whereas the willingness of firms to invest in polyvalent skills is somewhat impeded by the institutions surrounding VET in liberal market economies, Japanese firms are typically deeply involved in the skill formation of their employees and entering firm-based training (which is provided in firms, sometimes also in the form of job rotation schemes, in-house training centres and firm-supported vocational schools) remains a viable educational option vis-à-vis academic university education. Higher firm involvement is made possible because firms in segmentalist skill regimes rely on a specific combination of institutions that alleviate the poaching problem faced by their counterparts in LMEs. Employees are typically tied to a specific firm or group of firms in the long run, which provide incentives to their employees to invest in skills because of their strongly developed internal labour markets (Sako 1991) and benefits provided by the firm in the form of housing, pension or health benefits. The certification of the skills formed via this approach is weakly developed when compared to the *collective skill formation regime,* which also reduces employees' mobility to a certain degree due to the lower signalling value about workers skills. Finally, the Japanese economy is typically dominated by large firms or firm conglomerates, which developed rather strong mechanisms of cooperation (Thelen & Kume 2003) thus reducing the poaching problem further. So, even in the absence of strong public commitment, the development of a firm's involvement in the formation of broad and transferable skills is possible if it depends on a particular institutional configuration that underpins employer coordination and, especially, strong internal labour markets.[7]

France and Sweden embody the main characteristics of a *statist skill-formation regime*. Diametrically opposed to the segmentalist regime, employer involvement is low but public commitment to and the role that the state has in skill formation are highly developed. The largest role for the formation of vocational skills is played by the public education system, which offers a highly specific vocational track alongside the classical path of general, academic education. In Sweden, for example, young pupils can choose between over ten routes of vocationally oriented subjects at the upper secondary level. However, the strong role the state plays in this regime has somewhat crowded out employer involvement in skill formation and dual training programmes are limited to very few sectors and employers. In turn, the skill formation that takes place within firms is very firm- (or industry-) specific and used to complement the general vocational skills primarily developed by the public education system. In further vocational training, the role of the state is also pronounced in the Swedish case, which is generally commended for the use of highly developed active labour-market policies (Bonoli 2012, Esping-Andersen 1999). However, skill production might not always be optimal under the condition of extensive state involvement without a high level of firm involvement as there can be 'difficulties in securing the updating of school-courses at a time of rapid technological change' (Crouch 1992: 39), which is why during the 1980s and 1990s there were repeated attempts to give firms a larger role in skill formation. These, however, were largely unsuccessful (Crouch 1992, Crouch et al. 2004 [1999], Lundahl 1997).

7 For more detailed accounts of skill formation in Japan, see Aoki (1994), Dore and Sako (1998) and Thelen and Kume (2003).

The fourth ideal-typical regime is adequately titled *collective skill-formation regime*, as the responsibilities for skill formation are shared between different stakeholders and as there is a strong degree of firm involvement and public commitment in initial VET. Moreover, these systems are based on the involvement of other collective actors such as employers' associations, chambers of commerce and trade unions. As described by Busemeyer and Trampusch (2012a), real-world examples of this regime are Germany, Austria, Switzerland, the Netherlands and Denmark, although in varying degrees regarding the balance of responsibilities between employers, associations and the state. Collective skill-formation systems are best characterized by a combination of four distinct factors (Busemeyer &Trampusch 2012a: 14–15): First, there is a high share of firms involved in training, which shoulder a sizeable portion of the training costs of skill formation. Second, intermediary associations such as employers' associations and trade unions play an important role in the administration and reform of collective training systems (with varying degrees of state support in these processes). Third, these systems are usually characterized by the provision of portable, certified occupational skills that are standardized and fully recognized on national labour markets. Portability had to be understood in the sense that skills are not only certified, but typically also polyvalent as pointed out in the sections above and thus of potential use in different occupations. Finally, vocational training takes place not only in schools but also in companies, usually in the form of dual training or apprenticeship schemes, which make up a significant proportion of post-secondary education.[8] However, these systems can be prone to conflict, precisely because they involve multiple actors and are based on administrative and political processes, which are only 'partly controllable by state authorities because labour market actors and their associations play an important role' (Busemeyer & Trampusch 2012a: 34).

8 Ryan (2000) gives a more technical definition of apprenticeships based on five aspects: a) a combination of school- and work-based learning, which involves more time at work and less training in schools; b) a contract between employers and apprentices, which regulates the duties between both parties; c) financing by an employer, who has the major responsibility for the on-the-job training, d) standardized curricula and evaluation procedures and e) an accredited occupational certificate.

The typology given above serves as an outline for the analysis of the variation of VET in LMEs, as it broadens the perspective on skill formation offered by the VoC-approach and thus allows for a more fine-grained perspective on the *varieties of skill-formation systems*. Moreover, it shows that *firm involvement* is one of the two crucial dimensions of initial VET. Regarding the polyvalence of skills, collective training systems are a viable way of initial vocational training, precisely because employers are strongly involved in processes of skill formation, which go beyond their immediate production requisites. Thus the main takeaway for the present study is that firm involvement is not a 'continuous variable' in the sense that the more freedom employers have to make their training decisions the more training they will offer, but quite the opposite: different skill-formation regimes offer distinct sets of resources and constraints that influence employers' training decisions. In this context, the present section has argued that collective skill-formation systems offer a particular combination of beneficial constraints that induce employers to invest in polyvalent, i.e. transferable skills. Firm involvement also offers the benefit that occupational profiles can be more easily updated in light of technological change, because firms as private actors usually have better access to this information than state actors (Crouch et al. 2004 [1999]).

Of course, a certain proportion of firm-sponsored training will take place in all ideal-typical regimes described above, for example by large firms that can allow for a proportion of training slack and that use training as a screening device for internal labour markets, which in turn makes training attractive to young employees and can possibly bind them to the individual firm reducing the danger of poaching. Yet, without beneficial constraints and firm-embeddedness in institutions that induce either segmentalist or collective skill formation, Streeck's (1989: 94) diagnosis that 'left to the market [...] there will also be high-quality training, but [...] limited to isolated "islands of excellence", and differences between firms will be enormous' is probable. As firm involvement is a crucial aspect in the formation of vocational, occupationally transferable and polyvalent skills, and as it largely depends on the institutional embeddedness of skill-formation regimes and beneficial constraints, the question of how the latter emerged historically is crucial. The next section will introduce two closely related additional criticisms of the VoC approach. Then, the remaining sections of this chapter introduce the study's many hypotheses about skill formation reforms and the emergence of collective skill formation in LMEs, before skill formation reforms are presented in case studies of the United Kingdom, Ireland and Australia.

2.2 Theories of institutional emergence and change: historical institutionalism and power resource theory

This section discusses the criticism that the VoC approach paints an unrealistic picture of institutional change in post-industrial democracies and is too strongly geared towards institutional stability in CMEs and LMEs. Closely related to this point, a critical reader might emphasize the fact that the volume of Hall and Soskice (2001b) and the contributions therein strongly focus on mechanisms of institutional reproduction but that especially the theoretical chapter by Hall and Soskice (2001a)

> does not go the extra inch to explore and explain why, when, and how particular sets of institutions come into existence. Nor does it go the extra mile to examine how these relate to the wider set of class experiences and interests that seem (to some of us, at least) to be endemic to capitalism in all its national manifestations. (Coates 2002: 662)

For the sake of clarity, I will briefly summarize these, before I argue that they can be reconciled with the VoC approach. However, in order to do this, we are well advised to pay more attention to the historical trajectories of skill formation. Thus, it is useful to connect VoC studies from a historical institutionalist (HI) perspective and to add theories of political partisanship to the toolkit we need for analysing the politics of VET reforms.

The notion of different political coalitions that drive institutional change is especially important in the light of more recent research on institutional change (Hall & Thelen 2009, Mahoney & Thelen 2010, Streeck & Thelen 2005, Thelen 2004). The original VoC view on institutional change was heavily criticized for being overly static and based on debatable functionalist assumptions that predict change only as an outcome of self-stabilizing equilibria (Coates 2005, Deeg & Jackson 2007, Pontusson 2005). However, as Hall and Thelen (2009) argue, we should analyse 'institutions as resources', thus paralleling assumptions of actor-centred institutionalism (Scharpf 2000c, 2000d), to detect the motivation and potential of political actors to drive institutional change. Here, institutional stability is not a given but springs from:

> a continuous assessment of [actors'] own scope for action and the intentions of those with whom they are interacting. [...] In the political economy, [stability] depends on a stream of action that is political in the sense that it entails conflict designed to test the limits of cooperative arrangements and of the processes of mobilization that bring other actors in line with those arrangements. (Hall & Thelen 2009: 12–13)

From this perspective, 'the achievement of coordination appears as a political problem' (Hall & Thelen 2009: 13), as actors have to invest continuous support for forms of (market- or strategic-based) coordination to sustain institutional stability. A closely related question pertains to the motivations of actors, who are involved in the *politics of political change*. The notion of comparative institutional advantage within VoC is strongly focused on the competitive advantage that institutional complementarities offer to firms for different innovation strategies. However, actors might not only be interested in the efficiency institutional configurations have for economic competitiveness but, overwhelmingly, in the distributional implications these institutions have for them. We cannot readily assume that institutions are always designed in order to bring about societally optimal outcomes, but that actors are well aware of distributive advantages different forms of institutional design might have for them. Following Knight (1992: 40) 'the main goal of those, who develop institutional rules is to gain strategic advantage vis-à-vis other actors'. Thus, economic benefits are one kind of reason among others for institutional development, even if a certain degree of institutional functionality is needed for the competitiveness of a political economy (Becker 2007: 261). Economic considerations might figure prominently in discourses about political reforms, but they are one only among various 'reference frames' (Becker 2007: 261), i.e. – for example social or general welfare aspects – that support institutional changes in politico-economic systems, which can be 'marked by conflict and dysfunctionality' (Becker 2007: 263) and thus have 'space for development in different directions' (Becker 2007: 263).

Moreover, even when actors seek to increase institutional complementarities in order to strengthen competitiveness, they might not only always know which solutions would be functional to that end, implying 'limits of institutional design' (Pierson 2000c, 2004). These might originate, *inter alia,* because institutions usually have multiple effects, so the long-term effects of reforms cannot be readily foreseen; that they might also produce unintended consequences. Even if institutions are designed in order to complement a specific set of institutions and to create comparative institutional advantage, the environment surrounding the institutional configuration might change so that the institutions cannot perform their intended functions any more.

Before I move to describe the historical development of different skill-formation regimes and the implications a partisan politics perspective has for the study of skill formation reforms, a short note on types of institutional change is advisable. Models of institutional change that assume strong path-dependent effects have often treated exogenous shocks as punctuations of strong institutional equilibria (Baumgartner et al. 2007, Baumgartner et al. 2009) where long periods of stasis are disrupted by short periods of institutional change, commonly referred to as *critical junctures* in HI approaches (Capoccia & Kelemen 2007). Yet, younger contributions to HI have strongly questioned the view of institutional stasis stretching over long periods of time, being interrupted by relatively short periods of change (Mahoney & Thelen 2010, Streeck & Thelen 2005, Thelen 2009). Instead, these newer approaches point out that institutions might also change *incrementally*, where policy change in small steps can accumulate to effect institutional change.

In particular, Streeck and Thelen (2005) identify five mechanisms that can explain incremental policy change. First, *institutional displacement* connotes patterns of change in which a growing number of actors defect from dominant institutions thus leading to a rising salience of formerly subordinated institutions. Second, in processes of *layering* new institutions are attached to already existing institutions, which can gradually alter the structure and/or status of the former institutions. Third, *institutional drift* can occur when institutions need to be updated in order to continue to perform their intended function, but when political actors refrain from adapting the institution to the new challenges. Fourth, old institutions can be used to perform new or formerly negligible functions leading to a process of institutional *conversion.* Finally, institutional *exhaustion* describes the gradual breakdown of institutions over time via processes of depletion. These five types of gradual institutional change will be used as reference points in the country case studies in Chapters 3 to 5.

Back to the roots – historical institutionalism and the emergence of skill formation regimes

In line with the arguments above, we should devote attention to the actor coalitions that shaped the emergence of different skill formation regimes in the first place and to sequences of institutional development of VET. For this study, this pertains especially to the conditions under which employers became involved in systems of skill formation, contributing to the provision of polyvalent and transferable skills.

Thelen's (2004) meticulous study gives us an insight into the processes that shaped skill regime formation in the late 19th and early 20th centuries, a period that has received much attention in a number of recent publications that study its implications for the development of different models of capitalism and business organization (Iversen & Soskice 2009, Martin & Swank 2008, 2012). Thelen (2004) analyses the development of vocational training in the United Kingdom, the United States, Germany and Japan. Her historical institutionalist study traces differences between these countries' VET systems back to the settlement of early conflicts between guilds, employers and unions. More specifically, she focuses on two different lines of conflict, which were settled differently during two critical junctures, the first at the turn of the 19th century and the second in the period up to the early 1920s. The first juncture that is important for the fate of VET in the four nations was whether state actors tried to shore up the power of traditional artisans and their guilds as in Japan and Germany, or whether their early organizational structures were destroyed, as in the United Kingdom and the United States. In effect, the survival of independent guilds and artisans, who traditionally had the power of occupational certification, established the potential for conflict between early industrial employers and the guilds as representatives not only of skilled labour but also of independent organizations of capital. In contrast, where guilds were abolished they evolved into independent craft unions.

This early juncture had repercussions on the settlement of conflicts about skill formation certification in the early 1920s. Where the guilds survived, as in Japan and Germany, skill formation became contested across the class divide between big employers and early industrial unions, which developed a joint interest in breaking the certification monopoly of the guilds. In contrast, where guilds had developed into craft unions, the conflict about skill formation became contested along the class divide, as craft unions tried to use an approach that can be adequately termed as *politics of skill control*: craft unions typically tried to control the number of skilled workers by using training policies and regulations in order to drive up their own wages, which triggered employers to try to break the influence of craft unions over training or, as happened to a large degree in the United States, to limit the reliance on skilled workers altogether by replacing skilled workers with capital equipment (Gospel 1994, Thelen 2004).

On a close reading, Thelen's chapter on the British case somewhat turns the VoC assumption on the prevalence of general skills in LMEs on its head. Despite a low level of employment protection development and in the absence of any unemployment insurance, the workers organized in craft unions had a very strong interest in keeping skill formation as narrow and specific as possible in order to exploit their labour-market situation. In contrast, where workers were organized on a sectorial or industrial basis, they were much more willing to cooperate with employers in the area of developing broad and transferable skills, as worker mobility constituted an important power resource for their members. Moreover, they were more willing and better able to negotiate wage settlements that equalized pay among different sectors and occupations.

The crucial point taken from Thelen's (2004) study is that cross-class coalitions between employers and unions can be driving forces for institutional evolution and change in VET systems. However, her study also shows that we cannot readily form hypotheses on the formation of cross-class coalitions as they are heavily dependent on specific institutional configurations of national political economies and historically contingent trajectories.

Thus, in light of the fact that the development of cross-class coalitions can increase firms' involvement in skill formation, the question arises of how the development of cross-class coalitions in VET and in industrial relations was and can be influenced by political actors that want to reform VET systems towards stronger employer involvement. In this regard, we can make the connection to theories of partisan politics and power resources, which are essential in seminal works on the development of modern welfare states (Esping-Andersen 1990, Huber & Stephens 2001, Korpi 1983, Stephens 1979).

Power resources and the partisan politics of skill formation reforms

By now, it is a standard assumption in the study of mature welfare states that different states do not only react functionally to changed socio-economic conditions as posited by earlier theorists (Wilensky 1975) but that the processes of welfare-state expansion and reform are largely driven by different actors that try to structure institutions to the benefit of their core electorate. In the standard assumptions of early partisan theories, left-wing (social-democratic) parties represent the lower income strata, whereas right-wing parties represent the upper income strata (Hibbs 1977, Schmidt 1982). By now, the partisan political perspective is widely recognized as an important factor in the study of education (Ansell 2010, Boix 1998, Busemeyer 2007, 2009b, Busemeyer et al. 2013, Garritzmann 2016).

However, partisan theory has a second variant, which focuses more strongly on the combined strength of working-class interests (i.e. left parties and trade unions) vis-à-vis the strength of capital and upper-class interests as an important determinant for policy differences between welfare states (Esping-Andersen 1990, Korpi 1983, Stephens 1979). This classical perspective, which made a lasting impact on welfare state research, is strongly concerned about the distribution of social rights among citizens from different economic backgrounds and the impact of social policy on the role that markets play in the distribution of income. Moreover, it strongly suggests that political cross-class coalitions can be important driving forces in policy development *and* change.

Following Esping-Andersen's seminal work (1990), three ideal-typical welfare-state regimes with different distributional institutional setups can be distinguished, each of which is characterized by the long-term dominance of a name-giving political coalition. First, the *social democratic* regime was built on a cross-class coalition between small landowners, unionized workers and the middle class under the long-term government dominance of social democrats. This resulted in a strong role for the state in education policy and a strong redistribution of market-generated income via social policies. Second, the *liberal* regime was strongly influenced by the dominance of liberal and secular-conservative parties, which forged alliances between the middle and upper-middle classes and typically refrained from strong interventions into markets beyond a basic supply of education and social policies. Finally, the *conservative* (or corporatist) regime emerged from a long-term dominance of middle-class parties, often in the form of Christian democratic cross-class parties (van Kersbergen 1995), and gave a strong role to intermediary associations in education and social policy.

As pointed out at the beginning of this section, we cannot take for granted that politico-economic reforms of skill formation are strongly driven by considerations of economic efficiency. In fact, quite the opposite might be true, as employers, unions and governments as central organized stakeholders of skill formation systems might not only care about the outcomes that these systems produce but also about their distributional implications. It is a central claim of this book, which will be analysed in the following chapters, that independent of the ideal-type of capitalism, governments of different partisan colours have different preferences not only in terms of *policy* but also in terms of *politics,* i.e. which interests should be granted (privileged) access to policy-making.

If the claim that partisan governments and power resources should matter for the trajectory of skill formation reforms is accepted, the natural question is how they matter. The present study takes a middle position, analogous to the assumptions of public policy research (Esping-Andersen 1990, van Kersbergen 1995). Following different partisan political programs, we can expect *left* parties to favour redistributive public and supply-side oriented economic policies to pursue universalistic goals. Due to their strong organizational ties to the union movement, we can also expect them to push for skill-formation policies, which strengthen the role of unions as organized interests. Conversely, *secular conservative* parties should favour market-oriented approaches in education and economic policy based on ideas of individualism and private responsibility, and thus should favour strengthening the power of employers over unions and individual workers. Finally, *Christian democratic* parties favour segmented education and economic policies that distribute competencies to corporatist, *private-interest governments* (Streeck & Schmitter 1985) consisting of the intermediary organizations of capital and labour, according to the principle of subsidiarity, in order to preserve corporate affiliations and status differentials.

Below, I develop specific hypotheses about the intersection of partisan politics with the role of producer groups of capital and labour in policy-making, which can be selectively granted to them by governments. As pointed out above, the involvement of firms in the formation of transferable occupational skills has historically been underpinned by the formation of cross-class coalitions between capital and labour. Moreover the incentives for firms to invest in these types of skills are strongly conditioned by institutions of cooperative industrial relations. As I will argue in the next section, reforms of VET and industrial relations are in fact often intertwined and partisan governments can use *both areas* of reform in order to strengthen or dismantle the role of unions and employers, thereby granting them *institutional power* by allocating them an important role in VET governance and politics.

2.3 The politics of institutional change in skill formation

As pointed out above, the VoC approach has emphasized the centrality of skill-formation systems to competitive production strategies of LMEs and CMEs, and Germany was described as a prime example of a CME, thus a 'typical case' in the sense of Gerring (2007). In the same vein, Germany has figured prominently in studies of vocational training, which regarded its system of dual apprenticeship – or, in the terms of this book, *collective skill formation* – as a role model for the formation of intermediate skills (Culpepper 1999b, Finegold & Soskice 1988,

Crouch et al. 2004 [1999], Green 2001, Soskice 1994). These studies have characterized the institutional infrastructure of the joint, multilayered regulation of dual apprenticeships by social partners and governments as favourable to a high-quality training system underpinned by beneficial constraints that shore up the willingness of firms to invest in polyvalent skills (Soskice 1994, Streeck 1989, 1991, 1992, 1998).

However, the central focus of this book is the question of how collective apprenticeship solutions – and the related emergence of beneficial constraints – can emerge in LMEs (Finegold & Soskice 1988) and how these can be explained politically. How did the central stakeholders of apprenticeship systems (i.e. partisan governments and organized interests) politically influence the development of apprenticeship institutions in LMEs and how far did they move into the direction of collective skill formation? How sustainable are such developments in LMEs? Below, I claim that the institutional stability of apprenticeship reforms in LMEs heavily depends on the continuity of cross-class coalitions between capital and labour. Cross-class coalitions can minimize the frequency and intensity of conflict between the central stakeholders about collective skill formation via apprenticeships.

As we lack comparative research on the political determinants of VET reforms in LMEs, my main empirical contribution consists of three theory-guided case studies. These depict different institutional developments of VET and its politics in Australia, Ireland and the United Kingdom since the end of the 1970s in order to understand the processes that shape developments towards collective skill formation under unlikely conditions. To repeat the empirical puzzle this book is trying to solve: why did apprenticeships face a heavy decline in the United Kingdom, whereas the institution of apprenticeship remained relatively stable in Australia until the mid-1990s and even grew in Ireland? These divergent developments are at odds with earlier studies of skill-formation regimes. Moreover, the country cases refute claims that social protection reforms are necessary for specific skill formation (Estévez-Abe et al. 2001), as the three countries share similar liberal welfare-state arrangements (Castles 2010, Esping-Andersen 1999) and low labour market regulation (OECD 2004).

As a working hypothesis, the study builds on the central assumption of the VoC literature, which holds that mechanisms of strategic coordination contribute to specific skill formation in CMEs. As *collective skill formation regimes* display strong cooperative industrial relations and mechanisms conducive to the involvement of firms, these factors can be assumed to be crucial for the development of dual apprenticeships. Their joint governance by employers, unions and the state and their embeddedness in the wider context of macroeconomic institutions make investments in specific and portable skills attractive to apprentices and training firms alike. So, the main question is how these mechanisms are created and sustained politically under conditions that are commonly deemed to be hostile towards cooperative arrangements between capital and labour.

For the cases discussed here, previous evidence has pointed to parallel developments in apprenticeship systems and industrial relations. In the United Kingdom, unions have been effectively excluded from industrial relations since the Thatcher government (Howell 2005, Rainbird 2010, Rhodes 2000) and, despite recurrent reforms, the apprenticeship system declined (Finegold & Soskice 1988, Gospel 1995, Marsden & Ryan 1990, Rainbird 2010). On the other hand, in Ireland, apprenticeship has grown and industrial relations were governed by social partnership arrangements between trade unions and employers since 1987 until the crisis in 2009 (Baccaro & Lim 2007, O'Donnell et al. 2011, Teague & Donaghey 2009). It is generally acknowledged that social partnership contributed to the successful reforms of Irish apprenticeships (O'Connor 2006, Ryan 2005) but it is remarkable that the first steps towards reforms were initiated before the beginning of social partnership (Boyle 2005, O'Connor & Harvey 2001). Finally, like the United Kingdom, Australia has a long-standing history of apprenticeship training, but 'down under' it continues to be viable (Robinson 2001, Toner 2008) despite coming under pressure with the deregulatory industrial relations reforms of a liberal government in the middle of the 1990s (Cooney & Long 2010, Hampson 2004, Toner 2008).

As I will show, governments in all three countries have played a crucial role in structuring industrial relations and attempts to reform their apprenticeship and VET systems towards a collective model. Here, the question arises of why the governments have sometimes chosen to reform their skill formation systems towards a collective regimes, and why they did not try to move their systems towards a segmentalist or the school-based model described above (see section 2. 1). The scientific and political discourse and the economic conditions of the 1980s at least provide a partial answer.

Germany has figured prominently in studies of VET research on dual apprenticeship and was regarded as a role model for the formation of intermediate skills (Crouch et al. 2004 [1999], Culpepper 1999, Green 2001, Soskice 1994) because it contributed strongly to the competitiveness of the German economy via 'diversified quality production' (Streeck 1991), it produced low youth employment and it allowed the deployment of trained workers from shrinking to growing sectors of the economy in the course of deindustrialization. Apart from the impact of debates on the German model in policy discourses, the economic conditions of the 1980s effectively precluded a move towards the school-based system, as fiscal austerity – fuelled by high state debt and unemployment – did not allow for the creation of a cost-intensive vocational school track in secondary education systems otherwise dominated by an emphasis on academic skills. Moreover, the route towards a Japanese model of strong firm-based training, backed up by low trainee pay and strong career progression in internal labour markets, was stifled by high pay for untrained young workers (Marsden & Ryan 1990), wage accession principles based on worker seniority instead of VET certificates and – at least in Australia and Ireland – the prevalence of small and medium enterprises (SMEs), which are unsuited to provide strong internal labour markets.

Adding to these problems was the fact that craft unions were especially hostile towards the development of internal labour markets as it weakens their bargaining capacity if pay decisions are left in the hands of firms and they are excluded from collective bargaining. And last, but most important, all countries still had – albeit badly functioning – apprenticeship systems, which did not decline as early as in the United States (Gospel 1994, Thelen 2004) or were replaced by state-led vocational education in schools, as in France or Sweden, and could thus be addressed as objectives for policy reform.

What guides my analytical expectations is the suspicion that collective training systems are amongst the most complex spheres to reform by governments, as compliance with and active development of (newly) institutionalized rules for VET needs the support of the main stakeholders of the system outside government (firms, employer associations, unions and individual workers). Moreover, and more generally, training systems have an extraordinarily high conflict potential between private and public actors. To exemplify, to pursue production strategies that require a highly trained workforce, firms are dependent on the quality and type of skills that education and training systems provide. If apprenticeship systems place high financial burdens on employers and cannot provide incentives for a highly skilled workforce to pursue financially rewarding production strategies, employers will fail to comply with apprenticeship rules and eventually search for new production strategies that are less human capital intensive. On the other hand, education and training systems have to provide educational opportunities that go beyond the immediate skill requirements of firms. As pointed out above, training based on the logics of 'rational voluntarism' (Streeck 1998) of free markets will produce more suboptimal results of narrow and firm-specific skills than will systems jointly governed by the social partners (Finegold and Soskice 1988, Soskice 1994, Streeck 1989). If training is heavily geared towards the immediate skill needs of firms, it will fail to equip workers with general skills that are also relevant for other occupations and cannot, on a national economic scale, contribute to the development of 'high-skill' production strategies (Brown 2001) and might eventually contribute to a 'low-skills' equilibrium (Finegold & Soskice 1988).

To sum up, if VET systems are designed to satisfy private and public interests, the main stakeholders of the camps of business and labour will have to cooperate to sustain training institutions to prevent them from becoming too heavily geared towards either private or public interests. As the effects of training reforms need time to materialize – only new cohorts of trainees are educated according to the new standards – it is important that these coalitions are formed at the beginning of the reform process and sustained throughout the phase of implementation. This yields

Expectation 1: *Apprenticeship reforms towards the collective model can only be sustainable (i.e. policy change leads to institutional change) if they are underpinned by the emergence of a cross-class coalition of capital and labour.*

Before I outline the next expectation, a point of caution needs to be addressed. As training systems are embedded in the wider institutional context of the economy, the formation of cross-class coalitions is not assumed to be a sufficient condition for the sustainability of collective training systems. For example, bargaining decentralization can lead to the weakening of unions at the plant level and reduce their control over training content, which can in turn contribute to the decline of the on-the-job training component towards narrow, immediate firm-specific skill needs. At the same time it might lead to a decoupling of occupational status/skill and wages and reduce the incentives of firms to train because the poaching of skilled employees by competitors might become a bigger threat.[9] Under these conditions, it is plausible that cross-class coalitions supporting collective VET will only be durable if they are backed up by cooperative industrial relations that exhibit features of beneficial constraints (Streeck 1989, 1998).

The literature on the 'German model' of skill formation (Busemeyer 2009c, Finegold & Soskice 1988, Soskice 1994, Streeck 1989) also emphasized that strong intermediary capital and labour organizations and cooperative relations between them are not only beneficial to macro-economic coordination but also exert positive effects on the apprenticeship system. These findings have been corroborated by recent studies on the German apprenticeship system that point to the link between declining bargaining-coverage and lack of training slots due to changed industrial relations patterns and weakening employer organizations (Busemeyer 2009c, 2011). As the capacity for building social partnership and the impetus to pursue politics that go beyond immediate self-interests partly depends on the organizational strength and coverage of the social partners, we must analyse the intermediate organizations of capital and labour as crucial factors in the politics of VET reforms. If joint efforts to reform VET are successful this can have positive feedback effects on social partnerships. Thus, my second guiding expectation is:

9 Similar 'threats' are the influence of tertiarization and the change of financial markets towards profitability accounting and short-term capital investment. While the former pressures apprenticeships to adapt to service occupations, which mostly compete on price and not on quality, the latter can induce firms to focus on short-term competition strategies and reduce long term-investments in human capital.

Expectation 2: *Partisan governments can use VET policies in order to influence the balance of power between organized interests and influence the emergence of cross-class coalitions. Non-right-wing governments will use VET reforms to strengthen the role of unions in industrial relations and training politics. Conversely, right-wing governments will use VET reforms to weaken the role of unions in industrial relations and training politics.*

Regarding the initiation of policy change, the study builds on the classical PRT-perspective that the partisan composition of government matters substantially for the explanation of different policy agendas (Hibbs 1977, Schmidt 1982, 1996). While secular conservative parties are politically inclined to favour the upper classes and free-market policies, social-democratic parties and Christian-democratic parties can be assumed to employ social and educational politics that economically favour the working and the middle classes (Iversen & Stephens 2008). In this sense, Christian democratic governments have to be differentiated from secular conservative governments. Christian democratic parties can be expected to favour politics that already include the interests of labour and capital (van Kersbergen 1995) due to the principle of subsidiarity and should thus be favourable towards collective skill formation. This is supported by the fact that we find collective skill formation in countries with strong Christian-democratic parties: Austria, Germany, the Netherlands and Switzerland.[10] Here, the main question is how parties achieve well-balanced compromises between capital and labour.

The present study builds on this insight in arguing that partisan governments do not only directly structure the components of vocational education outside firms, but also largely define the 'rules of the game' under which industrial relations and conflict between capital and labour take place. The take-away from the present study is that we do not only have to analyse how governments directly influence VET policies but also how they structure industrial relations and to which organized actors they grant privileged access to policy-making.

10 This explanation is limited by the case of Denmark.

However, for non-right-wing parties a point of caution has to be emphasized, which is related to the changed logic of economic policy making in the context of the transformation from a system of 'embedded liberalism' (Ruggie 1982) towards an 'open economy' (Scharpf 2000a, b). Under these new conditions and mainly due to increased capital mobility, there are effective limits on the financial burdens that might be placed on large firms via taxes, social security contributions and mandated human capital investments, as firms, which do not profit from the institutional comparative advantage offered by a national economy, might relocate parts of their production to less cost-intensive national economies. This in turn means that apprenticeship systems have to be more responsive to firms' skill needs for production and to offer the option to update occupations and apprenticeship in line with economic changes, than was the case under the conditions of 'domestically dominated' economies. The same applies for small and medium enterprises, which might not have the capacity to relocate their production but will only support more elaborate curricula of apprenticeships if governments offer them support via joint training facilities that are able to fulfil the requirements of updated curricula.

Under these conditions, there might be effective limits to the constraints that might be placed on firms via training requirements. Thus non-right-wing governments might have to offer some kind of compensation to businesses in order to entice them to cooperate in training reforms towards collective skill formation, of which one example could be securing wage restraint on the part of the union movement. More generally, as the involvement of *both* sides of producer interests matters for the development of sustainable collective solutions towards apprenticeships, parties will not only have to incorporate the relevant interests of voters and interest groups they are traditionally affiliated with, but will also have to include the interests of adversarial groups into policy-making and thus potentially contribute to the formation of cross-class coalitions.

Finally, the expectations above have to be placed in an historical context because we have to account for earlier developments to understand how much scope for political action there is and which actor-constellations political legacies have left. Independent of the composition of government, it can be assumed that the scope of government policy will be determined largely not only by institutional veto-points of the national polity such as second parliamentary chambers or strong constitutional courts, but also by political legacies of the past (Rose & Davies 1994) and path-dependent developments (Pierson 2000a, 2004). Furthermore, we have to be aware of other domestic and international influences that exert exogenous pressure on the politics of VET reforms, which will be taken up in the case studies where appropriate.[11] Thus, for the impact of reforms across time, I base my analysis on

Expectation 3: *Training reforms produce positive feedback effects. Institutional change toward the marketization of training in LMEs will make it harder for subsequent governments to pursue reforms towards collective skill formation. Conversely, institutional change towards collective skill formation will make it harder for subsequent governments to dismantle collective VET (i.e. marketization).*

This hypothesis is based on the assumption that historical 'critical junctures' (Capoccia & Kelemen 2007) remove a number of policy choices from the menu of options for subsequent governments. Furthermore, firms, individuals and unions may adapt their strategies towards training institutions in the medium term, even if they were no supporters of the respective reforms in the first place. This may be due to mechanisms of positive policy feedback, which change the incentive structure of a system's central stakeholders or the impact that critical junctures have on the relative power of involved actors. These two distinct possibilities will be further explored in the case studies in the following chapters, which analyse the partisan politics of skill formation reforms and their impact on the four defining dimensions of collective skill formation in each case under study.

11 Some additional factors can impact on VET and will be accounted for if they emerged as important factors in the case studies. They are socio-economic influences (budgetary pressure, unemployment, inflation, service-sector growth), international influences and reforms in spheres of the economy that affect the provision and politics of VET.

3. United Kingdom – much ado about nothing and the persistence of voluntarism?

From a contemporary perspective, the British case[12] can be seen as a paradigmatic example of a *liberal market economy* and a *liberal skill-formation regime*. Regarding the former, relationships between firms (and, on a larger scale, employer associations), governments and unions are governed by arms-lengths market mechanisms with very little sign of strategic coordination. Yet, until the early 1980s, there were frequent attempts at bargaining centralization, Keynesian demand management and greater cooperation in industrial relations (Howell 2005), leading Hall (1992) to argue that Britain represented more of a mixed than a pure liberal market economy. Similarly, Pontusson (2005) points out that its institutions were based on 'institutionalized class compromise', albeit without the strong business coordination found in CMEs. Concerning *liberal skill formation*, the education system is very much geared towards general academic education and higher education, which is primarily privately financed via tuition fees. Compared to higher education, VET plays a much smaller role in national skill formation, and has for most part, since World War II been based on voluntarist cooperation between employers, unions and the state (King 1993, 1997). In sum, we can nowadays detect few institutional characteristics of collective skill formation.

First, *firm involvement* in initial VET is low, with a significant proportion of training costs sponsored by the state via 'quasi-markets' in which private and public agencies compete for public funds and in turn offer training to employers. Second, the *involvement of intermediary associations*,

12 The process of devolution and decentralization in the United Kingdom has resulted in some differences in the institutional set-up of VET in England, Wales and Scotland. The following exclusively refers to the developments in England even if I at times use Britain or the United Kingdom this is meant to denote England. Moreover, the differences between England, Wales and Scotland are minor when compared to the other two cases, Australia and Ireland.

with the Confederation of British Industry (CBI) and the Trade Union Congress (TUC) as the respective peak organizations of capital and labour, in standard-setting and VET-governance is very limited and relegated only to an advisory role in most government decisions on VET. Third, but related to the former aspects, *training content for in-firm training and off-the-job training* (i.e. training standards and certification) is only standardized to a small extent due to huge differences between training providers and training standards. While occupational skills are certified, they are less portable because of the disparate training standards and a concomitantly lower signalling value of employees' skills. Finally, while *dual training* models that combine workplace training with off-the-job training exist, these offer very little educational content, which has led several commentators to characterize them primarily as labour-market programmes with a training component (Gospel 1995, King 1993, Marsden & Ryan 1990, Ryan & Unwin 2001).

However, following the theoretical approach of the book, the contemporary perspective is placed in a historical context in order to explain how England arrived at being a liberal skill-formation system. While Thelen (2004) has shown how class conflicts between artisans, employers and emerging unions at the end of the 19th century and the beginning of the 20th have shaped countries' development paths towards an increasing or diminishing role for VET, her focus on these early critical junctures must be taken with a grain of salt for the explanation of the development that followed after World War II and profoundly transformed the United Kingdom towards a liberal skill-formation regime. Historically, in the United Kingdom, collective approaches to VET did not have a fertile ground because skill and certification were heavily contested along the class divide between employers and craft unions (Dingeldey 1996, Thelen 2004). However, Gospel (1994) has shown that, despite this contestation, it did not lead to a profound decline in apprenticeships until much later and, in similar vein, Busemeyer (2015) argues that institutional patterns of VET and education-systems more generally had been very similar across Western Europe at the end of the war, while the critical juncture towards a liberal skill formation regime happened much later with the arrival of the Thatcher administration (Busemeyer 2015, Fuller & Unwin 2009, UK-10).

In line with these contributions, the case study shows how initial VET has developed in the United Kingdom towards becoming paradigmatic of a liberal skill-formation regime. Following the theoretical argument of the book, the main analytical emphasis is on how relationships between employers, unions and governments have shaped VET policies and especially on how governments used VET policies in order to mould the politics of institutional change in their preferred direction. The case study shows, *inter alia,* that, even in the contested area of VET, there were frequent attempts by both Labour and Conservative governments to transform skill formation towards more collective approaches, which, however, did not succeed. These developments are shown by carefully tracing VET and industrial-relations politics in three periods.

The first period analyses institutional changes up to the arrival of the Thatcher government in 1979. It is characterized by 'corporatist experiments' in VET and industrial relations undertaken by governments of both major parties, which, however, failed to shore up apprenticeships under the Industrial Training Boards (ITBs) and Manpower Service Commission (MSC) in the 1960s and 1970s, and did not lead to a stable development towards more coordination between employers and unions. The second period is characterized by marked reforms under the Thatcher governments (1979–1990), which developed the Youth Training Scheme (YTS) as a major employment programme, ended tripartite institutions of training governance and, more generally, curtailed union rights. The profound changes in industrial relations of this period and the transformation of initial VET away from collective approaches towards labour market programmes were the critical juncture that finally set the United Kingdom on a liberal path of skill formation. The third and final period of analysis takes stock of the reforms enacted by the Conservative government of Major and the 'New Labour' governments of Blair and Brown, up to 2008. While they resulted in increasing centralization and continuous reforms of VET institutions under the subsequent Conservative and New Labour governments, they had little effect on the expansion of high-quality, 'German-style' training despite much reform activity.

3.1 The historical background – contestation and failed state interventions

> In Britain the constellation of interests was such that skill formation was contested first and foremost across the class divide, between unions of skilled workers and employers tenaciously resisting craft controls at all turns. This competition, not surprisingly, proved destructive to apprenticeship when no system of joint regulation could be negotiated. (Thelen 2004: 145)

In England, the apprenticeship system traditionally rested on a tenacious balance between the interests of craft unions and employers. In light of little regulation put forward by national legislation, the standards of apprenticeships in terms of employment conditions, training content and apprentice pay were settled by voluntarist agreements between craft unions and employers in skill-intensive sectors. Skilled craft workers' unions sought to use their influence on training and restrictive workplace practices as a means to control the supply of skilled labour, and by this means its ultimate price on labour markets (Dingeldey 1996, Thelen 2004, UK-10).[13] Employers, who 'were suspicious of craft unions' skill control' practices (UK-2), ferociously tried to limit union involvement in training and workplace organization, traditionally rallied around an agenda of 'defending firm autonomy' (Thelen 2004: 146) and, where they succeeded in struggles with craft unions, they used apprentices and training regulations as they saw fit for their immediate production needs.

Thus, firms and craft unions alike were not concerned so much with training content or collective approaches in the institutional regulation of training but instead sought to use apprenticeships as a bargaining chip in

13 Notably, British craft unions were eager to protect rigid job demarcations as an attempt to control the supply of skilled labour by limiting the flexibility of production processes. This stands in stark contrast to union strategies aimed at multi-skilling and equipping workers with general skills in order to maximize their employability in many occupations and – in turn – to make them less dependent on the present employer. On this issue, Williams (1963: 204) argued that Britain 'is the only European country in which the unions believe they are protecting their members by refusing to allow one worker to undertake jobs normally done by another [...] In other countries [...] unions are anxious for their members to have as wide a training as possible so that they have greater security of employment by the ease with which they can move from one branch of the work to another.'

their strategies to defend managerial prerogative or the wages of skilled workers. The lack of statutory regulation also helped to shore up the traditional structure of apprenticeship, as the completion of apprenticeships was not based on competences attained or the passing of formal (school- and firm-based) exams but on the time that was served as an apprentice (Gospel 1995, UK-10). In the period before the Second World War, this had led to frequent skill shortages, high apprentice wages and serious poaching problems for the few firms that adhered to high training standards, which led contemporary commentators to the conclusion that the approaches to skill formation between employers and unions were based on very short-sighted strategies (Zeitlin 2005, 2008). Until the early 1960s, the post-war governments of Labour (1945–1951) and the Conservatives (1951–1964) showed very little initiative for reforms in the area of VET, and also followed a rather non-interventionist approach towards decentralized industrial relations (Howell 2005).

Despite the contested nature of training between individual employers and craft unions, more consensual positions were evident between the peak organizations of capital and labour and also between the two main political parties. Regarding the former, the British Employers' Confederation (BEC) (which became the Confederation of British Industry (CBI) in 1965) and the Trade Union Congress (TUC) issued a joint report that recommended creating National Joint Apprenticeship Councils, with unions very keen to preserve their influence on training under these new structures and large industrial employers with the perception of unregulated industrial training as a hindrance to international competitiveness (Perry 1976). This initiative must be considered cautiously, as the BEC/CBI and the TUC traditionally are rather decentralized associations with little power over their individual members (Crouch 1993, Traxler et al. 2001).

With regard to political parties, education policy after the war was based on a cross-party consensus between the Labour Party and the Conservatives, who in principle agreed to expand secondary education as set down by the Butler Education Act of 1944. Yet this consensus was also based on rather loose regulations regarding the specific design of schools, which enabled a large variety of different schools to have only minimal emphasis on school-based VET (Busemeyer 2015). Moreover, both major parties left the apprenticeship system and voluntarism as its organizational basis untouched until the Conservative Party passed the Industrial Training Act in 1964, which created 27 Industrial Training Boards (ITBs) and made provisions for a system of training levies and grants in order to finance industrial skill formation as one of the two major innovations in training policy up to 1979. The second innovation was the creation of the Manpower Service Commission (MSC) by the Conservative Heath government in 1973, which was intended to become a major carrier for developing training and manpower policies. However, its institutionalization was accompanied by major changes to the levy grant system. The new provisions allowed firms to apply for exemption from the levy grant system, which they used frequently and thus undercut the collective dimension of VET finance (Senker 1992).

In the following, the political genesis of the two institutions is described in order to give a historical background to explain why these changes were not able to sustain collective approaches to skill formation (Ainley & Vickerstaff 1993, Evans 1992, Gospel 1995, Finegold & Soskice 1988, Fuller & Unwin 2009, King 1997). It is this context against which the changes under Thatcher and the subsequent Conservative and New Labour governments have to be understood.

The passage of the Industrial Training Act, which was intended to break with the voluntarist principles that apprenticeships rested on, followed after 'a "great debate" on training between 1958 and 1962' (Senker 1992: 28.).[14] The context of this debate was that governments became increasingly worried about Britain's poor economic performance compared to other European competitors, with an undersupply of training identified as a central factor for this shortcoming (Senker 1992). A major source informing the debates in policy and business cycles was the Carr Report, which was published early in 1958 and stressed the need for greater industry involvement in skill formation by succinctly asking 'whether industries have sufficiently reckoned the cost of not training – in terms of increased labour turnover, lower output, greater scrap and the like' (NJAC 1958).

While the Conservative government in principle acknowledged the responsibility of employers for industrial training, a central question was how to get more employers involved in its provision. Here, the government

14 At the same time a tripartite Industrial Training Council (ITC) was set up, but to encourage training it relied mostly on exhortation (Senker 1992).

pondered two main alternatives: first, a subsidy to employers for training apprentices and, second, a compulsory training levy. The first possibility was quickly discounted because in this case 'the question of government supervision would raise its ugly head ... [and] a proposal to introduce a system of inspection would lead to considerable opposition within industry' (John Hare, Minister of Labour, September 1960; cited in Senker 1992: 29). Subsequently, the government pursued the idea of a training levy, which was underpinned by the publication of the White Paper, Industrial Training: Government Proposals in 1962. As it set out in paragraphs 5 and 6, the voluntarist underpinnings of training and the uneven distribution of training were identified as major problems:

> A serious weakness in our present arrangements is that the amount and quality of industrial training are left to the *unco-ordinated* [sic!] decisions of a large number of individual firms. These may lack the necessary economic incentive to invest in training people who, once trained, may leave them for other jobs. While the benefits of training are shared by all, the cost is borne only by those firms which decide to undertake training themselves ... The Government has therefore decided that the time has come to strengthen and improve the existing partnership between industry, the Government and education authorities in the provision of industrial training. (Ministry of Labour 1962: 3–4)

The central proposal of the White Paper was the establishment of boards with members from government and both sides of industry that were to be responsible for training within individual industries. At this point, it became evident that the government was moving strongly in favour of legislative reform, and unions and employers alike publicly welcomed the White Paper. Senker's (1992) interpretation is broadly consistent with the well-known argument of Hacker and Pierson (2002: 283–285) about expressed policy preferences[15] of actors once an issue is locked in on the public policy agenda and approaching governmental decision making:

15 Hacker and Pierson (2002: 283) argue that we should take public statements of stakeholders cautiously as 'a group's actions often will not reveal its preferences but rather its strategic calculations of what is the best that can be accomplished given existing circumstances. An actor's expressed policy preferences may in fact be "induced" or "strategic" – that is they reflect accommodations to circumstances that constrain what can be achieved.'

> Having accepted that the tide was now moving strongly in favour of legislation, unions and employers all wanted to ensure that they were in a position to influence legislation and policies, and to secure effective representation of their interests in future arrangements. (Senker 1992: 32)

The boards envisaged by the White Paper were the centrepieces of the Conservative government's Industrial Training Act 1964, which was passed with the full support of the Labour opposition and with support from broad segments of employers and unions alike (Perry 1976, Senker 1992). The establishment of the first ITBs, which were expanded to 27 VET areas, began in the following summer and was continued by the incoming Wilson Labour government, when it took office in October. The Boards generally had a tripartite structure and were composed of educational, union and employer representatives, with the latter being appointed by the Secretary of State for Employment after consultation with employer organizations and trade unions. The government also created the Central Training Council (CTC), composed of six union and six employer representatives, for consultation on training policy. However, the CTC only had an advisory role and no statutory powers or control over ITBs, which was heavily criticized by the unions (King 1993).

With the benefit of hindsight, the Industrial Training Act was quite a remarkable endeavour at changing the structure that had traditionally underpinned vocational training in the United Kingdom.[16] In fact, the provisions of the Act even came earlier and went further than the legislation of German VET at that time (Busemeyer 2015), especially in its financial dimension. Under the new structures of tripartite governance of the ITBs and CTC, the principle mechanism designed to improve the poor supply of training slots were ITBs' statutory powers to raise a training levy in their respective sector. A part of the levy was intended to cover ITBs running costs but the bulk of it was to be redistributed as grants to firms providing satisfactory training and to cover their off-the-job training costs. In principle, for their sector, ITBs were responsible for developing training standards and were allowed to set their own levels of levies and grants, which were negotiated by the Board members from both sides of the industry. The power to raise a levy opened

16 Indeed, Corina (1975: 195) described the Industrial Training Act as featuring among the 'largest-scale attempts at structural change in Britain'.

up the possibility for a more even distribution of costs between those firms that trained and those that relied on poaching skilled labour from their competitors. But, more generally, the Industrial Training Act was a device for government to exhort non-training firms to invest in skill formation (Mukherjee 1970: 32–33, cited in Senker 1992).

Despite the new tripartite structure to regulate training on a sectoral basis and the levy-grant system as the principal mechanism to increase training investments, the Industrial Training Act had some shortcomings that hampered its effectiveness in expanding vocational training (King 1993, Pemberton 2001, Senker 1992). First, it did not fundamentally alter the statutory basis for apprenticeships. Training remained based on the principle of time serving, with no compulsory technical education. Assessment standards for apprentice certification were not set on a comprehensive basis as the economist Gertrude Williams had suggested in her seminal study on apprenticeship in Europe, pointing to reform lessons for industrial training in Britain (Williams 1963). Thus, training provision 'remained essentially decentralized within the individual firm' (Ziderman 1978: 41, cited in Senker 1992: 33).

Second, a central difference lay in the size of the new sectoral organizations. At the end of the 1970s the two largest ITBs – the Engineering Industrial Training Board (EITB) and the Distribution Industry Training Board (DITB) – covered 2.8 million and 2.25 million employees respectively while the Air Transport and Travel Industry Training Board (ATTITB) did not even have one-twentieth of their size with 123 000 employees under its scope (Senker 1992: 56–59). This also meant that the levy decision was strongly influenced by the prevailing power relations between unions and employers in the individual training boards. As the boards were quite autonomous from central government, the levies and approaches towards developing training standards grew extremely variable from board to board (Corina 1975). Moreover, the sectoral structure of the boards inhibited common approaches to skills that crosscut economic sectors. Finally, while the levy/grant system acted as a stimulus to training and to the equalization of training costs among different firms, small firms[17] were very critical towards the new ITB structure from the

17 One interviewee (UK-9) argued that this also applied to larger employers, which were especially critical of the administrative burdens connected to paying levies and collecting grants.

start and especially critical towards the levy-grant system (Anderson & Fairley 1983: 196, Perry 1976, Senker 1992). A central complaint among small firms, which were – qua size – underrepresented on the ITBs, was that the training boards' standards for collecting levies and distributing grants were not suited to the needs of small firms, many of which had to pay the levy but few received grants.

This provided an impetus for a discussion about the exemption of small firms from the levy in 1967, which was finally decided within the reform of the Industrial Training Act in 1973. This reform, described further below, came as a mixed blessing as, on the one hand, it instituted the tripartite MSC that was intended as corporatist centralized body with the aim of developing a comprehensive training and labour market policy, but on the other hand it increasingly undercut the effectiveness of the ITBs.

Discussions about the levy/grant system had already begun under the Wilson Labour government. A committee that inquired into the usefulness of the levy/grant system acknowledged that it was ill suited to small firms and recommended to exempt them from the levy, but in principle acknowledged that it had increased training efforts of firms across the board.[18] The tide of discussion turned, however. After the 1970 general election, a Conservative government had returned into office, which was committed to 'closely examine the work of the Industrial Training Boards and the operation of the levy/grant system so as to root out unnecessary bureaucracy' (Senker 1992: 39). The consultative process that followed led to the publication of a Green Paper in 1971, which recommended the progressive phasing out of the levy/grant system, as had been demanded by parts of the employers' camp since its inception (Perry 1976: 285–286, Senker 1992: 40–42). When it seemed that the government intended to follow this proposal, it encountered the expected resistance by unions, but parts of the employers' camp also joined in.

A CBI review of the Industrial Training Act recommended sustaining the levy/grant system. It stated that despite 'all the faults and shortcomings of the present system, the CBI considers that it can provide a sound basis for developing [sic] future strategy in industrial training' (Senker 1992: 43). A joint letter by the CBI and the TUC urged the

18 The Bolton Committee in principle advocated the continuation of the ITB levy/grant structure (Senker 1992).

government to proceed with caution and requested more consultation before an eventual reform, signalling the willingness to react swiftly if the government was to push through with its proposals. The CBI's position also reflected a cautious approach towards dismantling the ITB system, as a more centralized approach to training, which the unions had long been lobbying for, still did not seem entirely impossible (Ainley & Vickerstaff 1993, Evans 1992, Perry 1976).

The final compromise embodied in the reform of the Industrial Training Act in 1973 was intended to appeal to *both* camps of the conflict. The levy/grant system was effectively replaced by a levy/grant/exemption system, under which firms had to demonstrate that they were training according to their own needs in order to be exempted from the levy (Perry 1976), while the levies that could be imposed were limited to a maximum of 1% of the firm's payroll (Senker 1992: 45). A further development came close to levies being effectively abandoned as firms could easily escape the levies under the new regulations (Lee 1989, Senker 1992). Moreover, widespread exemptions seriously undercut the funding for ITBs training services and administrating the exemption proved far more onerous for the ITB staff than the administration of levies and grants had been. The new exemption regulation also weakened the institution stability, as VET reforms need a rather long time until their benefits occur to employers and workers (UK-3).

On the other hand, as an appeal to trade unions and an exchange for wage moderation, a national training agency had been discussed within the consultations of the ITB reforms and the changes to the levy/grant system. The new agency was to take over the Training Opportunities Scheme (TOPS)[19] from the Department of Employment, but also coordinate training that did not lie in the ITBs remits, i.e. cross-cutting occupations and training services for firms not belonging to an ITB. It was also to provide financial support for those ITBs whose finances were not sufficient due to ceasing levy/grant schemes.[20] The CBI opposed the training agency, but it was adamantly supported by the Trade Unions (Sheldrake & Vickerstaff 1987: 56–57), and incorporated into the

19 TOPS was to provide VET for adults who wished to acquire new skills and financed accredited off-the-job training (Stevens 1999).

20 Indeed, most ITBs increasingly had to rely on funding by the MSC after 1973 (Senker 1992).

functions of the tripartite MSC that the Employment and Training Act of 1973 had created.[21] The MSC was essentially composed of two agencies – an Employment and Services Agency (ESA) and a Training Services Agency (TSA), whose relationship to the ITBs was rather loose at first (UK-9). As early as 1975, the TSA came forward with a report that stressed the inadequate amount of industrial training provided by employers under the existing institutional arrangements (Training Services Agency 1975). In order to counter chronic skill shortages that became evident throughout economic cycles, it made a radical proposal for a substantial change in training finances, arguing that:

> the best hope for improvement in the supply of young persons with long-term transferable skills would be through measures which enable individual employers to be refunded the full cost of all training off-the-job, at any rate in the first year, through a collective funding arrangement of some kind, and which make decisions about numbers subject to some form of influence beyond the short-term outlook of individual employers. (Training Services Agency 1975: 23–25)

This proposal for a different funding arrangement and more control about the training intake ran quite radically opposite not only to the recently decided move to levy exemption, but also to individual firms' prerogatives in making training decisions. While the TUC expressed strong support for the proposals, the Labour government that had come into office after a miners' strike had brought down the Heath government in 1974, 'was not prepared to press ahead in the face of employers' opposition' (Senker 1992: 49).[22] With collective funding effectively taken off the menu of options, the MSC was left to approach employment and training policy in a largely uncoordinated fashion (Senker 1992). When unemployment worsened throughout 1976, the MSC became increasingly occupied with youth unemployment and special temporary work programmes. As a major programme that complemented TOPS, the MSC introduced the Youth Opportunities Programme (YOP) in 1978

21 A ten-member commission managed the MSC with three representatives from the CBI and TUC each. Further members were two local authority representatives, an academic and a government-appointed Chairman. The same pattern was reproduced in regional area manpower boards.

22 Interestingly, in early 1976, the MSC tried again to lobby for a collective funding arrangement in *Training for Vital Skills: A consultative document*.

as a temporary work experience scheme that consisted of a one-year training and work experience for the young unemployed. The spending for these two programmes rose rapidly, but:

> did little to improve skills, however, since the funds were concentrated on temporary employment, work experience and short-course training measures and the demands for quick action prevented any long-term manpower planning. (Finegold & Soskice 1998: 30)

More important, these programmes already signalled the beginning of *training as employment policy* broadly continued and enlarged under Thatcher's three consecutive governments.

The limited effect of the ambitious training reforms of 1964 can be seen as evidence that policy change does not necessarily lead to institutional change if it does not alter the preferences and/or behaviour of key actors (Vossiek 2017). Despite the introduction of the ITB system, it failed to radically alter the post-war configuration of conflict between employers and (especially craft) unions over training – essentially leaving the voluntarist training framework intact. This applies for Labour *and* the Conservatives – for both VET hardly fell into the remit of governmental responsibility (UK-11). Both refrained from creating VET statutory regulations regarding training duration, provision and content and thus underwrote that training remained based primarily on the principle of voluntarist regulation between employers and unions.

However, despite the shortcomings of the institutional structures of the ITBs and the MSC, other secular developments worked against the goals of shoring up industrial training and bringing its quality and standards on par with continental competitors. First, manufacturing had already begun to decline when the reforms were enacted and this process continued throughout the 1970s and 1980s (Gospel & Druker 1998, Lee 1989). This decline contributed to shrinking apprenticeship places (UK-9), which receded from roughly 220 000 in 1970 to a mere 73 000 in 1985 (Lee 1989: 159).[23]

Second, the VET reforms were only loosely connected to reforms in industrial relations (UK-1), which could have potentially created beneficial constraints and could have helped to create incentives for

23 These numbers should be taken cautiously, as YTS already started in 1983.

employers to invest more heavily in VET and human capital. While there were frequent attempts to move industrial relations to stronger bargaining coordination immediately after the war and up until the 1970s (Crouch 1993), these efforts were hampered by little employer coordination and a growing shop-steward movement over which the central unions had little control and which contributed to fragmented wage bargaining. This led to frequent wage hikes because individual craft unions held a strong bargaining position and worked against TUC strategies to exchange wage moderation for welfare state reforms (Rhodes 2000). It also meant that wage differentials between apprentices and skilled worker had narrowed substantially as craft unions had pushed up apprentice wages in order to prevent the substitution of skilled workers by cheaper apprentices (UK-2). This, in turn, reduced employers' willingness to invest in apprentices (Marsden & Ryan 1990). In the same vein, fragmented bargaining structures hampered ITB's effort where industrial sectors switched from multi-employer to single employer bargaining (UK-1), which meant that the levy system was not underpinned by equalized wage floors for skilled workers that could have been additional safeguards against poaching. Put differently, 'apprenticeship had ended' in the late 1970s (UK-9).

Desmond King (1995: 161–165) argues, in a similar manner, that the links between training and labour market policies remained weakly developed before the advent of the Thatcher governments. In line with the present argumentation, he traces this back to the prevailing preferences among organized interests and partisan governments. The 'tenuous nature of the political coalition[s] promoting reform' (King 1995: 161) meant that the ITB initiative failed to break the reluctance that the FBI/CBI as well as the trade unions held towards training with the prevailing conflict between job control and managerial prerogative on the employers' side and wage control strategies by skilled workers' on the unions' side.

When Labour governments held office (1964–1966, 1975–1979), they only had narrow electoral majorities. Difficult economic circumstances and close ties to the union movement prevented a more holistic approach towards training and industrial relations policies (Minkin 1991). When the MSC was instituted in 1973, a more comprehensive approach to training seemed possible but the introduction of the levy/grant/exemption system undercut the effectiveness the ITBs had in reforming VET, especially with regard to the involvement of firms. Mounting unemployment in the aftermath of the first oil-crisis also meant that the MSC's resources were increasingly devoted to programmes for the unemployed, which worked against comprehensive VET reform. Changes in VET under the Thatcher government have to be seen in the context of this 'failed revolution' (Pemberton 2001).

3.2 The critical juncture – Thatcher's anti-union politics and employment-led restructuring (1979–1990)

> Government economic policy was dominated by the belief that controlling the money supply and public expenditure were the keys to reducing inflation and restoring competitiveness. Education and training accounted for approximately 15 per cent of the budget and thus needed to be cut if spending was to be curtailed. The cuts included: across the board reductions in education funding, a drop in state subsidies for apprenticeships and the abolition of [...] training boards [...] The financial rationale for the cuts was underpinned by the then strongly held view of the government that training decisions were better left to market forces. (Finegold & Soskice 1988: 31)

When the Thatcher government took office in 1979 it was prepared to change the institutions of the British political economy. This entailed, *inter alia,* welfare state retrenchment (Pierson 1994, Rhodes 2000), stabilization of the pound with monetarist policies (Hall 1992), the curtailment of the public sector with a massive privatization of public utilities (Rhodes 2000) and, most important for the focus of the present study, fundamental reform of industrial relations away from largely unsuccessful attempts at neo-corporatist coordination and towards a purer form of interest group pluralism and coordination via markets.

The prime mechanisms for achieving the latter were the dismantling of tripartite institutions, and, more specifically, the curtailment of union power, which was directly attacked by stripping off union wage-bargaining and strike rights with the intention of breaking the seemingly uncontrollable shop-floor movement that had often hampered neo-corporatist wage coordination in the post-war decades (Howell 2005, Rhodes 2000). These politics of class warfare against the unions allowed employers to reach wage settlements with non-unionized workers and thus enhanced business power to arrive at lower wage levels. On the policy level, this strategy was complemented by instituting a regime of 'workfare' (Jessop 1993) in employment policy that introduced in-work benefits, cut replacement levels of unemployment compensation and tightened eligibility criteria to access these benefits (Pierson 1994, Rhodes 2000).

Despite these direct measures to free the economy from the grip of unions and to make coordination more market based, the Thatcher government also used training policies as an *indirect method* to reign in powerful unions. As pointed out previously, training constituted a source of power for (craft) unions to exert pressure in wage bargaining by controlling the number of skilled workers. Moreover, unions had traditionally used apprenticeships to shore up their own power base by recruiting young workers as members. In training policy, neither ITBs nor the MSC had provided effective challenges to the institutional underpinnings of apprenticeships as the main form of industrial training – these institutions were simply too 'weak and facilitated the maintenance of existing priorities amongst employers and *trade unions*' (King 1993: 220, emphasis added).

As I will show, the Thatcher governments progressively stripped away union influence from training and thus weakened the vestige of power that the unions had traditionally possessed in wage bargaining. However, the government had to move cautiously as it needed the unions' cooperation via the MSC in order to deliver labour market programmes in the face of economic turmoil and mounting (youth) unemployment. In the initial stages of training reform it therefore had to refrain from a direct attack on union control. Only later did it achieve a reduction in union power over VET via consecutive training reforms throughout the 1980s, which left their mark as they lastingly removed the unions as central players in training politics.

Apart from the inherited voluntarist legacy in training, one has to account for the economic problems that the Thatcher government faced when it came to power in 1979 in order to understand the events in training policy and politics throughout the 1980s. During the 1970s the economic situation had dramatically worsened, especially after the first oil crisis had hit in 1973. Without a stable mechanism in wage bargaining to underpin Keynesian anti-cyclical policies, 'stagflation' ensued and unemployment continued to rise. These developments had their peak in the famous 'winter of discontent' in 1978/79, when public and private sector workers joined forces in reaction to high inflation and falling real wages, which caused militancy and strikes to rise to unprecedented levels. However, not all voters from a working class background were content with these protests against falling wages and the defence of wage differentials. Rhodes concludes that what the working class movement got out of this strategy 'was Margaret Thatcher' (Rhodes 2000: 35). Faced with high inflation, a stagnating economy, high rates of unemployment (OECD various-a, various-b) and failed attempts to reach agreements on wage restraint in a decentralized bargaining system, the Thatcher government embarked on a course of deregulation based on neoliberal premises (Gospel 1995; King 1993; 1997; Rhodes 2000).

In the second half of the 1970s, apprenticeships had already begun to decline significantly (UK-9) as a side effect of the economic turmoil Britain found itself in. Alongside general unemployment, youth unemployment rose significantly and the new government was pressed hard to tackle the problem, as it was a primary concern to voters (UK-9, Finegold & Soskice 1988: 32, Senker 1992: 54) and the MSC could provide training as a means to address the 'potentially explosive issue of unemployment' (Ainley & Corney 1990: 49). This can be seen as a primary reason, why the MSC was kept intact – it had the institutional capacity to deliver programmes targeted at unemployed (Evans 1992, Senker 1992, UK-9). Until its demise in the late 1980s, it remained the major carrier for unemployment programmes and training, which was transformed from classical apprenticeships towards employment programmes with a training component (Ryan & Unwin 2001). Similarly, the government increasingly directed the MSC's budget and thereby limited resources to plan and implement the envisaged training reforms. In the terminology of institutional change, this was a case of *institutional conversion* as the MSC – originally installed to shore up and reform apprenticeship training – now became directed to other purposes.

Leaving the MSC intact was more of a strategic move than a sign of commitment towards tripartite, collective structures in VET governance, which were progressively dismantled in order to strengthen the independence and flexibility of individual employers in skill formation

(Evans 1992, King 1997). Regarding governance, one of the first reforms of the new government was to abolish most ITBs in 1982, thus ending the levy/grant/exemption system as the primary financial mechanism to induce employer participation (Rainbird 2010, Senker 1992).

Quite naturally, as institutions where the unions still played an important role and as there were few institutional alternatives for training delivery, the MSC had not endorsed the abolition of ITBs, but instead recommended to keep six ITBs[24] (Senker 1992: 57). Against this view, there were critical voices from businesses and contemporary researchers arguing that the ITBs had not been effective and, in some cases, even helped to shore up restrictive trade-union practices via traditional and rigid apprenticeships (Senker 1992: 60–65). The passage of the 1982 Employment and Training Act withdrew funding for the running costs of the ITBs and allowed for the Secretary of State for Employment to abolish two thirds of the ITBs.[25] The remaining ITBs, where in some case the industry had a united front and massively opposed the government's plans to abolish their respective ITB (UK-12), now had to finance their running costs by a non-refundable levy.

The sectoral differences among ITBs and the resistance they put up against eventual dismantling were also influenced by power relationships within the ITBs – dismantling was easier where union representation was low and in most ITBs of the service sector, where employers had traditionally been very reluctant to train (UK-12, UK-4). Stripped of financial support from the MSC and government, most of the remaining ITBs vanished in the course of the 1980s or evolved into voluntary Industry Training Organisations (ITOs) without statutory power. Construction was the only sector where a tripartite council is still responsible for training governance and makes use of a levy-grant system (UK-12). Thus, the Act of 1982 was the first hard hit for the unions, as statutory representation at the sectoral level of training governance had been abolished and this had taken away their influence over training provision and design. The government not only weakened unions in training governance via

24 The ITBs recommended for retention were engineering, construction, hotel and catering, road transport, clothing and allied products, and rubber and plastics processing.

25 All ITBs except those recommended for retention (see above) and the ITB for off-shore petroleum (Senker 1992: 62)

the abolition of the ITBs, but also devised training policies whose design worked *in favour* of a growing employer prerogative in training.

Based on the MSCs New Training Initiative (NTI) in 1981, a permanent VET programme for Britain's school leavers was envisaged that could reduce youth unemployment and add to national skill formation. While the MSC envisaged the creation of a permanent programme as part of a long-term strategy of skill formation and industrial restructuring, government saw it as welcoming opportunity to signal its commitment to fight youth unemployment (Senker 1992, UK-9). On a larger scale, the NTI was based on three central pillars: to devise a training programme with certification standards that did not rely on time serving, to combat youth unemployment, and to reform continuing VET for adults. But it also promoted the view that training would best be provided by individual firms free of the ITB's obligations and that initial vocational training should be supported by payment rates to training firms, especially for the off-the-job component, in order to boost employer-take up of training (UK-9).

As the central outcome of the New Training Initiative, the Youth Training Scheme (YTS)[26] was launched in 1983. It was the follow-up programme to its predecessor, the YOP, which had grown to 550 000 places in just four years of existence and had attracted growing 'criticism [...] for its failing job replacement rates and poor quality training' (Finegold & Soskice 1988: 32). For the government, YTS was an opportunity to hollow out union power and to introduce a

> modernized apprenticeship system that would *at last* replace the outmoded, skill-specific craft training of the ITBs. In its stead, the New Training Initiative would produce the flexible, multiskilled workers of the future, able to move across old craft boundaries to apply core skills in a variety of circumstances. (Ainley & Corney 1990: 53 cont., italics added by author)

The YTS was devised as guaranteed training and work experience for unemployed 16 and 17 year olds and started with a surplus amount of 100 000 out of 460 000 training places in 1983 – however, the particpant numbers quickly rose so that by the start of 1986 'over a *quarter* of all 16 year olds in England (nearly a half of those not in full-time education) were on YTS schemes' (Senker 1992: 55). Thus,

26 YTS was renamed Youth Training (YT) in 1988, but I will use YTS to denote the programme for the whole case study.

> YTS effectively segregated the population of 16 year old school leavers into a relatively small group of apprentices (at that time 15 per cent of the 16 year old school leavers) and the vast majority either entering YTS or going into employment with very little training. (Senker 1992: 55).

In 1986, the scheme was extended to 2 years for 16 year olds, which gave them an additional 7 weeks of off-the-job training entitlement, while one-year YTS participants were guaranteed 13 weeks' off-the-job training, each to be taken in MSC approved courses. But the 'real innovation' of YTS was its financial structure. First, for YTS-participation, the trainee received an allowance, sometimes supplemented financially by an employer, who had to provide a guarantee of training provision. In this manner, the programme effectively shifted the financial responsibility for training towards the state and the trainees in a large proportion. Due to the training subsidy, wage costs for young trainees were lowered substantially, which created an incentive to replace costly, skilled workers with cheaper trainees – at least for semi-skilled production tasks. Second, it also introduced the logics of a competitive training market between public and private providers (UK-9). The essential question was who was able to deliver the off-the-job content of YTS, which was resolved by the MSC contracting out training delivery to public and private managing agencies (UK-9). Thus, despite a rhetoric that finances were provided to directly support employers, in reality the MSC bought training.

In effect, the introduction of YTS offered an institutional challenge for previous apprenticeship programmes. Training take up moved from being demand-driven by employers' skill needs towards being supply-driven by the number of unemployed youth receiving an allowance. In sum, YTS largely freed employers from their traditional obligations towards apprentices (King 1993; 1997). Commenting on the design of YTS and its effects on the relationship between apprentice and employer, Toner argues that

> it broke the historical nexus between apprenticeship and employment as a 'trainee' was no longer an employee of a firm from whom they received a wage, but the responsibility of a training intermediary in receipt of a government allowance. (Toner 2008: 427)

The allowance system encouraged employer take up by lowering the costs of training, and employers used YTS as a screening device (Senker 1992: 55) or in – some cases (construction, hairdressing, and engineering) – to finance the initial stages of apprenticeships (Finegold & Soskice 1988: 32). However, YTS was increasingly seen as a diluted version of the old craft apprenticeships, and its quality only increased slightly when the scheme was extended to 24 months (UK-9). For employers, YTS had little value in terms of the actual skills that trainees possessed after YTS participation, as the training delivery was mostly focused on employers immediate short-term production needs and not on the formation of broad and high skills (UK-4). Rather quickly, many researchers pointed to the fact that YTS should be qualified as a labour-market programme given its low requirements for educational content standards and variable quality of training delivery (Stevens 1999, Unwin & Ryan 2001; UK-4, UK-9) and Marsden and Ryan held that 'low quality remain[ed] the scheme's Achilles' heel' (1991: 271).

Furthermore, attrition rates were comparatively high and some employers used the opportunity to replace apprentices with trainees subsidized under government allowances (King 1993). The unions had been very critical of this possibility from the start (UK-9), thus contributing to the decline of traditional apprenticeships, to which YT offered no substantial alternative (Rainbird 2010). Moreover, between April 1986 and January 1988 not even a quarter of those trainees leaving YTS 'had gained any qualification' (Senker 1992: 55).

The failure of the MSC to provide sufficient quality training was especially problematic because at the 'peak of its glory' the MSC had a substantial budget of which almost half was spent on the YTS (Evans 1992). In order to address varying training standards, the government created the National Council for Vocational Qualifications (NVQC)[27] in 1986, with the task of creating a framework for National Vocational Qualifications (NVQs). Its task was finalized when NVQs were introduced in 1990. These set the benchmark for qualifications at five levels, ranging from level 1, indicating skills for semi-skilled occupations, to level 5, which signals professional and management qualifications. Technician, craft and supervisory skills that traditionally had been imbued by 'classical' craft apprenticeships were set at level 3. However, despite advancing a coherent framework for skills and qualification, the NVQs facilitated an ever-growing variety of certified training, which enabled employers to pick and choose only those qualifications immediately

27 The Qualifications and Curriculum Authority subsumed the NVQC in 1997, but this did not result in a substantial change in NVQ policy.

relevant to their short-term interests (Ryan & Unwin 2001), which will be discussed in greater detail in the next section.

Politically, the second Thatcher government confronted a weak opposition as the Labour Party had split in 1981, which facilitated VET reform away from collectivism and a major dismantling of the unions' wage-bargaining rights. With YTS increasingly displacing what remained of traditional apprenticeships, the government went to finalize its legacy of removing unions from training politics. It dismantled the last remainders of collective approaches in training by abolishing the tripartite MSC and the Training Commission (TC)[28] in 1989. The context of this decision was the government's plan to link unemployment benefit reception with participation in Employment Training (ET) in 1988, which had first been put on the political agenda with the government's White paper on the NTI.

Unions had already been very critical towards the government's unemployment and industrial relations policies when it launched ET as the major new unemployment programme in 1988 (King 1993). The programme included the formulation of personal action plans at Jobcentres, and the combination of most training programmes into a single scheme. The new element of ET was the linkage of training with the receipt of unemployment benefits, meaning that refusal to participate in ET could result in benefit loss. When the unions straightforwardly rejected the programme at the TUC general conference (UK-9), the government reacted with the abolishment of the MSC (Ainley & Vickerstaff 1993: 550–551, King 1993).

The MSC was redesignated as the Training Agency and located within the Department of Employment. This absorption has since greatly weakened the capacities of non-state actors to pursue policies that diverge from the government's training strategy (Gospel 1995). This was also facilitated by the low priority that the CBI assigned to training (UK-9) as the only major political player except for government that was still included in national training governance. Employers formally continued to play a major role when the government established Training and Enterprise Councils (TECs) as new intermediary governance structures for the delivery of governments' training schemes in 1989. The TECs were already been announced in the White Paper *Employment in the 1990s*, which not only admitted that YTS did not have the

28 The Training Commission was the follow-up organization to the CTC.

envisaged effect on skill formation but also focused on the obligations of employers to provide sufficient training and on a vision to support local skill formation networks among firms:

> [E]mployers are increasingly complaining that they do not know where the skills are to come from to meet tomorrow's needs – especially the technical, technological and white-collar skills, in new and developing products and services. This is at least partly because some employers took a short-term view and cut back training intakes in the recession so that the supply of trained people has been inadequate during the current recovery [...] Several countries, notably *Germany* [...] also have more locally based training systems with the close and continuous involvement of employers and employer institutions. Such systems are more likely to be attuned to the shifting pattern of employer needs [...] than the more *inflexible arrangements* at national and industry levels. It is at the local level that jobs and the need for particular skills arise (Secretary of State for Employment 1988: 28–29, *italics* by author).

The White Paper recommended a new, three-tiered structure with TECs as the prime agents for training policy at the local level, complemented by non-statutory Industrial Training Organizations (ITOs) at the sectoral level, steered via the central Training Agency. However, the TECs had a very weak financial and statutory basis. Their task, to end short-termism in the formation of vocational skills (Secretary of State for Employment 1988: 60), was not only contradicted by the composition of TECs but also by their short-term funding (Wood 1999).

Regarding the former, TECs were statutorily weak, employer-led sectoral bodies, which were composed principally of business representatives who 'by law [were required] to be the chief executives of companies' (Crouch 1995: 299), but did not necessarily attain a great degree of input from employer organizations (UK-9, UK-12). Nor did TECs have any authority to sanction firms that did not train or that trained poorly (Crouch 1995: 300) as the ITBs had at their disposal with the right to collect training levies. Financially, the TECs were funded on a very short-term basis in line with results of training achievements (certifications, apprentice placements), and competed inter-sectorally for the public training budgets, having a large degree of discretion in the allocation of received funds (Wood 1999). The competition between TECs for training funds was further instance of a move towards a 'training market', which remained a fundamental idea of the reform instituted by later governments. Yet, the measures:

> which [were] used to judge TEC performance create incentives for them to perpetuate the low-skills equilibrium; they can best satisfy their targets by providing narrow, employer-specific training, concentrating on low-cost, low-capital intensive courses (e.g. hairdressing over engineering), and focussing on those low skilled occupations, such as retailing, where high turnover rates make it easier to place people in jobs [...] Those TECs that seek to develop a strategy for investing in higher-level skills must also overcome the short-termism built into their contracts with the government which are assessed and renegotiated each year with no guarantee of future resources. (Finegold 1992: 242, cited in Crouch 1995: 300)

With regard to training providers, whose courses TECs bought to provide the off-the-job components of training, this also set incentives to focus on offering training pitched at a low skill level, which proved to be detrimental to the offer of high skill vocational courses in an increasingly crowded training market (UK-5).

Within the new governance structure of the Training Agency and TECs, the exclusion of unions was cemented as a new status quo. Unions were no longer represented by statute, and their involvement depended on the invitation of the Department of Employment or the Training Agency. As the last of its steps to remove unions from training politics, in February 1989, the government ended the unions' right to be consulted over proposals for training programmes at unionized workplaces. King (1993: 230–31) depicts the general development of training politics and policy away from tripartism towards greater employer and industry prerogative over the contents and structures of training, as an irony of history:

> since historically it was the failure of this sector [industrialists and employers] adequately to train that forced government intervention in the first place. Previous reluctance to train stimulated the government's intervention through the Industrial Training Act of 1964 whose framework of industry training boards and levy/grant system was intended to transcend employer recalcitrance.

In sum, the historic legacy of the Thatcher administration consists of the following aspects.

The institutional reconfiguration of the VET administration broke decisively with the last remnants of collective skill formation institutions. Union influence on training politics was progressively dismantled from 1979 to 1990. At the same time, union representation was ended by abolishing the ITBs and the MSC, resulting in less *involvement of intermediary associations* in training policy. However, the break with tripartism did not lead to more *firm involvement,* despite the political rhetoric of making the system more employer led, which had backed the introduction of TECs in 1989. On the contrary, the state increasingly took on financial responsibilities for training with the introduction of YTS as an employment policy with a training component that enabled the substitution of apprentices (and notably also skilled workers) by youth receiving a training allowance.

In terms of training content, YTS and NVQs did not lead to a decisive number of youths holding *certified occupational skills* as its regulations put training content largely at the discretion of the individual employer and attrition rates were immensely high. For the few apprenticeships that remained the government did not devise any statutory regulations. The loose regulations of YTS also meant that the *dual principle* of workplace and off-the-job training was undercut, especially as the system moved further towards the training market. Thus, the reforms did end union influence but did not break decisively with the voluntarism prevalent in the history of British apprenticeships. Moreover, the comparatively low status of apprenticeship training when compared to higher education was reduced even further as 'training became associated with programmes for the unemployed rather than with skill enhancement' (King 1993: 222).

3.3 Major, New Labour and 'old politics' – persistence of voluntarism and market-based training (1990–2008)

> It is now clear to all but the most dogmatic that an approach to training based purely on market forces will not work. We have reached the limits of voluntarism. (Tony Blair 1991: 3, cited in King & Wickham-Jones 1998: 440)

> For too long the UK's levels of participation and achievement have dragged us down the international education and training league. (Government White Paper: 'Helping Business to Win', President of Board of Trade et al. 1994: 30)

> Training in Britain takes place in a free market. (Department for Education and Employment and Foreign and Commonwealth Office 1997: 2, cited in King & Wickham-Jones 1998: 440)

Set against the massive impact that Conservative politics had on industrial training in Britain, the reforms under the Major and Blair administrations can be described as instances of *policy change* that did not produce *institutional change*. The logic of the institutional structures that developed under the Thatcher administration remained resilient, despite huge reform efforts and continuous institutional re-engineering under the successive governments (Keep 2006, Rainbird 2010). The Conservative Major government tried to resuscitate apprenticeships with the introduction of Modern Apprenticeships (MA) in 1994, which were to offer a higher quality route of dual VET.

When New Labour came into power in 1997 it underscored the principle that training is based on a free market and did little to revive unions' influence on training politics (King & Wickham-Jones 1998, Rainbird 2010, Steedman 2010). From a traditional partisan politics perspective this is especially puzzling as Labour traditionally had strong ties to the union movement (Wrigley 2002). However, New Labour had reoriented its course during the mid-1990s and adapted to the institutional legacies of a liberal market economy that had been finalized in the Thatcher decade. Thus, it did not strongly challenge market-based coordination, decentralized industrial relations or employer prerogative in training. Instead, it attempted to buffer socio-economic distortions of the liberal market by alleviative social polices. Thus, training essentially became a non-partisan issue from the mid-1990s onwards (UK-10).

The following section describes and analyses the policy reforms that the post-Thatcher government took, focusing on reasons why attempts at reinvigorating collective skill formation were largely unsuccessful. This concerns the policy reforms of apprenticeships as well as the administrative structure, as voluntarism and low-quality training have prevailed strongly and training governance has not decisively changed after Thatcher.

Reforms under Major (1990–1997)

Throughout the economic slump of the 1980s, manufacturing had continued to decline and this led to a reduction of apprenticeship places (UK-4, UK-9, Gospel 1995). Parallel to the rise of YTS as the major scheme to combat youth unemployment, higher education had continued to grow throughout the 1980s, which made it increasingly difficult for those firms that wanted to train to find suitable apprentices (UK-4). However, skilled workers and youth willing to train were in high demand once the economy recovered from the early 1990s onwards. Critical voices among business representatives grew louder as they felt or perceived skill shortages (UK-6) with the employment-geared design of YTS contributing little to skill formation. Lobbying by business for a higher quality VET programme than YTS increased and the new government was keen to respond to employer demands (UK-2, UK-3, UK-6). Moreover, voices within the treasury about the economically detrimental effects of low skills and skill shortages grew louder (UK-9). Finally, the unions changed their stance towards VET governance, when the TUC gave up its refusal to cooperate with TECs (Dingeldey 1996: 705).

As a reaction, in 1994, the Conservative Major government introduced Modern Apprenticeships (MA), which were set at NVQ level 3, to provide higher quality training than YTS and to polish up the prestige of VET, which had become primarily associated with training for the unemployed (King 1993, UK-3). In the 1994 White Paper 'Competitiveness: Helping Business to Win' (President of Board of Trade et al. 1994) the government clearly announced its vision to bring training up to standards that would enable businesses to compete internationally (President of Board of Trade et al. 1994: 30). It also acknowledged the limited impact of YTS on skill formation and appealed to employers to offer training places:

> [YTS] continues to be the main route for young people leaving school at age 16 or 17 [...] In 1992/3 50 per cent of those leaving YT gained a qualification or a credit towards one, mainly at NVQ level 2 or higher. [...] [But] [t]here is still a need for more skilled people at technician and modern craft level. The Government is working with employers, TECs and ITOs to introduce 'Modern Apprenticeships' for 16 and 17 year olds from 1995. These will offer work-based training to NVQ Level 3. TECs will work with local employers to organise the supply of places. The Government has challenged employers to invest in this important skills area and make training places available. The aim is that by the end of the decade there will be 150,000 new apprentices training in England at any one time, and over 40,000 young people each year achieving qualifications at NVQ level 3 or above. (President of Board of Trade et al. 1994: 38–39).

The same document also announced the government's intention to invest additional finances into MA, with an extension to 18 and 19 year olds (President of Board of Trade et al. 1994: 47), and to offer all 16 and 17 year olds training credits to 'obtain YT or Modern Apprenticeships from an employer or other recognized training provider' (President of Board of Trade et al. 1994: 39). The final design of the MA also tried to avoid some aspects that had been prevalent in the 'old, time-served system' (UK-2): with a duration of 24 month it set a limit to apprenticeship duration and a minimum of 100 hours off-the-job training had been made compulsory. Moreover, joining a union in order to attain an apprenticeship place was 'de facto' no longer necessary (UK-2).

Additionally, MA aimed to provide a more structured job entry (UK-3), and the White Paper made frequent references to collective skill-formation systems such as those of Germany, Austria and Switzerland. A further aspect that separated MA from YTS was that the apprentice and the employer had to sign a training contract that gave the apprentice employed status. The envisaged volume of 150 000 apprenticeship places is noteworthy when compared to 220 000 apprentices in the 1970s, especially when taking into account the industrial decline. In sum, the introduction of MA was a substantial attempt at reinvigorating VET with the formulation of a new training framework alongside YTS, which some commentators deem 'ironic' as the previous government had deliberately dismantled the underpinnings of traditional apprenticeships (Gospel 1995: 36).

Despite the government's ambitious reform agenda to put apprenticeship back on the skill-formation map, this goal was undercut by some long-standing problems of British VET. First, despite the appeals to business to take on more responsibilities in the creation of intermediate skills, MA essentially remained based on employer voluntarism – while it provided carrots in the form of financial incentives, the regulatory framework did not include any sticks that could have compelled business to change its prevailing attitudes. Moreover, the YTS still continued to be funded alongside MA, which, after its inception, never grew to participant numbers that would rival the volume of apprenticeships in collective VET systems.

While MA had lower attrition rates, provided better training quality and promoted employer involvement in the financing and provision of training (Gospel & Fuller 1998), it never became the biggest programme in British VET. At the time of the Major government this was also influenced by continuing high numbers of unemployed youth, which existed alongside the shortage of skilled workers, which business perceived. At the same time, while YTS offered a training path below the standards of MA, higher education expanded increasingly throughout the 1990s and attracted many youth who would have been candidates for MA (UK-6, UK-9). Thus the number of potential 'modern' apprentices (level 3 of NVQ) shrunk, despite employers demand for apprentices at this level (UK-6).

Second, MA was still based on the essentially loose regulations of the NVQ system, which grew up in a haphazard way since the finalization of the NVQ framework in the 1990s (Raggatt and Williams 1999, UK-3, UK-5, UK-9). In contrast to the occupational principle (*Berufsprinzip*) classically found in the Germanic countries, which values broad occupational skills (Deissinger 1994, 2008) and regulates training input, the NVQ system is essentially output / competency based in that it allows trainees and firms to combine modules, which are certified if the skills as stipulated by the NVQs can be performed (UK-3). This design facilitates a short-term employer focus on skill formation as NVQs can be combined that reflect only the immediate production needs of the respective firms (Ryan & Unwin 2001), and thus did not counter short termism as one of the long standing VET problems in the UK.

Moreover, the NVQ system is based on the logic of a competitive market, where provider choice was thought to enhance the quality of training standards (UK-5). As different bodies devised and awarded NVQs, an ongoing difficulty has been that awarding bodies in fact used very different standards of competency assessment (UK-5). This, in turn, contributed not only to problems with training standards but also to ambiguities regarding the reliability of assessment (UK-9) and skill content (UK-5) and a lower 'real portability' of skills due to certification opacity. While the NVQs were intended to develop higher quality training standards, their effect in this respect remained quite limited. Even in sectors that were traditionally known to provide high-quality and comparatively broad training, such as engineering and construction, the development of NVQs essentially followed the top-down regulations of

NVQ standard setting with very little additional resources available and did little to update skill profiles (UK-12), in that:

> The resources available [...] for designing qualifications have been devoted to meeting NVCQ criteria rather than to up-dating them in accordance with the requirements of new technology and organisation. In these circumstances, it is hardly surprising that the contribution which the NVQ system has made to the development of intermediate skills in engineering and to up-dating training to help workers to cope better with organisational and technological change has been modest. (Senker 1998: 93)

Finally, when Labour returned to office in 1997, it continued broadly along the lines of the previous conservative governments in apprenticeship policies, left the NVQ system intact, and largely refrained from reintegrating unions into training governance. From a traditional partisan politics perspective on training this is especially puzzling given the fact that the Labour Party and the trade unions had been traditional allies in training policy, despite the little effect that the collectivist institutions of the 1960s and 1970s had in changing the preferences of employers and unions and on the delivery and quality of VET. How the Labour government only slightly modified training policies and politics in the period from 1997 to 2008 and especially why it refrained from decisively breaking with the legacies of the Thatcher government is the content of the next section.

Reforms under New Labour (1997–2008)

While the New Labour governments did not fundamentally challenge voluntarism and the reliance of the market for training provision as the basic underpinnings of VET (Fuller & Unwin 2009, Keep 2006, Unwin 2010), it did engage in reforms of training policy and training governance. The basic pattern of VET reform remained at first focused on youth unemployment but was later extended to older workers. Steedman (2010: 2) has dubbed this 'social inclusion over skills' as the government focused increasingly on raising the number of apprentices and devising adult entitlements to training (UK-5) while changing very little in terms of the regulation of apprenticeship content and standards or the governance mechanisms underpinning VET. New Labour's apprenticeship policies were broadly in line with its 'third-way' strategy of cushioning the negative effects of employers' options to 'hire and fire' workers as deemed fit in a loosely regulated labour market (Gray 2004). However, the expansion of VET programmes to older, low-skilled workers in order to lower social inequality (Payne & Keep 2011) was not complemented by a boost in the quality of VET provision.

In parallel, New Labour set the ambitious target of increasing higher education participation to a half of each school-leaving cohort and expanding disadvantaged children's' access to higher education (Ansell 2010). The expansion of higher education – without reforms in the quality and regulation of VET provision – and the growth of adult apprenticeships (Ryan 2005, Steedman 2010) meant that training remained subordinated to higher education and an increase of VET quality continued to have a lower priority than social inclusion (UK-1, UK-9, UK-11), a process that had already started with YTS and ET under Thatcher.

Moreover, despite strong policy rhetoric to make VET employer-led and more relevant for firms, the reforms under New Labour failed to boost firm involvement as the increase in apprenticeship numbers was driven by an expansion of public funding (Steedman 2010). More generally, New Labour's course in training effectively represented a lasting shift from demand-side to supply-side oriented policy as is also meticulously documented for other areas such as the overall strategy of human capital investment (Boix 1998), industrial relations (Howell 2005), labour market policy, or social protection (Rhodes 2000).

Before I depict the reforms undertaken by New Labour, I first address the fundamental U-turn that the Labour Party took in its strategy towards VET policies, as at the beginning of the 1990s it had still been committed towards more intervention in training policy and based its financing proposal for training on a levy-system very similar to the ITB system prior to 1973 (King & Wickham-Jones 1998). Most astonishingly, Labour turned away from a diagnosis of training failure long held in the party, namely that 'employers left to themselves will not invest enough in training' (TUC-Labour Party Liaison Committee 1985: 13; in King & Wickham-Jones 1998: 444), when it moved away from state intervention towards a competitive training market, with an important role for employers via the TEC system, before its election in 1997. Instead of more regulation, it announced plans for the creation of Individual Learning Accounts (ILAs) (King & Wickham-Jones 1998: 447) and thus effectively shifted the responsibility for training from firms to individuals – to be supported by entitlement by public grants – and only appealed to employers that they 'have the primary responsibility for training their workforces in job-related skills' (Labour Party 1996a: 9, cited in King & Wickham-Jones 1998: 447).

One of the first reforms under New Labour was the introduction of Foundation Apprenticeships (FAs), which complemented its 'New Deal for Young People', a major employment programme that offered young unemployed (16 to 24 year olds) work experience, subsidized employment and voluntary work programmes. The programme was piloted in 1998 and later expanded to older workers under the label 'New Deal'. Because of the low status of YTS, the reform towards FAs had already been planned by the outgoing Major government (UK-9, UK-10) and was essentially introduced without altering its content by New Labour. Foundation Apprenticeships as the 'natural extension of YTS' (UK-9) were set at NVQ level 2 – like YTS – and continued broadly along the same regulatory lines. Off-the-job content remained lightly regulated, and, while the participating youth now enjoyed full-employed status (also the case in MA), employers continued to receive public subsidies to fund training delivered by a public of private provider operating in the training market. Like, YTS the volume of training delivery remained more important than training quality (Fuller & Unwin 2011, Steedman 2010), which spurred new criticism among scholarly observers of VET reform (Ryan 2005, Ryan & Unwin 2001).

In 2001, the government essentially engaged in 're-branding' (UK-9) the two apprenticeship programmes, when it renamed MA as Advanced Apprenticeships (AA) and FA as Apprenticeships (A). Apprenticeships (formerly YTS/FA) had a minimum duration of 12 month leading to a National Vocational Qualification (NVQ) at level 2, and Advanced Apprenticeships (AA) (formerly MA) had a minimum duration of 24 month leading to a an NVQ at level 3. As pointed out above, the introduction of MAs aimed at a greater commitment by both trainees and employers, in particular to work towards qualifications at NVQ level 3 (technician, craft, and supervisory skills) or above. Under this framework, apprentices normally have an employment contract and employers receive a subsidy for training costs. Noting a fundamental disparity between the two forms of apprenticeship found today, Ryan et al. (2007) argue that only AA meets the criteria normally applied for the generic meaning of apprenticeship, while Apprenticeships fall short of these criteria, due to lower educational standards and a different funding structure between state, apprentice and employer.[29] Concerning the educational content, reservations about the quality of apprenticeships still persist and attrition rates remain very high, especially for Apprenticeships (Ryan & Unwin 2001, Rainbird 2010).

These programmatic reforms were accompanied by changes in training governance in 2001 as the government introduced the Learning and Skills Council (LSC), which was complemented by Sector Skills Councils (SSCs) and Local Learning and Skills Councils (LLSCs), the latter gradually replacing the TECs, which had been run in a business-like way but had not significantly contributed to higher quality training standards or delivery (UK-9, UK-10). The SSCs were made responsible for the core funding in their respective sectors and developed training standards in cooperation with standard setting organizations (SSOs) of the training market such as RSA, City & Guilds, EDExcel or even training providers that have their training certified as NVQs. Despite this institutional reform, employers were still overrepresented within training governance and guaranteed a statutory minimum of seats in these bodies. This did not apply to unions (Keep 2006).

The LSC/SSC system fulfilled[30] the tasks of collecting labour-market information, identifying skill and productivity gaps, updating national occupational standards, and allocating the publicly funded training and vocational education in cooperation with colleges, training providers, universities and planning bodies to ensure that they understand the sectors' needs. However, firm involvement is still based on

29 They also point out that statistics on apprenticeships can be skewed as training that combines work-based learning, off-the job training and technical education and aims at NVQ-levels 3–5 might not be eligible for public funding and thus not included in statistics (Ryan et al. 2007: 129f).

30 In 2009, the coalition government replaced the LSC with the National Apprenticeship Service (NAS).

the voluntarism that has dominated training in the United Kingdom for most of the 20th century (King 1993, 1997).

A fundamental problem of this system is that these institutions can only set financial incentives but due to the loose statutory framework of the 'British Training Market' (Ryan & Unwin 2001) they are ill suited to influence skill decisions and provision made by individual firms via coordinating institutions. Moreover, as funding came to be set centrally within the respective department for employment, even the CBI lost some of its influence on training policy, especially in the funding dimension. Similarly, employers, which are represented within training governance, have little leeway to modify these national targets, based on estimates of the government department. In the absence of joint decision-making and shared responsibilities between the social partners, Keep described the national governance mechanism as the state

> acting in isolation and [the targets are] then imposed on a multiplicity of actors in which sanctions are often lacking and wherein the state has no hold whatsoever over the actions of one key group of actors – employers. (Keep 2004: 12)

What this is referring to can be termed the *paradox of the British training state*. Since the Thatcher government, the amount of responsibility for the funding of training moved increasingly towards the state as training was increasingly used for social policy purposes, epitomized by programmes such as YTS and the New Deal for Young People. But, with the introduction of competency-based assessment by the NVQs in the early 1990s, the setting of skill standards and assessment was devolved to the sectorial level as consecutive governments – with or without the cooperation of the social partners – refrained from introducing a nationally standardized curriculum. As a consequence the state has little control over the actual content of training at the level of VET provision. Training content remains the prerogative of the firm, and the trainee can be certified as long as NVQ-defined competency standards are met. As educational contents vary strongly due to the decentralized nature of standard setting this leads to huge variations in skill levels and standards between different sectors.

As Labour moved towards the social inclusion agenda by extending apprenticeships to older workers, the long-standing problem of employer voluntarism was not broken, but was even exacerbated as state-sponsored training was used to fund already employed, but not formally qualified workers, for example under the guise of Train to Gain. In 2002, the big supermarket chain Morrisons employed 10% of all apprentices in the UK (52 000) of whom the majority were over 25.[31] Criticisms of using state funding for existing employees in large numbers mounted (UK-4) as the firm used the money to fund training that 'would have been done anyway' (UK-5). The climax was finally reached when a whistle blower told the BBC that apprenticeships, that were signed off as completed could not have been really certified as the firm 'did not employ an assessor then'.[32] This example shows that training has become diluted when compared to a generic apprenticeship (UK-5, Ryan & Unwin 2001).[33]

For the development of training under Major and the New Labour governments we can detect a broad continuity in training politics and policies. First, despite the New Labour reforms towards the LSC/SSC/LLSC system, employers still continue to be the dominant group in training governance institutions, which at the central level of decision making is not characterized by a large *involvement of intermediary associations* from both sides of the industry. With the move towards a training market, training providers are new actors that populate the field of VET policy, but due to their commercial nature, whether they represent workers' and/or employers' interests must be seriously questioned. Later, the New Labour government moved towards reinvigorating a role for unions in training by allowing statutory time-off for union learning representatives (ULRs) to cater for workers' training needs (McIlroy 2008). However, in light of the rather loose institutional framework of a training market, which is suited to short-term employer needs, it is questionable whether this will enhance cooperation towards high-skill apprenticeships in the workplace.

Second, the low involvement of unions in contemporary British VET policy is exacerbated by the developments in apprentice numbers and their sectoral composition. Most apprenticeships are at lower skill levels (NVQ level 2); only 60% are done by under 25-year olds and level 2 apprenticeships are also found in occupations that classically

31 http://www.bbc.com/news/uk-17564255
32 http://www.bbc.com/news/uk-17564251
33 *The Economist* 26. April 2014: 29–30.

had high training standards (NVQ level 3) (UK-6). Moreover, most apprenticeships are now concentrated in the service sector, where union membership is at best modest and unions no longer have the capacity for workplace monitoring (UK-2). Thus, even under the New Labour government we saw no signs of union revitalization in the sense that unions were strengthened as strategic partners. On the contrary, the use of apprenticeships as an employment and social inclusion policy – the latter with the extension of initial VET to older, formally unskilled workers – not only cemented the low status of VET but also worked to provide 'cheap labour' (King & Rueda 2008) to employers, especially in the service sector. In this way, apprenticeships have grown in size but not in substantive quality and remain an inferior alternative to higher, academic education.

3.4 Conclusion

With hindsight, it can be argued that the United Kingdom has rather moved *towards* than away from a liberal model of skill formation for intermediate skills. The tripartite formal institutions of the 1960s and 1970s that were designed to improve the amount and quality of training did not fundamentally alter the scope and design of training, effect a shift in the preferences of employers and unions, orchange the voluntarist underpinnings of post-war training arrangements. In parallel, industrial relations have hardly moved towards cooperative relations between capital and labour since the end of the 1980s. Even today, there is no statutory union representation in workplaces, nor has there been a move towards more centralized wage bargaining. At the policy level there is no extensive statutory definition of apprenticeship under the NVQ system and training is heavily geared towards the interests of individual firms, as they have much leeway in apprenticeship training at the workplace. The main problem in politics under all governments irrespective of the governing party, is that training reforms are heavily geared towards the freedom of employers in implementing apprenticeship rules, while excluding unions. The constant failure to bring adversarial industrial relations on more cooperative terms has not allowed for the formation of a cross-class coalition that could have underpinned a joint approach to high-quality apprenticeships.

To sum up, the central problems for a way towards a system of collective skill formation in the United Kingdom seems to lie deeper at the roots of industrial relations than apparently assumed by central policy makers. Despite continuous efforts to reform the English system towards this goal there has been little institutional change. Lacking any system that might introduce 'beneficial constraints', which force employers towards high-skill strategies, the British state might end up in a continuous cycle of institutional innovation with little effect on employer provision of training (Keep 2006). After the abolishment of the unsuccessful tripartite institutions during the 1980s and without other policy options (levies, statutory rights to collective bargaining, regulated labour markets, an industrial policy that favours high craft-skills sectors), the voluntarist tradition of employer engagement prevails despite a strong role for governments in defining and funding apprenticeship.

4. Ireland – apprenticeships and social partnership as a sustainable model?

Ireland has some marked similarities to England regarding the institutional legacy of VET, because it inherited the voluntarist and contested tradition of apprenticeships when gaining independence in 1922. Irish attempts to provide statutory regulation for VET, to increase firm involvement and to reform industrial relations towards centralized wage bargaining did not produce institutional change, as those attempts were usually short lived. In a similar vein to the macroeconomic problems of the United Kingdom, which worsened after the first oil shock, in the 1980s, Ireland experienced 'extreme fiscal difficulties, high unemployment [...] and towering public debt problems' (Hardiman et al. 2008: 599). And yet, during the last 40 years, Ireland's small, open, trade-dependent economy has undergone a massive economic transformation. Ireland changed from agrarian backwardness and traditional manufacturing to a service-based economy that is focused on foreign capital investment and high-tech and internationally traded services, which might partly explains the intensity with which it was hit during the current economic crisis.

This transformation is frequently explained by the political reaction to the mounting problems of the mid-1980s. Consecutive Irish governments encouraged tripartite social partnership between employers, unions and the state, which – in substance – traded wage concessions and industrial relations stability for tax concessions, welfare and education reform by the Irish state (Compston 2003, Hardiman 2000, Roche 2007). This strategy also included the development of apprenticeships towards a more continental model of collective skill formation (Nyhan 2010, O'Connor & Harvey 2001, Ryan 2000) and broke with the UK-inherited tradition of voluntarist regulation between employers and craft unions that had prevailed since independence.

Under social partnership, the Irish economy grew rapidly and unparalleled by any other rich Western democracy – the Celtic tiger was born. Although it is challenging to disentangle the growth of apprenticeships and the beneficial economic conditions of the Celtic tiger, I will subsequently show how VET reform towards collective skill formation and social partnership were interrelated: VET played an important role in the emergence of social partnership, which in turn helped to underpin the reform towards dual apprenticeships.

This chapter traces the development of VET policies and politics in the case of Ireland against the background of historical commonalities with the United Kingdom. It places a special focus on the period of the 1980s and 1990s as this is the central period when Ireland started to move towards collective skill formation, at the same time when Thatcher embarked on her course to decollectivize industrial relations and to exclude the unions from British training politics. Some historical differences at the point of departure (ca. 1950) between the two cases should be mentioned, before I move to the description of the Irish case.

First, the two cases differed in their economic structure, as industrialization in Ireland lagged significantly behind its UK counterpart, from which it had inherited 'a weak, dependent industrial base' (O'Connor 2002). Agrarian employment was much higher and industrial employment much lower in Ireland compared to the United Kingdom (see OECD various), which depressed the demand for workers with manufacturing and vocational skills. Moreover, Ireland pursued a strategy of trade protectionism up until the early 1960s, taking manufacturing wages out of foreign competition. When the country embarked on a course of trade liberalization, it accompanied this strategy with the policy of granting low-capital income taxation to foreign firms and investors, which in turn contributed to the development of an economic cleavage between large, foreign-owned multinational corporations and an indigenous economic sector, which was mainly composed of SMEs. Second, due to its status as an economic laggard, when Ireland joined the EU this opened up the possibility of accessing the European Union's structural funds, which were also used on a large scale to invest in VET. Finally, when compared to the classical 'Westminster'-type two-party system of the United Kingdom, Ireland – for most of the time since the Second World War – should be more correctly described as a two-and-a-half party system (Mair and Marsh 2004) in which Fianna Faíl (FF) single party governments alternated with governing coalitions of Fine Gael (FG) and the Irish Labour Party (ILP).[34] In contrast with other European nations, the Irish party system was not primarily based on a cleavage between labour and capital, but according to the stance that the parties took in the critical phase before independence (Adshead & Tongue 2009). The religious cleavage is muted in the predominantly Catholic country and the two major, Catholic parties, FF and FG, occupied the centre position of the party system at different points of time (Mair 1986). Due to the traditional weakness of the ILP, the party system was tilted towards the centre-right, but the 'catch-all' party orientation of FF and FG also incentivized both parties to promote centrist policies in order to appeal to the median voter (Weeks 2010).

In terms of the three main parties' relations to organized interests, FG held closer relations to organized business than the other two parties. The ILP traditionally had very close ties to the union movement and was established as its political wing in 1912, but FF also regularly cooperated with trade unions and managed to gain 'traditional support bases amongst the working class' (Adshead & Tonge 2009: 97) and concomitantly showed 'goodwill towards the trade union movement' (O'Connor 2002: 155). The main peculiarity in Irish party competition was that, up until 1989, FF refrained from entering coalitions with other parties, despite only holding a parliamentary majority in the Dáil after four elections (1957, 1965, 1969, 1977). This resulted in frequent FF minority governments or in coalitions between FG and the ILP, which entered coalition 'as a necessary evil, the essential price for replacing Fianna Fáil in government' (Farrell 1983: 257, in Marsh & Mitchell 1999).

However, despite the common legacy in industrial relations and VET institutions with the United Kingdom, Ireland managed to move closer to a model of collective skill formation and social partnership in industrial relations when faced with the economic hardship of the 1980s. In the course of reform it moved away from a laissez-faire approach towards VET and introduced Standards-based Apprenticeships (SBAs)

34 The only exceptions were the 1948–1951 five-party government (FG, ILP, Clann na Poblachta, Clann na Talmhan, National Labour) under Taiosech (Prime Minister) Costello, and a three-party government of FG, ILP and Clann na Talmhan under Costello from 1954–1957.

at the beginning of the 1990s. This new system was only modest in size – in terms of covered occupations and the share of a youth cohort in dual training – when compared to the volume of dual training in collective skill formation countries such as Germany, Austria, Switzerland or Denmark, but displays some central characteristics typical of collective skill formation.

First, the involvement of firms in initial VET became underpinned by a training levy, which was used to sponsor the components of off-the-job training in Foras Áiseanna Saothai (FÀS) training centres and institutes of technology (ITCs), in which apprentices receive a training wage. Second, *intermediary associations* are involved in setting training standards. These include employer associations and trade unions, but representatives from the ITCs also cooperate in the development of training curricula for the designated apprenticeship trades. Third, this leads to a high level of standardization of training content and training duration. Apprenticeships usually take three-and-a-half years and provide *portable occupational skills*, which are *certified* by a National Craft Certification at the end of training. Finally, the SBA system is a highly structured dual VET system, with seven alternating training phases, of which phases 1, 3, 5, and 7 are done on the job, phase 2 at a FÀS training centre and phases 4 and 6 take place at an ITC.

The following sections trace the evolution of Irish VET away from an ideal-typical model of liberal skill formation and towards a more collective system. The first period analyses the trajectory of voluntarist training policies and unstable, mostly pluralist industrial relations up to 1985. Up to that point, VET policies and politics were remarkably similar to parallel developments in the United Kingdom. The few training reforms initiated by FF governments failed to break decisively with the prevailing voluntarist nature of training, despite the introduction of a tripartite institution for industrial training (An Comhairle Oiliuna – AnCO), which introduced a levy/grant system, but largely failed to address low training quality and employer commitment. Moreover, cooperation in industrial relations could not be brought on a stable cooperative basis and VET was wound up in struggles over wage bargaining between employers and craft unions.

From 1985–1995 this situation fundamentally reversed after the tripartite National Economic and Social Council (NESC) published a landmark report. Subsequently, the report became the basis for negotiations between unions, employers and governments and led to the beginning of tripartite social partnership agreements, in 1987, about industrial relations, wage bargaining, taxation and training, which lasted until the present economic and financial crisis. Quite remarkably, while social partnership constituted an important base for the reform towards the SBA in 1993/4, industrial training had already been a major component in the NESC document. Governments used it strategically to shore up cross-class cooperation between employers and unions by facilitating joint approaches to training governance and the infusion of additional funding into the apprenticeship system.

The final section describes a third phase (1995–2008) after the critical juncture towards social partnership. This last phase saw incremental adaptations of the VET system, which, however, failed to address the problem of imbalances in training growth, heavily tilted to the construction trades. This contributed to a staggering reduction in training numbers, when a housing bubble that had been swelling throughout the 2000s burst with the arrival of the financial crisis.

4.1 The historical background – the inheritance of British training

> With few exceptions, arrangements in Ireland for the recruitment and training of apprentices are haphazard. In general, little attempt has been made, on a national basis [...] to provide for the systematic training of apprentices in practical skills or for their release from work to attend appropriate technical school courses. [...] In brief, the effectiveness of the present arrangements for the recruitment and training of apprentices depends mainly on the outlook of individual employers and it is questionable whether sufficient employers adopt a progressive outlook on the subject. (An Ceard Chomhairle 1961; in McCarthy 1977: 7)

> [L]ike its UK counterpart, Irish apprenticeship was in the 1980s an archaic, publicly unregulated and declining institution, restricted mostly to craft occupations in industry and construction, that certified apprentices according to time-served rather than vocational competence. (Ryan 2000: 59)

When it gained independence in 1922, Ireland inherited the voluntarist tradition of apprenticeships from the United Kingdom (Field & O Dubchair 2001, McCarthy 1977, Ryan 2000). These were based on 'informal regulations between employers and unions' (IRE-1, Nyhan 2010) at the occupational level. Hence, apprenticeship regulation was very similar to traditional indentured apprenticeships and 'theoretical training was primarily seen as the responsibility of the apprentice' (IRE-1). However, despite a need for structured off-the-job education (IRE-3) and political attempts to install more structured training, the theoretical component of VET remained 'fairly unregulated' (IRE-8, Murphy 1977). The time-served nature of apprenticeships also meant that wage progression of apprentices was not based on actual skills, but on seniority within a firm (IRE-1, IRE-3).

This structure of apprenticeships, which were traditionally located in sectors with a strong craft legacy such as construction and manufacturing, was underpinned by historical conflict lines between employers and craft unions similar to those of the United Kingdom (*cf.* Chapter 3). Employers perceived training as a net production cost and 'not an investment' (IRE-5) and were reluctant to train beyond immediate production needs. Craft unions, which were still organized around the principles of British unions after World War II (IRE-6, IRE-8), sought an advantage in wage bargaining by limiting the supply of skilled labour via controlling the access to apprenticeships (Costine & Garavan 2001, IRE-1, IRE-6). The union strategy was complemented via 'closed shop' politics and the defence of strict occupational demarcations that stood in the way of a broad approach of multiskilling apprentices (IRE-1, IRE-6). Put differently, instead of proactively trying to reform vocational training policies 'the overriding priorities of trade unions have lain elsewhere, a fact chiefly manifested in their pre-occupation with maintaining or improving pay and working conditions' (Costine & Garavan 1995: 38).

In turn, employers, which had little incentive to train apprentices in broad occupational skills, only trained them in a narrow, firm-specific range of skills and mainly used apprentices for the productive work at hand (IRE-6), while trying to limit their own dependence on skilled labour. Day or block release for off-the-job education existed but this was most likely to be found with larger employers, as smaller and medium-sized employers perceived theoretical training mainly as a cost (IRE-5, IRE-6) and needed apprentices to be productive in day-to-day work routines (IRE-3). Thus, even where certification of apprentices existed, certificates had 'little exchange value' as they did not properly signal the skills of the worker (IRE-6).

As in the United Kingdom, governments were reluctant to interfere strongly in the area of training because they saw training as the primary responsibility of the organized interest of capital and labour (Nyhan 2010).[35] Politicians usually 'only paid a lip-service' (IRE-7) to apprenticeship policies, with the partial exception of the ILP due to its strong linkage with the union movement (IRE-1). Consequently, until 1960 apprenticeship politics remained 'a system driven very much by unions and employers' (IRE-5).

The early legislation in VET did little to challenge this voluntarist heritage. The Vocational Education Act of 1930, which set very loose guidelines for the regulation of state-provided vocational education, foresaw only an advisory role for employers and unions in national VET policy (IRE-2). While it instituted Vocational Education Committees (VECs) on a local level in order to direct local training policy for full-time second-level training, with 'very limited exceptions the social partners were not formally involved' (Murphy & Coldrick 1988: 30). One year later it was complemented by the Apprenticeship Act of 1931, which provided for the formation of apprenticeship committees and represented 'the first systematic effort' (Heraty et al. 2000: 185) to regulate apprenticeship standards in terms of training duration, wage levels and training courses. Regarding the latter, it compelled employers to release their apprentices for training courses, but only under the condition that they took place during normal working hours and were held within three miles of the workplace (Heraty et al. 2000: 185).

Moreover, no compulsion existed for employers to send their apprentices to courses organized by the VECs. In sum, these early provisions could not break voluntarism and McCarthy concludes that the 'Act failed because it left it optional to the [apprenticeship] committees to make a rule requiring employers to train and instruct apprentices by them *in a particular manner*' (McCarthy 1977: 6, italics by author). Thus, the acts improved apprenticeships, where employers and unions could forge agreement, but the training standards hugely varied

35 For exceptions to government inactivity, see O'Connor and Harvey (2001: 333–334) and Nyhan (2010: 46–47).

between occupations and regions (cf. McCarthy 1977: 6, IRE-2). In addition, early corporatist initiatives before and after World War II that could have underpinned more cooperative relations between training employers and unions largely failed (O'Connor 2002, O'Leary 2000).

After these early initiatives, training reform came to a halt for almost 30 years. Compared to other West European economies, Ireland was lagging behind in growth, which led to high unemployment and strong emigration, so in 1959 the FF government led by Taiosech (prime minister) Seán Lemass repealed the Apprenticeship Act of 1931 and replaced it with new legislation. At the national level, the An Cheard Comhairle (ACC – apprenticeship board) was put in place as a regulatory institution, which was composed of employer, trade union and state representatives. Its primary objective was to coordinate and regulate the apprenticeship system regarding the following aspects: educational standards necessary for entering apprenticeship and their recruitment by employers, provisions regarding day release and on-the-job training standards, monitoring of on-the-job training and standardization of the system of apprenticeship examination (Government of Ireland 1959).

The first two aspects, in particular, are noteworthy because no state regulation existed regarding the intake of apprentices, which was formerly basically controlled between craft unions and employers (IRE-5). In effect, the state had little capacity to adequately plan the capacities for off-the-job education (IRE-5). Moreover, the system failed to break with the tradition of qualifications based on time serving as it had little monitoring capacities (McCarthy 1977). Thus in an early report, the ACC questioned the

> effectiveness of the present arrangements for the recruitment and training of apprentices [which] depends mainly on the outlook of individual employers and it is questionable whether sufficient employers adopt a progressive outlook on the subject. (An Ceard Chomhairle 1961; in McCarthy 1977: 7)

Moreover, the ACC stressed the necessity for greater cooperation between employers and unions at the national and the local level in order to improve the quality of the VET system in terms of training standards and practice (An Ceard Chomhairle 1961; in McCarthy 1977: 7). Almost 10 years later, a report echoed that the reforms had failed 'to improve on-the-job training and to regulate [apprentice] intake' (AnCO 1973: 6).

Despite these problems, further reform was also needed in conjunction with the historical decision of the Lemass minority governments of 1959 and 1961 to meet the 'dire economic situation' (IRE-2) with a 'historic U-turn' (O'Connor 2002: 162). It gave up protectionism of the domestic market, switched to a policy of attracting foreign capital by low capital tax policies and applied for Ireland to join the European Economic Community (EEC) in 1961. On the party political side, these moves met little opposition due to the 'evident exhaustion of protectionism' (O'Connor 2002: 162). The strategy of opening up the economy was based on a planning approach contained in three programmes for economic expansion and the creation of tripartite consultative bodies in the areas of manpower planning, pay determination and industrial relations reforms. Regarding the two latter aspects, Lemass hoped to entice unions to a voluntary policy of wage moderation and hoped to break union rank-and-file militancy in wage bargaining (Crouch 1993, Hardiman 1988) with the inclusion of consultation and economic planning, which worked reasonably well as the economy expanded and near full employment was reached up until the early 1970s.

Yet, the opening up of the economy had a more direct effect, which underscored the necessity of training reform (IRE-2). In line with the strategy of attracting foreign capital, the policies of state agencies shifted markedly towards infrastructure and human capital investment (IRE-5). International companies that located parts of their production to Ireland brought in higher standards of training and new technology that necessitated broader skills than usually offered by the contemporary apprenticeship system (IRE-5). Moreover, the need for VET reform was stressed in the tripartite National Industrial and Economic Council's (NIEC) 'Report on Manpower Policy' (NIEC 1964), which recognized the need for an active approach to the labour market and skill-formation policy in order to create economic growth. This resonated well 'amongst the developmental wing of the then ruling Fianna Fáil party and the trade unions' (Boyle 2005: 24) but unequivocal support was prevented by craft unions (IRE-8), who were sceptical about the prospects of VET reform.

After consultations in the Dáil, in line with the proposals of the NIEC, a new Industrial Training Act was passed in 1967, which replaced the ACC with AnCO. This new attempt to reform haphazard apprenticeship structures and to end voluntarism and employer neglect for training had three important components.

First, like its predecessor, AnCO was composed in a tripartite manner with an executive council composed of five union and five employer-association nominated representatives, one nominee of the minister for education as well as two nominees and one independent chairman appointed by the Minister for Labour. This representative pattern was reproduced in seven statutory apprenticeship advisory committees (AACs) that had the task to offer counsel on VET regulation in different sectors. The reform increased the options of the social partners to contribute actively to apprenticeship reform, but now had become underpinned by the discourse around the need to improve VET in order to stimulate economic growth and to attract foreign capital to Ireland by broadening the availability of skilled workers (Boyle 2005: 23). As the formal responsibility for training lay with the Labour Ministry and not with education, the technical and practical components were strongly emphasized vís-à-vís general, academic education when AnCO was created (IRE-2).

Second, the legislation gave AnCO the power to set a statutory framework for apprenticeship regulation, i.e. guidelines for the definition of apprenticeship certification and on-the-job-instruction as well as off-the-job training. Third, in terms of training finance, it instituted a levy/grant system to finance off-the-job training, which was intended to distribute the costs of off-the-job training more evenly between the state and employers and, more importantly, between training and non-training employers. Regarding the levy, it gave organized interests a stronger role in the financial aspect of VET policy as the sectorial committees could set more fine-grained training regulations and could adapt the levy to the specific sectoral needs.

While this process was similar to the changes in the United Kingdom (i.e. the creation of ITBs in 1964 and MSC in 1973) and expanded the cooperative arena between unions and employers more firmly (IRE-8), the new reform did not yet put Ireland on a development path towards collective VET, as it did not cause a large-scale change of the social partners' essentially voluntarist attitudes towards training.

First, while the new legislation gave AnCO the power to compel employers to release their apprentices for off-the-job education, many firms simply did not release their apprentices. This was strongly contested between the unions and employers (IRE-5). Drawing on data from an annual AnCO report, McCarthy (1977: 18) reports that on average roughly 40% of apprentices had not been released for off-the-job training during the period from 1968 to 1973. This was especially pronounced among smaller employers that needed apprentices to fulfil their immediate production requirements (IRE-2, IRE-7). Moreover, small workplaces generally lacked genuine union representation that could have exerted additional pressure on employers to release their apprentices (IRE-2).

Second, training was still not based on competences achieved but on time serving between four and five years, which most unions accepted for access to a union card and employment in closed shops (IRE-5, IRE-7). This practice was still possible as no agreement could be reached to make certification mandatory in order to achieve craftsperson status (AnCO 1968). Moreover, due to the structure of AnCO and its AACs, training regulations for off-the-job education still varied vastly among occupations and few common standards were in place (IRE-1, IRE-7). Finally, at its inception, AnCO had very limited financial means to provide off-the-job training (IRE-1) and pointed to inadequate facilities in terms of workshops and schools in its first annual report (AnCO 1968).

This was somewhat ameliorated when Ireland joined the EC in 1973. AnCO received grants from the European Social Fund (ESF) (Nyhan 2010, IRE-5) that were used to build a network of AnCO Training Centres for practical education and to establish Regional Technical Colleges (RTCs)[36] that offered post-secondary vocational training and day-release educational elements of apprenticeships (Nyhan 2010, O'Connor & Harvey 2001). However, the patterns of VET provision by employers and the politics between social partners and governments remained essentially unchanged.

Here, as with the English reforms of the 1960s, policy change in the regulation and governance of VET did not lead to real institutional change, despite the provisions of the 1967 Industrial Training Act and the Creation of AnCO. This was also evident for another change, proposed by the AnCO in 'Apprenticeship – A New Approach' (AnCO 1973),

36 These were redesignated as institutes of technology (ITCs) in 1999.

which had been devised on a social partnership basis in AnCO's executive committee. Even the introduction of a statutory phase of one-year off-the-job learning in AnCO's training centres, which took place prior to on-the-job training with an employer, did not fundamentally alter this situation (IRE-6).

This was a first step towards a greater coherence of skill-standards but it 'was a mixed blessing in that cut at the heart of the concept of apprenticeship [...] [being] sponsored and implemented by employers' (Nyhan 2010: 48). Despite an increase in off-the job education, the one-year learning prior to apprenticeship did not trigger institutional change insofar as many employers simply recruited their apprentices after the first state-sponsored year (O'Connor 2006) and the new provisions had little effect on the problem of limited day or block release by employers (IRE-2, IRE-7). Moreover, the levy for training was heavily contested between unions and employers, with a cross-cutting cleavage between employers of different sizes similar to the United Kingdom. Larger companies usually trained more apprentices than small firms and were thus not too critical about the levy, which they regarded as a cost that they would normally meet with their usual training expenses, but SMEs chafed under the levy as an additional cost (IRE-5).

In essence, this situation remained unchanged until the late 1980s, when VET appeared at the forefront of industrial relations reforms. Since the lifting of protective trade measures, FF governments had regularly tried to appeal to the union movement to moderate wage agreements with employers in order to decrease industrial strife (Crouch 1993, Hardiman 1988, O'Connor 2002) to make the strategy of economic expansion via the attraction of foreign capital more viable. Yet, attempts at bargaining centralization failed to produce peaceful and cross-sectorally coordinated wage setting. Industrial relations on a local level were frequently and heavily contested between unions and employers, leading to industrial strife and wage hikes in sectors that experienced skill shortages. This happened despite several national understandings on wage and pay policy during the 1970s and early 1980s, which were short-lived experiments of corporatism (O'Connor 2002, Power 2009). In contrast with this, the mid-1980s became a focal point in Irish industrial relations and VET reform, and marked the beginning of lasting cross-class cooperation (until 2009) in both policy fields. The next section places these developments in the historical context of the failed attempts of the 1970s and early 1980s and analyses how and why governments, employers and unions departed on a course towards more cooperation and which role VET reform played in this process.

4.2 The critical juncture – cross-class cooperation towards economic challenges and training reform (1985–1994)

> The government [and the social partners], conscious of the grave state of our economic and social life, have agreed on this Programme to seek to regenerate our economy and improve the social equity of our society through their combined efforts. (*Programme for National Recovery,* Government of Ireland 1987: 5)

In the early to mid-1980s, Ireland saw soaring unemployment and high levels of net debt and inflation, which put both governments and their industrial partners under pressure to search for solutions to the severe economic crisis. In this context, training and industrial relations politics took a profoundly different direction from the English case. While the latter saw the removal of the social partners from training policy, the dismantling of tripartite VET and manpower governance and the deregulation of industrial relations, Ireland followed a consensus-seeking approach in policy reform. Social partnership between organized interests and governments emerged, which in turn led to a long-lasting return to centralized wage-bargaining and strong political cooperation and moved Ireland closer to collective VET.

As I show, the critical juncture for these developments was the emergence of the common perception of macro-economic problems, which congealed around two papers published by the tripartite NESC (NESC 1985, 1986) respectively, which was the basis for the beginning of social partnership in the decision for a Programme for National Recovery (PNR) in 1987. The PNR propelled the increase of cooperative approaches in training and led to subsequent reforms towards a more collective VET-system. How these changes came about and which aspects led to a changed behaviour of governments, unions and employers is the main focus of this section. In line with my hypothesis on the nexus between non-right-wing governments and industrial relations reform, VET played an important role in the emergence of cooperative approaches between employers and unions.

The time before social partnership started was politically turbulent in terms of both industrial relations and economic development (IRE-10, Hardiman 1988, McCann 1993, Murphy & Hogan 2008, Power 2009, Roche 2009). Despite attempts of FF governments and a coalition between FG and the Irish Labour Party (1973–1977) to institutionalize wage moderation via bargaining agreements between peak employers and unions before the PNR, these settlements failed to deliver industrial peace during the 1970s. The expansion of the Irish economy also crucially depended on public investment, which successively built up debt to a level that became unsustainable during the 1980s.

After successive governments had failed to reign in industrial unrest, the political climate changed at the beginning of the 1980s (IRE-10) due to mounting unemployment and the 'escalation of public borrowing' (O'Connor 2002: 164). The outgoing FF government (1979) had attempted to counter industrial strife about wage settlements by concluding two National Understandings for Social and Economic Development with the trade unions and the major employer federations in 1979 and 1980. These involved the government directly in pay setting and were two-tier agreements, where moderation in pay setting was to be compensated by investments in employment creation, infrastructure, education and training, welfare and public housing (IRE-10). But these understandings did not translate into real job or wage growth in the context of recession, rising inflation and mounting debt. In turn, a third agreement between the government, unions and employers failed in 1981 because of disagreement about its pay component, which was 'mainly because employers' organizations refused to enter into national pay negotiations' (Power 2009: 54). The Confederation of Irish Industry (CII) and parts of the union movement had still been still in favour of continuing with the national agreements, but the major opposition came from the Federation of Irish Employers (FIE) and smaller employer associations (IRE-10). The principal disagreement between unions and employers was the cause of unemployment: While unions held up their wage claims and argued that unemployment was caused by too little demand, employers asserted that excessive wage claims of the unions were its primary cause (Culpepper 2008, Roche 1994).

The incoming government coalition between FG and ILP refrained from addressing this impasse and instead focused on reigning in inflation and curbing public expenditure, which effectively ended the period of incipient corporatism under the national understandings (IRE-10, Compston 1994, Hardiman 1988). The end of the corporatist experiment was accompanied by political turmoil: The period of late 1981 and 1982 saw no less than three elections at a time 'when the strength of Fianna Fáil and Fine Gael and Labour combined was delicately balanced' (Marsh & Mitchell 1999: 40). In the first two elections neither FF nor a coalition of FG and ILP could gain a parliamentary majority. The first minority government was formed as a coalition between FG and Labour, but collapsed when it could not gain a parliamentary majority for a budget that proposed cutting subsidies and introducing new taxes. The tiny Workers' Party brought down the FF minority government that followed, before the election in November 1982 brought a comparatively comfortable majority for a renewed coalition of Fine Gael and Labour that held office until 1987. But the new political stability did not lead to macroeconomic stability. The return to decentralized bargaining did not translate into job growth or falling unemployment and – while it reduced strike militancy – wages still continued to outpace inflation and widened the pay differentials between workers (Roche 1994). In this context, the strategy of attracting foreign multinationals became a fruitless approach, and the coalition's effort to stimulate growth by 'using fiscal policy exacerbated the problem, causing public debt to reach 136.6 per cent of GDP by 1986' (Ornston 2012: 127). Thus, even in the context of the highest emigration since the 1950s, unemployment skyrocketed to a staggering 17% (Ornston 2012: 127). In sum, the combination of high unemployment, strong inflation, meagre growth and high debt presented the biggest economic crisis in the post-war years, bringing Ireland into a situation where it was 'weeks away from IMF taking over control' (interview with IBEC official, cited in Baccaro & Lim 2007: 28, also: IRE-8, IRE-10).

Retrospectively, the dire economic situation opened up a window of opportunity for more thorough reforms of industrial relations and VET. The economic crisis created conditions that proved difficult for an immediate VET reform and for the expansion of apprenticeship given the depressed demand for skilled manufacturing workers and adversarial industrial relations. Nonetheless, VET was already an important topic within two central publications of the tripartite NESC[37], which the literature generally regards as the focal documents that formed the basis for the turn to social partnership in 1987 (Compston 2003, Hardiman 2000, 2002, O'Connell et al. 1999, Roche 2007 Teague & Donaghey 2009a, b). That VET is not discussed in these contributions illustrates the extent to which Irish VET has been ignored in comparative political economy.

In 1986, the NESC, with members drawn from the traditional social partners, senior civil servants and government nominees, published a report titled 'A Strategy for Development 1986–1990: Growth, Employment and Fiscal Balance' (NESC 1986), which became a focal turning point for Irish industrial relations (Culpepper 2005, O'Donnell et al. 2011). In contrast to earlier reports, which had addressed the situation of the Irish Economy and proposed short-term reforms, the 1986 report deliberately addressed Ireland's situation in a 'medium term framework' (NESC 1986: xiii), as its 'Council was [...] of the view that the major imbalances which had built up in the economy could not be redressed in a short space of time' (NESC 1986: xiii). In this vein, the report switched the attention away from immediate financial and economic problems towards an analysis of low growth rates as the key problem with the sluggish economy recovery and performance:

> What is crucial for the attainment of sustained economic growth in an Economy such as Ireland's is the capacity of the internationally trading sectors to produce goods and services and to sell them competitively on export markets, or on the domestic market in the face of competition from exports. In the short term this can be achieved by securing the maximum degree of cost-competitiveness and in the medium term by defending competitive advantage while at the same time expanding the productive capacity of the economy. (NESC 1986: 185)

The NESC identified unemployment and imbalances in public finance as the two major challenges facing Ireland and recommended taking measures to accelerate the growth in economic output, primarily via the development of the export-oriented sectors, but also to redress and retrench public expenditures in a way that the latter are 'shared

37 In 1973, the NESC became the follow-up institution to the NIEC.

equitably across all sections of society' (NESC 1986: 305). The tripartite nature of the NESC and the agreement on a common medium-term outlook that essentially took a perspective on Ireland 'as a small, open' economy (Culpepper 2008, Hardiman 2002) facilitated compromise among employers once the NESC's recommendations entered the political stage. The NESC proved to be an important institution on the way to social partnership as it was this institution in which

> employer and union leaders developed a shared analysis of the nature of the country's economic problems… [They agreed] that moderation in pay increases would be essential to improve competitiveness and, thus, generate the necessary economic improvement. (Hardiman 2002: 8)

The other important report for VET and industrial relations reform was also produced by the NESC in its 1985 discussion paper on 'Manpower Policy in Ireland' (NESC 1985) that in turn formed the basis for a Fine Gael and Labour Party coalition government White Paper on VET and manpower policy reform. The government White Paper described the apprenticeship system as 'costly, inefficient and inflexible' (Department of Labour 1986: XX).

Based on this analysis it proposed major changes. A new apprenticeship system should be based on standards achieved rather than on time served; it should ensure a satisfactory balance between supply and demand for apprentices and reduce the public financial cost by more effectively spreading the cost for off-the-job training between firms and the state. The report also demanded that 'the interests involved in apprenticeship takes [sic!] a more flexible and long-term view of the requirements' (NESC 1985: 273) of VET reform. While the paper signalled a principal willingness for the infusion of more government money into apprenticeships, which unions and employers had been calling for throughout the 1980s (IRE-1), it also envisaged a strong role for the social partners in the process of reviewing apprenticeships (IRE-5, IRE-6). However, this review process should be connected to the broader process of manpower policy (IRE-10), and not organized as piecemeal as under the old regulations of AnCO and the AACs. The White Paper recommended that the more comprehensive involvement of the social partners should take place under the remits of a new agency for manpower policy that was to bundle the training and employment functions formerly spread among AnCO and other governmental agencies in order to give a more effective response to training and employment needs in the context of high youth and adult unemployment (IRE-6, IRE-10, IRE-13).

Taken together, the two reports acted as important catalysts for the reconfiguration of VET in Ireland and the way the macroeconomic challenges should be governed. For VET, they stressed the need for more coherent manpower policies including apprenticeships, which had traditionally been of little interest to governments of different party compositions, except for those including the electorally comparatively weak Labour Party (IRE-8). The NESC 1986 report, in particular, was central for a move towards social partnership in tackling the challenges of low growth, high inflation and unemployment and a dire state of public finances (IRE-7, IRE-10, Hardiman 2002, Culpepper 2008).

Despite putting VET reform back onto the political agenda, it was still unclear how the apprenticeship system was to be reformed towards a standards-based system and who was to pay for the new system. This entailed, *inter alia,* the challenge to break the traditional impasse between craft unions and employers. This changed when apprenticeship reform became connected with the broader process of social partnership and led to the introduction of a new, standards-based apprenticeship system in 1993/1994. This process occurred under the new institution of FÁS (FÁS/Training and Employment Authority), as a new tripartite agency for manpower policy, which replaced AnCO in 1987 and gave a new role for the social partners in apprenticeship politics and in VET governance.

In 1986, the government decided that the old AnCO structures were to be this transferred to the new FÁS institution. This became incorporated in the 1987 Labour Services Act. The creation of FÁS resulted from a merger of AnCO, the National Manpower Service (NMS) and the Youth Employment Authority (YEA). The NESC report, the government White Paper on Manpower Policy and a NESC-commissioned consultants' report (Danaher et al. 1985) had criticized the multiplication of institutions in the field of manpower policy and the failure to 'create a coherent active labour market policy' (Boyle 2005: 44). The reports suggested bundling youth and adult employment programmes under a single agency with a stronger role for the Department of Labour.

The principle that the Minster of Labour appointed the members of the FÀS Board upon recommendation was continued, and the social partners remained equally represented. However, FÁS represented a new institutional opportunity to approach the reform of the apprenticeship system, as the main body within FÀS responsible for apprenticeships, the National Apprenticeship Advisory Committee (NAAC), became strongly driven by the social partners (IRE-1, IRE-2, IRE-3, IRE-6, IRE-8). The advice of the NAAC, which was always chaired by a either a union or an employer representative, was also sought after much in the process of apprenticeship reform and emerged as a central driving force in the evolution of the Standards-based Apprenticeship (SBA) model that was introduced in 1993/1994 (IRE-6, IRE-8).

It is noteworthy that the creation of FÀS preceded social partnership. Research unambiguously holds that social partnership and economic governance by tripartite pacts between union, employer associations and governments have provided the basis for the successful reforms of the Irish apprenticeship system (Nyhan 2010; O'Connor 2006; Ryan 2000), this fact has received little attention except in Boyle's (2005) meticulous study of Irish reforms of active labour-market policy. Boyle traces the agreement on FÁS back to the emergence of a political cross-class coalition between central FF and Labour politicians who worked across the government-opposition divide, which marked an 'important part of the prehistory of social partnership' (Interview 13, cited in Boyle 2005: 32). This coalition consisted of the more populist wings of FF and the ILP and was strongly connected to the union movement. It focused on progressing an active manpower policy as had been set out by the NESC in 1986 (Boyle 2005). This coalition remained central in the support of an active manpower policy, even as the FF governments (1987–1992) abandoned the course of Keynesian politics they had still followed at the beginning of the 1980s. Foras Áiseanna Saothair was reorganized once the social partnership had stabilized and became the institutional forum in which the reform towards the SBA-model took place.

The year 1987, which saw the emergence of the FÀS, also marked the beginning of the social partnership between employers, unions and governments that lasted until the economic crisis of the late 2000s. It was based on tripartite pacts that entailed agreements over a wide area of policies such as fiscal and tax policies, public expenditure, social policies and – most importantly – the return to centralized wage bargaining with pay floors for the private and the public sector and low-paid occupations (Hardiman 2002, O'Donnell et al. 2011), thus bringing an end to the long-standing problem of bargaining contestation and wage-driven inflation. Why had social partnership emerged as an economically but also *politically* viable solution? Which incentives did it hold for governments, employers and unions?

Although the debate around the policy proposals of the NESC 1986 report had already begun under the outgoing FG/ILP coalition, it came to a halt when Labour withdrew from the coalition because it did not agree with cuts that its bigger coalition partner envisioned for the next budget. After the dissolution of the Dáil, the next elections results were challenging for coalition formation because neither of the big two parties was able to secure a parliamentary majority. Fianna Fáil was elected as the strongest party in early 1987, but fell three seats short of a parliamentary majority and still adhered to the principle of not entering coalitions (Marsh and Mitchell 1999). With the rise of the right-wing Progressive Democrats (PD) and the left-wing Workers' Party, government formation generally became 'much more difficult after the 1987 election' (Marsh & Mitchell 1999: 51).

Fianna Fáil secured office by attracting the support of some independent Dáil members, but was immediately faced with tough choices due to the dire state of public finances and economy in order to prevent a total economic collapse (Baccaro & Lim 2007, Hardiman 2002, Marsh & Mitchell 1999, Ornston 2012). The option to impose a tight budget with severe cuts, in a 'monetarist' fashion, was complicated by the fragile majority of the FF minority government, because it had traditionally relied on working class support, which made it hard not to hit parts of its own constituency (Hardiman 1988). Based on earlier experiences, it was generally perceived that

> the trade union movement possessed considerable labour-market power and disruptive capacity, and governments generally acted on the assumption that if ICTU perceived that the vital interests of the trade unions were under threat, it would have the capacity to make such a strategy very difficult to implement. (Hardiman 1988: 215)

Thus, the incoming FF government steered a delicate course, when it introduced a very tight budget, which was very similar – except for an even tighter public borrowing requirement – to the FG proposal that had led to the dissolution of its coalition with the ILP. However, the unions did not react as anticipated because they faced the problem of mounting unemployment (Roche 1994). For them, the strategy of fighting for and obtaining wage increases under decentralized wage bargaining had not delivered real earnings benefits to its members. On the contrary, despite nominal wage increases, inflation and a progressive income tax burden had resulted in losses in real-take home pay of between 7% and 11% (NESC 1986). Moreover, ICTU officials became increasingly worried that the government might engage in politics similar to the politics of 'class war' against the unions that they had observed in the United Kingdom under the first and second Thatcher governments (IRE-8, Baccaro & Lim 2007: 34, Ornston 2012: 134). Ornston captured this in an interview with an ICTU official who pointedly expressed the mood of the trade union movement:

> We were looking at Margaret Thatcher and we said, 'Holy shit, this is heavy stuff. We can't have that happen here. What if it does?' We read British papers. We watched British television. We, on the union side, said that we have a crisis. Real earnings fell by 8 per cent in less than a decade; unemployment was very high; inflation had hit 24 per cent in the early 1980s; and manufacturing was being decimated, particularly indigenous industry. (ICTU representative, cited in Ornston 2012: 134)

Other aspects also contributed to the new stance that unions took on the verge of social partnership in late 1987. First, the emergence of the PD as a new party on the right of the political spectrum indicated that the political system could be moving away from accommodating union preferences into politics (Roche 1994). In addition, more pronounced splits in the union movement began to emerge due to changes in policy: the failure to proceed with a scheduled pay raise for senior civil servants after the new Finance Minister had been in office for just two days was a first warning sign that the government was serious about fiscal rectitude (Ornston 2012: 134). When further public expenditure cuts were announced, public-sector unions became increasingly worried about job security and real-take home pay and expressed their willingness to negotiate on wage moderation. In contrast, some craft unions in the private sector argued that decentralized bargaining remained more beneficial for them (Teague 1995). Finally, throughout the economic slump of the 1980s, union membership had begun to decline (Roche 1994), which was partially met by amalgamation between traditional craft unions. This move towards union centralization and more industrial unionism made strategies of union particularism increasingly difficult (IRE-1, IRE-8).

In sum, these contingent developments made it gradually more difficult for the union movement as a whole to focus on the domestic purchasing power of their members as the main issue in wage bargaining (Culpepper 2008). This strongly contrasted with the employers' stance that inflation and excessive wage demands were a core cause of Ireland's weak international competitiveness. On the political front, unions had lobbied for job creation via government spending on construction and via capital investment (Culpepper 2008),[38] but this view had been contradicted by the NESC's 1986 report's analysis that wage moderation, balanced public finances and investments in skills were the major policies necessary for the restoration of international competitiveness and were imperative for economic growth (IRE-10).

The unions' counterparts, the major employer associations, were 'the most reluctant of the social partners to embrace national tripartite pay bargaining' (Roche 1994: 397), even after the unions had moved towards this option.[39] Notwithstanding that some of the organized employers had 'walked away' from centralized wage bargaining and the national understandings around 1980 (Hardiman, 1998, Power 2009), employers were still in doubt that the government could sustain fiscal rectitude when faced with serious opposition and still saw decentralized wage bargaining as their best option (Culpepper 2008, Roche 1994). However, as the unions moved towards the position of centralized wage bargaining and the government signalled its willingness to adopt this solution for the public sector, employers were presented with a new set of options. With coordinated wage bargaining for public jobs on the horizon, private sector employers slowly began to shift their position towards centralized wage bargaining after the unions had repeatedly pointed out

38 Also see *Irish Times*, 30 January 1986.

39 For other interpretations see Baccaro and Lim 2007: 35, Hardiman 1988.

that they were willing to keep their side of the bargain: If employers still opted for decentralized wage bargaining, coordinated bargaining in the public sector could lead to spill-over effects into the private sector and further damage cost competitiveness (Culpepper 2008).

A basic compromise on the centralization of wage bargaining finally emerged after the new government had succeeded in its advocacy of a tripartite agreement by courting employers (Roche 1994) and trade unions (IRE-9). This strategy was essentially based on a tight coupling of fiscal rectitude and promises to both social partners for public investment and tax reductions to compensate them for their agreement. *Politically*, this strategy became possible for the FF minority government because the FG leadership had committed to 'support the next Fianna Fáil budget as long as Fianna Fáil continued to follow a sound economic programme' (Marsh & Mitchell 1999: 51) in its Tallaght Strategy, which gave FF a de facto parliamentary majority on the major economic issues.

Finally, the government managed to reach consensus with the major social partners, who jointly signed the PNR in late 1987 as a response to the 'deep social and economic crisis' (O'Donnell & Thomas 2002: 175). However, union participation had only been secured by a narrow margin. Participation in the PNR was put to a vote at the ICTU general conference, which resulted in favouring participation in the PNR; although the majority of unions were against the agreement, block voting procedures within the congress favoured the public-sector and larger unions, which voted in favour of the PNR (Baccaro & Lim 2007: 35). The programme addressed four broad areas of policy reforms, which were the:

> (i) creation of a fiscal, exchange rate and monetary climate conducive to economic growth; (ii) movement towards greater equity and fairness in the tax system; (iii) diminishing or removing social inequities in our society; and (iv) intensification of practical measures to generate increased job opportunities on a sectorial basis. (Government of Ireland 1987: 5)

In the PNR, the social partners agreed to centralize wage bargaining, which contained binding commitments on wage moderation in both the public and the private sector. Wage moderation on part of the unions was to be compensated with promised tax cuts over the three years of its duration, amounting to roughly 225 million pounds (Hardiman

2002: 19). This was coupled with a low interest-rate and low inflation regime and buffered by a non-accommodating exchange- rate policy and control of public expenditure via expenditure retrenchment, which, however, did not include social welfare transfer payments (O'Donnell & Thomas 2002). The PNR did not include an explicit paragraph that addressed education reform specifically, but rather it contained a declaration of intent to invest in educational expansion (Government of Ireland 1987: 14–15). Moreover, a Central Review Committee (CRC), consisting of representatives of the PNR's signatories,[40] was established in order to monitor progress and to review its policies.

The specific design of the PNR offered benefits to government, unions and employers. For the government, it was the basis for the implementation of fiscal rectitude and budgetary consolidation without having to fear that unions would engage in oppositional politics. Despite the Tallaght strategy of FG, FF still remained in the position of a 'weak government' (Baccaro & Lim 2007, Power 2009) in terms of its electoral support and was faced with the possibility of electoral punishment for engaging in austerity politics. Moreover, due to the dire economic situation, it was quite unclear at the time whether national recovery could be achieved and within which time horizon. Fianna Fáil's attempt to strike a bargain with unions and employers can therefore be interpreted as a cautionary exercise in 'blame avoidance' (Weaver 1986). With the responsibility for the PNR widely shared across employers, unions and, tacitly, the FG, a potential failure of the PNR might have resulted in a loss of fewer votes than a strategy of 'crash through or crash' akin to unilateral decision making under Thatcher. Furthermore, as the working class was a central part of the electoral support for the FF, getting the unions on board acted as an additional safeguard. The unions had to defend the PNR towards their members as a sound policy, which reduced the FF government's risk of confronting 'strong and militant

40 Aside from government, three groups of actors were PNR signatories. The trade unions were represented by the ICTU as the peak labour association. The Federation of Irish Employers (FIE), the Confederation of Irish Industry (CII) and the Construction Industry Federation (CIF) represented employers, and the Irish Farming Associations, the Irish Co-operative Society and Macra na Feirme represented farmers.

public service unions, whose members would be immediately affected by spending cuts' (Roche 2007: 397).

For unions, the PNR offered compensation for modest pay settlements by way of cuts in personal income taxation and the potential for economic growth and out of the unemployment crisis (Culpepper 2008: 16, O'Donnell et al. 2011). Moreover, it offered them a viable option to regain influence within politics, as they had been kept 'at arm's length' by the outgoing FG/Labour coalition (Hardiman 2002: 9). This option of shoring up political power can be seen in the context of the British union movement's fate in the face of the post-oil-shock economic crisis and as Irish unions had been given to understand that they could 'either [be] part of the solution or part of the problem' (Hardiman 2002: 9). The economic crisis and membership losses also provided an option for unions to progressively work out a deal with employers and the government (Baccaro & Lim 2007, Rhodes 1998, 2001). The creation of tripartite institutions such as the CRC, but also the NAAC gave them 'institutionalized access to government ministers and key civil servants' (O'Donnell & Thomas 2002: 173).

Finally, employers had only bought into the PNR after they were assured that the unions would keep part of their bargain and because wage coordination in the public realm might have negative spill-over effects on the private sector. Moreover, employer representatives were concerned that unions would want extra wage increases at the company level and that this type of wage drift might erode nationally bargained wage restraint (Roche 1994). Their initial reservations about the reliability of the union movement's promises were also refuelled after the social partnership had taken off. In 1989 the inflation rate agreed in the PNR was exceeded and the UK-based Manufacturing Science and Finance Union (MSF) and the Amalgamated Transport and General Workers Union (ATGWU) called for a special ICTU general conference in order to withdraw from social partnership, but they were defeated by the bigger public sector unions and the biggest general union (Services Industrial Professional and Technical Union – SIPTU (Baccaro & Lim 2007: 35).

However, social partnership was also largely compatible with general business aims and employers could obtain a good deal (Hardiman 1998, Power 2009) as social partnership was a vehicle that could deliver modest and predictable wage increases as well as industrial peace, while also delivering an investment-friendly regime of low inflation and low interest rates (O'Donnell & Thomas 2002). Moreover, stable low corporate taxation rates and the retention of managerial prerogative at the firm level acted as additional incentives to cooperate in social partnership, which only impinged 'marginally on managerial prerogative within individual enterprises' (O'Donnell & Thomas 2002: 180) and still allowed for the pursuit of firms' flexibilization strategies.

After its inception, the PNR muted some of the critical voices within the union and employer camps, as it delivered increasing levels of growth, which were helped, albeit fortuitously, by an 'international economic upturn and a drop in the inflation rate, and turned a modest pay-and-tax-cuts deal into an increase in real disposable income' (Hardiman 2002). The industrial peace and wage moderation brought about by the PNR also gave employers a more positive outlook towards tripartism under social pacts (Baccaro & Lim 2007: 36).

Public opinion was also rather content with the first results of the PNR and election polls indicated that an overall Dáil majority was possible for FF. After the government had been defeated in the Dáil after losing a motion concerning the provision of funds for sufferers from AIDS, Taiosech Haughey used this as an opportunity to call for an early general election. In this 1989 election, FF stabilized its vote share at 44%, but fell short of an absolute majority by seven seats, which finally made it give up its traditional 'non-coalition stance'. It formed a minimum winning coalition with the right-wing PD, a former breakaway of FF, but this did not change the government's willingness to continue on the path of social partnership.[41]

Yet, rather than stimulating and consolidating economic growth, the PNR had been largely unsuccessful in reducing unemployment, which became a central issue in the second round of social partnership negotiations. The consultations preceding the Programme for Economic and Social Progress (PESP) of 1991 therefore not only focused on wage moderation via centralized bargaining and the further consolidation of public finances but also placed far more emphasis on employment and training policies.

41 For a more detailed account of the coalition formation between FF and PD consult Marsh and Mitchell 1999: 54–58.

On the topic of employment, the PESP proposed an advanced version of the Social Employment Scheme (SES), which had underpinned the cross-party coalition between FF and ILP in the run-up towards the PNR (IRE-6). The new Community Employment Development Programme, which was consolidated into Community Employment in 1994, was an area-based approach to active labour market policy that introduced job opportunities with FÁS and delivered training for the unemployed in local communities. The scheme quickly grew to 20 000 places 'making it Ireland's most important ALMP measure' (Weishaupt 2011: 278). However, in contrast to the United Kingdom, the scheme did not act to replace traditional apprenticeships as it primarily targeted the older unemployed.

Regarding VET, apprenticeships emerged as an important part of the employment and training strategy contained within the PESP. It referred directly to the 1986 government White Paper on manpower policy and restated its objectives of creating a new apprenticeship scheme that was to 'be based on standards achieved rather than time served; [to] ensure a satisfactory balance between supply of and demand for apprentices; [and to] reduce the financial cost to the state while maintaining quality' (Government of Ireland 1991: 64). The PESP also contained agreements on long-standing problems of apprenticeships in Ireland – especially the uneven quality of occupationally fragmented training – as regulations still did not stipulate mandatory training requirements and standards in order to be recognized as a skilled craftsperson. As a new approach, it was agreed that a National Crafts Certificate would be a compulsory requirement in order to become a recognized craftsperson and that the duration of apprenticeships was to be determined by trade-specific training requirements (Government of Ireland 1991: 64). Moreover, the new system would contain fixed periods of workplace and off-the-job training, a structured system of apprentice intake and the PESP included the target of increasing the number of apprentices by 1000 per year, with the option of expanding the system into further trades. Finally, employers and trade unions would be given strong representation to oversee the process of apprenticeship reform within FÀS, especially via the NAAC.

The inclusion of apprenticeship reform as a central component of the PESP changed the incentives for employers and – especially craft – unions (Boyle 2003), and offered a venue in order to overcome the impasse between union strategies of 'skill control' and employer neglect of training. Even after they were given more representation and influence over training policy via the NAAC when FÀS had been inaugurated, unions had still resisted major changes to the training system, especially where they could blur skill profiles (IRE-1). However, in the new context of pay moderation, strategies of skill control lost their attraction and unions came to realize the need for off-the-job education and skills certification in order to secure their members' employment opportunities in a rapidly changing labour market (IRE-3, IRE-5). Moreover, the infusion of additional government funding into the off-the-job component of VET offered an additional incentive (IRE-7, IRE-9). As social partnership had delivered modest growth under the PNR without substantial income losses for private sector workers, it would also have been a daring strategy to resist changes to the apprenticeship system, where negotiations took place on par with the employers and the government and unions could play a strong role in the evolving policies under social partnership (IRE-6, IRE-8). With stronger regulations for apprenticeship intake, if an agreement on a new system could be reached this could prevent employers from hiring apprentices as unskilled workers after the first year of training at AnCO and pave the way to a more structured labour market entry for skilled workers (IRE-2, IRE-3, IRE-6).

The latter point also offered an incentive to the FF-PD coalition. If employer involvement could be strengthened in the course of reform, state-sponsored funds for off-the-job training would be used more efficiently (IRE-6, IRE-8). A critical point of the earlier AnCO-reforms, which should provide for a more structured entry into the skilled trades, had been that at the end of the 1980s employers still 'preferred to poach skilled workers from other companies or to cherry pick those coming off the state sponsored (AnCO/FÀS) first year off-the-job apprenticeship' (Nyhan 2009: 462). The FÀS expansion of training capacities also necessitated a more controlled intake of apprentices in order to plan the spending on training personnel (IRE-3, IRE-6, IRE-8). Moreover, the European funding that Ireland received could still be used for investments in training (IRE-6).

Finally, employers were 'tied into' social partnership, which had paved the way to cross-class cooperation on the national level. They were sympathetic to an apprenticeship system that was based on competences achieved rather than time served but they and their representatives on the NAAC were still reluctant to pay more for training and the implementation of a new scheme:

> Employers were supportive of the idea of a qualitatively superior apprenticeship system that was standards-based rather than time-served, but they wanted the state to pay for it. While desiring a new [...] system, employers did not wish to have to bear its costs but did wish to be able to 'cherry pick' the results of the system by being able to avail of a new cadre of highly trained apprentices. If US corporations were to be allowed to pick skilled labour coming out of the RTC's 'off the shelf' at taxpayers expense, why shouldn't Irish employers be allowed to do the same? (Boyle 2005: 48)

At this time point, employers still perceived training as a cost and not as an investment (IRE-2, IRE-7, IRE-8). This applied especially for smaller employers, who were afraid that more structured off-the-job training phases would reduce their ability to use apprentices for productive purposes (IRE-8). Thus, in negotiating the new system, employers argued for an increase in government funding as a crucial necessity (IRE-1, IRE-7).

Nevertheless, the creation of FÀS together with tripartite social partnership arrangements provided a fertile ground for an agreement in 1991 between the Irish Business and Employers Confederation (IBEC), ICTU and the FF government, which was mostly negotiated within the NAAC and the board of FÀS (Boyle 2005; IRE-3). Based on the social partner discussion document 'Apprenticeship – A New Approach' (FÀS 1989) the paragraphs on apprenticeship reform that were included in the PESP were hammered out. At that point in time the FÀS leadership was still sceptical about how to convince employers to reform the system away from their current short-term priorities, believing that 'employers would have to be cajoled, if not coerced, into a system from which they would, in the long-term, benefit' (Boyle 2005: 48). Yet, FÀS leadership and the Department of Enterprise and Employment found a solution by strategically coupling the renegotiations of the new, standards-based system to negotiations in the preparation of the tripartite PESP agreement of 1991. This convinced employers to partake in the new system, as they were to be part of all tripartite bodies to be created with the inauguration of new collective apprenticeship institutions (Boyle: 2005).

However, the commitment expressed by the social partners in the PESP still had to be institutionalized into a new system. The negotiations about its specific design dragged on under the umbrella of the respective committees within FÀS. In finally convincing the employers to partake in the system, even if they had to pay for a part of the general training, the cross-class party political axis between parts of FF and ILP was again decisive (IRE-6). At the beginning of 1993, a new coalition government between FF and the ILP had formed that possessed a considerable parliamentary majority with almost 61% of the vote share. Very central to the reform of apprenticeships were the Minister for Employment, Ruari Quinn of the Labour Party, and Mary O'Rourke of the FF as the incoming Minister for Education, who strongly cooperated with FÀS and the NAAC (IRE-6, IRE-8). In the discussions on financing and reform of apprenticeships towards a standards-based model, O'Rourke made direct references to Germany as a role model for apprenticeships and made clear that an efficient training system needed the strong support of employers:

> I referred also to employers who are not taking sufficient responsibility for training apprentices. The German system is constantly held up to us as the proper model for training apprentices. Compared to the German system where employers must provide adequate on-the-job training and release apprentices for off-the-job training, Irish employers for the most part were not committed to apprenticeship training [...] Then the question of a new apprenticeship system [...] was the subject of detailed discussions between the social partners during the negotiations on the current *Programme for Economic and Social Progress* in 1991. The system was to be standard based. To be recognised as a craft worker in future a person would have to have the national craft certificate. (O'Rourke 1993)

In 1993, when employers' public opposition towards a new system had ebbed, the government pushed through the SBA reform. Under the SBA, apprenticeships are statutorily regulated and combine seven structural phases of workplace learning and off-the-job vocational education. The SBA system, which was instituted first as a pilot project and then put in place on a regular basis with the Apprenticeship Act of 1994, covered up to 26 designated trades (FÀS 2012) in traditional manufacturing occupations, but mostly in building and construction. It became structured on a modular basis, where four on-the-job phases (phases 1, 3, 5, 7) alternate with statutory off-the-job training and education in

FÁS training centres (phase 2) and institutes of technology (phases 4 and 6). Thus, the time for off-the-job education amounts to roughly 21% of the whole apprenticeship time, but off-the-job instruction is strongly geared towards technical education with only 2% general education (Ryan 2000: 50).

Time is still an important element, as apprenticeships normally take four years until completion and apprentice pay is structured in four levels that correspond to the year of the apprenticeship. Under the provisions of the SBA, apprentices enjoy full employee status and are entitled to off-the-job education and training elements of the SBA. Regarding the funding of apprenticeships, employers fund the on-the-job phases while the state funds the off-the-job phases. However, employers also contribute a special levy of 0.25% of their payroll and apprentices are paid a training allowance to the rate of pay appropriate to the year of apprenticeship whilst on the off-the-job phases.

Concerning employer involvement and responsibility, under the new system they had to meet certain standards in order to be permitted to take on apprentices. This was decided on by the inspectorate of FÀS. It covered not only specific tools and training equipment but also the availability of a skilled craftsperson approved by FÀS as a trainer (Boyle 2005: 52–53). Moreover, apprentices have to reach specified standards during their phases of workplace training or they cannot progress to the next phase of the apprenticeship. Under the governance framework of the SBA, standards are set collectively by FÀS in co-operation with the Department of Education and Science (DES) and the NAAC.

From 2001 onwards, standards were set within the National Framework of Qualifications (NFQ), established on the basis of the Qualifications Act. The corresponding governmental agency, the National Qualifications Authority of Ireland (NQAI), which devised and regularly updates the NFQ, is composed on a tripartite basis (NQAI 2011), as is the Further Education and Training Council (FETAC), which is the awarding body for apprenticeship qualifications, which are normally placed at level 6 (roughly equivalent with NVQ level 3).

From its institutional configuration the system had changed very little since its inception and had grown spectacularly during the phase of the Celtic tiger. Starting with roughly 4000 apprentices in 1995, at its peak in 2007 the system contained 30 000 apprentices (FÀS 2012).

Research on the effects of institutional changes that have occurred in Ireland's apprenticeship system suggest that they have transformed it to a higher qualitative level, as is expressed by increases in the apprenticeship intake, higher completion rates and high satisfaction among major stakeholders (McCartney & Teague 2001, O'Connor 2006, O'Connor & Harvey 2001).

While many indicators point in this direction, a note of caution is appropriate, as the intake and completion rates were systematically skewed as to overrate the success of Irish apprenticeship reforms. A construction boom mainly drove the increased intake since the middle of the 1990s, until the boom burst in the current economic and financial crisis with devastating effects on the SBA. While the system was rated as very successful by many observers at the end of the 1990s (IRE-3, IRE-8), its small scale and focus on occupations relevant for building and construction have made the system vulnerable to economic cycles as I will show in the next section. However, Ryan (2000) was right that, in contrast to the fragmented system nowadays found in the United Kingdom

> [i]nstitutional development in Ireland has moved towards a continental approach in three respects: the linkage of apprenticeship to the education system, the development of social partnership for the design and administration of apprenticeship, and the adoption of a statutory framework to underpin the whole. The development has been consensual, taking the time necessary to win support and commitment from the social partners, helped along by generous public funding. (Ryan 2000: 62)

4.3 Standards-based apprenticeships and the 'Celtic tiger' – Incrementalism and path-sustaining adaptation (1995–2008)

After the reform of SBAs under social partnership, the development of apprenticeships proceeded rather consensually. The process was still underpinned by social pacts at the national level that continued to be based on wage moderation, bargaining centralization and compensation via tax and social policies, as a basic framework for generalized political exchange, which had cross-over appeal to governments, employers and unions. Foras Áiseanna Saothai continued to infuse more funding into the apprenticeship system and, due to its role as the planning and delivery agency of active labour market policies such as CE, it grew to become a central and powerful institution within the Irish economy (IRE-9, Boyle 2005). After SBAs' inception, employers became more appreciative of the new system over time, apart from some smaller employers, who lobbied for training geared to smaller firms' needs.

These calls were answered in 1997, when the incoming FF and PD coalition opened up a possibility for smaller employers to lobby for more employer-geared training and support outside the new apprenticeship scheme, which some perceived as unnecessary, demanding and inflexible. The new government, in turn, based on a White Paper on Human Resource Development, followed these business calls and in 1999 established Skillnets Ltd, which opened up new funding possibilities for an enterprise-led approach to training, especially geared towards SMEs (Maloney 2005). However, this new training possibility did little in the way of displacing traditional apprentices, but can at best be seen as a layering attempt in order to assuage small businesses. Compared to training expenditures of FÀS, the budgetary size of this programme is miniscule.

The gradual development of the new SBA-system proceeded in a consensual manner between incoming governments and union and employer representatives in sectors with training occupations. The few conflicts that ensued after 1994 were not primarily about the system as such, but rather within the system between FÀS and the ITCs (IRE-5, IRE-7) or between employers and the ITCs, when apprentices failed the theoretical test and had to repeat the respective off-the-job-phase (IRE-5, IRE-7). Moreover, despite attempts to broaden the system beyond the classical apprenticeship occupations and into the service sector, respective developments were rather limited, which turned out to be fatal for the apprenticeship system due to secular developments in the construction industry.

In general, the development of the Irish economy under the social pacts of a 'competitive corporatist' nature (Rhodes 1998, 2001) was characterized by stable employment and economic growth, where some employment decline in the traditional manufacturing sector was more than compensated by exponential growth in the modern high-tech sector (Ornston 2012), which was substantially dominated by foreign-owned companies such as IBM or Apple. However, growth did proceed without exerting too much upwards pressure on wages, which could have caused wage drift – a potential danger for the stability of the Irish economy (OECD 1999). The widespread adherence to moderate pay agreements was also helped by the fact that the representation of unions, which could have tried to bargain for a greater share of the MNC's profits, is comparatively low in the foreign-owned high-tech sector (Hardiman 2002: 13, Ornston 2012).

However, far greater wage drift occurred in the construction sector, which grew exponentially because of infrastructural investment underpinning the high-tech sector. As many SBA occupations and apprentice places were directly linked to the construction sector, these developments became extremely relevant to the structure of apprenticeship in Ireland. First, the spectacular growth in apprenticeships was mainly driven by building and construction occupations (IRE-7, IRE-9, FÀS no date), which made for the bulk of the 30 000 apprenticeship places in the mid-1990s. This also meant that money was increasingly infused into the system for the provision of the three off-the-job phases (IRE-2), as employers took more apprentices in as the government had planned for (IRE-2, IRE-3). In addition, wages in the building and construction industry, especially for skilled manual trades, showed 'spectacular gains' (Hardiman 2002: 13) from the middle of the 1990s onwards, which meant that now 'there [was] probably substantial wage drift' (OECD 1999: 73–74), which started to exert wage pressure into other sectors of the economy (IRE-3).

However, the frequent settlement of wages in the construction industry far above the moderate pay level agreed nationally meant that apprenticeships in these occupations were increasingly sought after (IRE-1, IRE-3). As economic growth started to shrink from its spectacular levels in the mid-to-late-1990s in most sectors, construction continued to boom, fuelled by cheap mortgages and low interest rates (IRE-6), which were further reduced as Ireland entered the European Monetary Union. This significantly increased the private demand for housing (Honohan 2009: 209–215). Critical voices from the ITCs that witnessed the substantial shift into building-related courses were not taken up by FÀS, which still continued to increase apprenticeship funding in order to tackle skill shortages in the booming building sector (IRE-2, IRE-3, IRE-4).

During the boom, the workforce employed in construction rose from 'about 7 per cent in the early and mid-1990s to over 13 per cent by 2007' (Honohan 2009: 212), and '20 per cent of GNP came from construction' (Kelly 2010: 1). When the housing bubble burst in the US and then reached Ireland, GNP contracted by 17% in 2009 (Kelly 2010) and apprentice numbers plummeted from their peak of 30 000 to 1500, leaving an oversupply of government-sponsored places for off-the job training (IRE-1, IRE-4). Under the crisis, social partnership, which had endured for more than 20 years, also collapsed and the next elections resulted in a devastating loss for FF, which reached an all-time low of 20% of the votes. This burst also inspired an overhaul of the apprenticeship system, which was still ongoing almost 10 years after the onslaught of the economic crisis.

4.4 Conclusion

Ireland and the United Kingdom had a similar heritage of apprenticeships that were primarily based in traditional manufacturing and crafts sectors and heavily contested among craft unions and employers. Governments of different parties traditionally did very little to bring in stronger statutory regulation in VET, which was essentially based on voluntarist and contested agreements between employers and unions. As in the United Kingdom, where ITBs and the MSC were used to shore up apprenticeship training, the reforms of the Irish Industrial Training Act of 1967 failed to transform the Irish apprenticeship system towards more cooperation between the state, unions and employers and did not succeed in producing a higher degree of cooperation in skill formation. However, in contrast to developments in the United Kingdom under Thatcher, which saw the displacement of apprenticeships by employment programmes such as YT and the marketization of training provision, from 1986 onwards, the Irish institutions of apprenticeship have moved towards a collective system of skill formation. Apprenticeship regulations and governance were historically marked by incremental reforms that effected little institutional change, but they have undergone strong institutional change towards a collective approach since the mid-1980s, which was underpinned by the emergence of Social Partnership in 1987.

Two crucial institutional innovations transformed Irish training towards collective skill formation. The first was the creation of FÀS, which represented a new governance framework for labour market policies and vocational training and gave unions and employers more influence over the content of training politics. The second, on the policy level, was the introduction of the SBA in 1994. This was the central innovation, which based training on statutory regulation of training content, provision and certification. As pointed out above, these developments have brought Ireland closer to a model of collective skill formation in four central dimensions.

First, *firm involvement* in initial VET is underpinned by a training levy, which is used to sponsor components of off-the-job training in FÀS-training centres and ITCs. Apprentices receive a training wage during these phases. Second, *intermediary associations* are involved in setting training standards, as employer associations, trade unions but also representatives from the ITCs cooperate in the development of training curricula for the designated apprenticeship trades. Third, this also leads to a high degree of standardization of training content and training duration. Apprenticeships usually take three-and-a-half years and imbue *portable occupational skills*, which are certified with a national craft certificate at the end of training. Finally, the SBA system is a highly structured dual training system, with seven alternating training phases of which phases 1, 3, 5, and 7 are done on the job, phase 2 at a FÀS training centre and phases 4 and 6 take place at an ITC.

This process was underpinned by a political cross-class coalition between employers, unions and governments, who came together to agree on national policy priorities with the signing of social partnership pacts. This cross-class coalition provided a fertile ground for developing training away from its voluntarist legacy. However, the unsustainable housing and construction boom led to a collapse of apprenticeship training and, more generally, social partnership in the late 2000s. In this context, it might be argued that the apprenticeship system became ‘a victim of its own success’ (IRE-4), as no actor had a firm preference to change a system that was deemed very successful and one of the most crucial educational policy innovations of social partnership (IRE-5, IRE-8). Until the recent crisis, the policy reforms in apprenticeships had proven institutionally sustainable during governments of different partisan compositions and were even developed further under social partnership. The next years will be a crucial test if the cross-class coalition underpinning the apprenticeship development in Ireland proves resilient after the breakdown of partnership in industrial relations more generally.

5. Australia – joint economic restructuring and a slow shift to marketization

Compared to the other two cases, Australia occupies a middle ground between collective skill formation and VET delivery via competitive training (quasi-) markets. It offers apprenticeships *and* traineeships. From the mid-1980s to the mid-1990s, employer associations and unions strongly cooperated with a Commonwealth Labor government in order to reform traditional craft apprenticeships towards a system of nationally certified, dual training that produced portable skills. This came to be known as the National Training Reform Agenda (NTRA). Traditional apprenticeships were also complemented with traineeships – a development similar to England – and training provision partly shifted to a 'training market' in which public and private providers compete for government funding. Compared to apprenticeships, traineeships are set at a lower duration, educational level and content and were introduced in 1985 as an attempt to combat high youth unemployment. At first introduced outside classical apprenticeship occupations, traineeships nowadays permeate all occupations and have grown more strongly than reformed apprenticeships, especially since the mid-1990s. In comparison to England, the distribution of training between apprenticeships and traineeships is reversed, i.e. most training in Australia still takes place at a higher level of the Australian Qualifications Framework (AQF).[42]

Before I analyse the trajectory of apprenticeships in Australia between *collective skill formation* and VET delivery in a government-sponsored quasi-market, some particulars of this Antipodean state should be addressed that set it apart from the other two LMEs.

---

42 It is *per se* difficult to compare national qualifications frameworks, but intra-framework comparisons should be admissible. In England, most training offered via AA or Apprenticeships is level 2 and not level 3 of the NVQ framework; in contrast, most training in Australia is set at certificate level 3 of the AQF and not below.

First, in contrast to the unitary state structures of Ireland and the UK, Australia is a federal polity with divided competencies among the Commonwealth and the states/territories.[43] This has frequently led to differing governments with different party-political backgrounds in the states and the Commonwealth, and has led to the emergence of a strong federal Senate. In combination with rigid constitutional amendment procedures, this often proved an effective barrier to competence shifts between the different state levels. The federalist structure was also a constraint hindering the development of a formal welfare state throughout the 20th century (Castles & Uhr 2005) and made training reforms 'a daunting task' (Lundberg 1994: 5), as education and training legislation have been competences of the federal states. This complicated VET reforms throughout Australian history, and especially during the NTRA when training entered the stage of 'high politics' (Ryan 2002: 95) between the Commonwealth and the states, but section 96 of the Australian constitution provided an inroad for federal influence over training politics, which can make money available to the states and territories under certain conditions.

Second, Australia – together with New Zealand – is a peculiar case of 'incongruent development' (Castles 1985: 6) of the labour movement's strength and its parliamentary representation by a social democratic labour party: 'In both countries the labour movement has been exceptionally strong in terms of any international comparison [...] and yet democratic socialist parties have only infrequently held office' (Castles 1985: 7). In 1960, union density stood at 50.2% and thus almost 10% higher than contemporary union density in the United Kingdom (40.4%) (Visser 2009). The strength of organized labour was complemented by the fragmentation of organized business, with the first single national employer organization, the Confederation of Australian Industry (CAI), only being established in 1977 and thus almost 50 years after the formation of the Australian Council of Trade Unions (ACTU) (Lansbury & Wailes 2011: 124). However, Labor governments at the Federal level have been the exception rather than the rule and federal governments were clearly dominated by The Liberal-National coalition,

43 States: New South Wales, South Australia, Tasmania, Queensland, Victoria and Western Australia. Territories: Northern Territory and Australian Capital Territory. For simplicity, I refer to both as 'states'.

consisting of the Liberal Party of Australia, the Liberal National Party of Queensland, the National Party of Australia and the Country Liberal Party.[44] From 1900 until 1980, the Australian Labor Party (ALP) only held office for roughly 20 years. This weak record is especially due to the period after the Second World War, with only two Labor governments being formed under Prime Minsters Chifeley (1945–1949) and Whitlam (1972–1975). However, Australia also holds the record for the 'world's first democratic Labour government being formed in Queensland in 1899' (Castles 1985: 18) and the world's first national Labor majority government in 1910. Moreover, during the decades from 1910 to 1950

> Australia appears to have possessed the strongest labour movement of the world, with the Australian Labor Party (ALP) averaging some 43% of the vote in the sixteen elections held and trade union membership as a percentage of the total labour force averaging in excess of 30%. (Castles 1985: 21)

The historical strength of labour did, however, not translate into an expansion of the formal welfare state before the Second World War. Instead, Australia's 'radical welfare state' (Castles & Mitchell 1993) was based on protecting high levels of real earnings by industrial awards. Moreover, as I detail below, the change in VET away from the English roots of indentured apprenticeships towards more structured dual training models did not occur until the 1980s, when VET was linked to larger reforms of the Australian political economy.

Third, Australian exceptionalism in terms of welfare state development in comparison with other western welfare states[45] is also due to an early policy innovation: the development of a system of industrial arbitration courts, which became the central pillar of the radical welfare state and 'social protection by other means' (Huber & Stephens 2001: 172). In 1904, the Commonwealth Conciliation and Arbitration

44 The names and composition of the parties that traditionally formed the 'Liberal-National coalition' have changed throughout history, but for simplicity, I will use 'Liberal-National coalition' throughout the text.

45 Again, New Zealand is another exception to the pattern of Welfare State Development in Western Welfare States (Castles 1985, Castles & Mitchell 1993, Huber & Stephens 2001).

Act established a Commonwealth Conciliation and Arbitration Court,[46] following the example of New South Wales, which had established a similar institution for industrial arbitration in 1901. The court comprised a judge, a union and an employer representative, and was given powers for the settlement and enforcement of industrial disputes over wages and strikes. Most importantly, the court held the power to make wage awards binding for whole industrial sectors. The court was also granted the power to make federal awards for the 'prevention and settlement of industrial disputes extending beyond the limits of any one State' (Archer 1992: 387). By 1912, all states had institutionalized similar structures for industrial arbitration. The foundation of the federal court enabled the pivotal decision known as the *Harvester Judgement* in 1908, which established the general concept of a basic wage for an unskilled worker above which the court could award an additional wage margin for skilled workers. In the decision, Justice Higgins:

> established a needs-based criterion for setting the basic (or minimum) wage that should be paid to an unskilled worker. [...] Arguing that an average man must support himself, his wife and three children, Higgins set the basic wage at 42 shillings a week. Since this was above the prevailing minimum rate being offered by state tribunals, many unions sought to be covered by a federal award. (Archer 1992: 387–388)

Besides introducing the basic wage, the arbitration system also spurred union development as only organized associations were entitled to be under the courts jurisdiction, which led to the trebling of union membership between 1906 and 1914 (Clarke 1992: 188–189; in Huber & Stephens 2001: 172). Arbitration became the basic mechanism for settling industrial disputes and acted as a functional equivalent to multi-employer bargaining (Gospel 1994) as organized interests had to coordinate wage bargaining with reference to a potential decision of the court, which would be binding. By the mid-1950s, almost 90% of the working population was covered either by federal or by state awards (Archer 1992: 388). This nearly full coverage secured high real-wage incomes for the majority of the working population, and was only

46 Later renamed Conciliation and Arbitration Commission, Industrial Relations Commission and Fair Work Australia. For the sake of clarity, I will refer to the institution as Australian Industrial Relations Commission (AIRC) throughout the text.

supplemented with a weak formal welfare state with a strong reliance on means testing.[47]

Finally, until the 1970s, Australian economic policy followed the logic of 'domestic defence' (Castles & Mitchell 1993, Easton & Gerritsen 1996) consisting of strong trade barriers, reliance on the export of raw materials and selective immigration policy aimed at skilled workers. In Australia protectionism lasted almost 15 years longer than in Ireland. Up until the 1970s, Australia was highly competitive in exporting raw materials and agricultural products on world markets. The rents generated from competitive exports were used to shore up incomes of workers and rents of employers in domestic manufacturing, which employed the majority of skilled workers and was strongly protected by trade barriers.

Taken together, these peculiarities have been highly influential for the development and reform of apprenticeship in Australia, which I depict in the following sections. The first section describes the development of VET and apprenticeships up until the mid-1980s and draws parallels with the English and Irish developments before their respective critical junctures. Compared to the other two cases, the basic interests in apprenticeships and technical training among governments, craft unions and employers were broadly similar with little institutional development away from craft-based indentured apprenticeships that were contested along the class divide.

The second section describes how reforms towards *collective skill formation* emerged in the 1980s in the context of economic problems of high unemployment, falling terms of trade and sluggish growth that confronted the new Labor government under Prime Minister Bob Hawke, who was elected to office in 1983. During this period, the Labor government strongly cooperated with the ACTU and economic policy-making was based on eight Price and Income Accords, which were used to manage a liberalization of the Australian economy away from the model of domestic defence, which had become unsustainable under the conditions of the inceptive global open economy. In the late 1980s, training reforms under the NTRA became a central pillar in the programme of economic modernization as an unlikely cross-class coalition between metalworking employers and the unions had formed. Employers sought government support in order to make their formerly sheltered

47 This has led some scholars to characterize Australia as the ideal-type of a *wage-earner's welfare state* (Castles 1985, Castles & Mitchell 1993).

businesses internationally competitive, while unions attempted to gain from skill premiums and skill certification in order to shore up real wages. While this cross-class productivity coalition succeeded in initiating VET reform towards more collective skill formation, it became fragile when the later years of Accord politics witnessed a decentralization of industrial relations that worked against the unions' goal of coupling the restructuring of industrial awards with training reform.

As I show in the last section, the institutions created in the phase of the NTRA were resilient in the sense that they moved training towards a system of nationally accredited vocational qualifications. However, the same institutional heritage also opened the way for the marketization of training provision and the development of a 'segmented training system' (Cooney & Long 2010), which occurred most strongly when the coalition government returned to power in 1996.

5.1 The historical background – regulation by states and industrial arbitration

> For most of its history, Australia has been a nation short of industrial and technical skills. [...] [S]killed labour in the Australian colonies was from the outset scarce and its possessors, even convicts, were able to secure a premium for its application. (Ryan 2002: 3)

> Despite the way some unions used the craft-based vocational system as a bedrock for organising practise, the apprenticeship system had a number of deficiencies. [...] [U]nion control of craft labour markets was based on strategies of exclusion [...] and unions used trade recognition boards to limit the number [of] new entrants to the craft. (Ewer 2000: 38–39)

> Australia [...] used high tariffs and import licensing to generate local full employment. These trade policies, in turn, accommodated the relatively high and indirect wages in the manufacturing sector that arbitration created. [...] In Australia, the Tariff Board literally told industrial firms, 'You make it and [we'll] protect it.' (Schwartz 2000: 73)[48]

48 The citation within the citation of Schwartz (2000: 73) is from Capling and Galligan (1993: 105).

Like Ireland, Australia inherited its apprenticeship structures from the United Kingdom. Apprenticeships were time served, normally set at seven years duration and based on an indenture between employer and apprentice (Goozee 2001, Ray 2001). As in the other two cases, they were dominated by craft unions, which used them to limit the numbers of skilled workers in their respective trades in order to extract wage premiums (Ryan 2002); because of this they were reluctant to increase the theoretical content of training and tried to limit educational mobility via strong occupational demarcations (AUS-9). As the unions' counterpart, employers were wary of the craft unions' practices of skill control (AUS-22), but pressures and scope for substituting skilled labour by capital were lower than in the United Kingdom due to the small size of the domestic product market and its protection via tariffs (Gospel 1994: 513). Moreover, two other peculiar institutional aspects of the Australian economy helped to shore up the classical apprenticeship system and the investment in vocational skills by employers: federalism and the system of industrial arbitration.

In Australia's federal polity, the competences for formulating training regulations such as educational content and apprenticeship governance (and generally education policy) were classically situated at the state level (Goozee 2001, Ray 2001, AUS-15, AUS-22, AUS-29). This makes it historically more appropriate to characterize VET in Australia as a state-based training system firmly rooted in 'state economies' (AUS-22). While the federal government was responsible for general economic conditions such as tariffs or industrial relations that transcended state barriers, 'it was for long a settled opinion that the Commonwealth had no role or powers in education' (Birch, in: Ryan 2011).

This separation of competences stifled the evolution of a national system of training regulations until the late 1980s, the phase of the NTRA (AUS-2, AUS-25). Moreover, as each state had and continues to have its own apprenticeship training act (AUS-15) and its own funding regulations for off-the-job and publicly provided training (AUS-15, AUS-25), different regulatory systems with different training curricula and certification mechanisms evolved, which reduced worker mobility in occupational labour markets, except for the case of national industries or where reciprocal agreements on training existed between the states (AUS-8). This development reduced labour mobility between the states and, concomitantly, the options of employers to poach skilled labour outside of 'a few concentrated urban labour markets' (Gospel 1994: 513). Thus, early training legislation at the state level developed at different paces (Goozee 2001), but by 1943 all of the six big states had created apprenticeship authorities 'to oversee both the employment and training areas of apprenticeship' (Goozee 2001: 16).

Moreover, the states had created apprenticeship 'committees to advise on matters for particular trades, [...] [which] proved to be extremely important in the development of apprenticeship in Australia' (Ray 2001: 8). These committees were regularly composed of union and employer association representatives (AUS-25) and worked together with states' apprenticeship authorities and industrial relations departments on matters such as apprentice day release, certification and provision of off-the-job technical education, which typically took place in state-financed technical colleges.

In terms of industrial relations, the apprenticeship system was deeply embedded within the system of arbitration and 'legally binding awards served to restore and codify apprenticeship rules and [made] them legally enforceable to employers' (Gospel 1994: 513). Arbitration covered, *inter alia,* apprenticeship wages, training contracts, apprentice numbers, working conditions and the provision that young people may only be employed under an apprenticeship (Gospel 1994, Ray 2001: 7–8, AUS-2, AUS-15), which limited their use as cheap labour. As apprenticeships were included in the award system, governments were usually not involved in their regulation as a third party, except for aspects not covered by the awards system such as finance and delivery of off-the-job education. Moreover, the awards system shored up trade-union power and 'thus provided further institutional support for apprenticeship' (Gospel 1994: 513).

The awards system also created the first 'national regulations' for apprenticeships in those cases in which the awards were set at the federal level, such as in metalworking or the electrical trades, and thus fell under the auspices of the AIRC. As I show in the next section, the organized interests in metalworking became pivotal players in reforming apprenticeships into a national system in the late 1980s and early 1990s. Traditionally the inclusion of craft apprenticeships into awards enabled craft unions to bargain more about working conditions more generally, thus using 'training as a bargaining chip' (AUS-3) in a very similar manner to unions in Ireland and the United Kingdom. Additionally, the awards system acted as a 'proxy for multi-employer bargaining and a form of market-wide regulation' (Gospel 1994: 513) evening out differences in apprenticeship remuneration and conditions among different employers. In setting low wage differentials within trades, awards also served as additional safeguards against poaching and provided incentives for employers to train (AUS-7). The state itself also supported training as public utilities and national railways were major employers of apprentices (AUS-7, AUS-25).

In sum, until the mid-1980s, the structure of apprenticeship in Australia remained stable and was dominated by indentured craft traditions also found in the United Kingdom (AUS-2, AUS-15, AUS-25). Training conditions were basically set between employers and craft unions, which used the apprenticeship system to increase their bargaining power. However, apprenticeship regulations in terms of remuneration and pay were underpinned by the system of industrial arbitration by the AIRC and state arbitration courts, and thus had a more formal institutional background than training in Australia's European Anglophile counterparts. Another difference in the basic structures of training in Australia were the limited competences of the Commonwealth in education policy. It is historically more appropriate to speak of state training systems compared to national training policies in the United Kingdom and Ireland.

Despite this basic configuration, the slow shift to a service-based economy necessitated an expansion of training provision into non-industry/non-manufacturing occupations by the Australian states. They expanded the provision of formal technical and vocational education beyond the apprenticeship system in state-based training institutions, which were later renamed technical and further education colleges (TAFE) (Goozee 2001). But, in contrast to the apprenticeship system where working conditions and pay scales were regulated by industrial awards, 'where structured training arrangements existed in the service sector, [...] they were not reflected in the job classifications described by relevant industrial awards' (Ewer 2000: 39). This also applied for non-trade workers within manufacturing, for which 'no skill recognition and training system existed of any kind' (r 2000: 39). As I will show next, these inequities between workers with apprenticeship certificates and those without became a focal point of the NTRA in the 1980s.

Politically, the traditional strength of the labour movement in Australia did not translate into ALP governments at the federal level, which, from 1949 onwards, with the exception of a short-lived ALP government from 1972 to 1975, was dominated by the Liberal-National coalition. Training seldom emerged as a salient issue on the federal political agenda up until Whitlam's ALP government (1972–1975) (Goozee 2001, Ray 2001, Ryan 2002, 2011), and when it emerged, the competences of the states in (technical) education were an effective barrier to policy reform. Thus, despite the formal task of the Commonwealth to foster industrial development, when the Australian Apprenticeship Advisory Committee (AAAC), which was composed of the heads of state training commissions, educators and the Commonwealth department of Labour, was founded as a first national advisory institution on VET in 1956

> only the most minimal role for the Commonwealth was envisaged by any party, and [...] technical training was construed as narrow skills training for industry, mostly within the apprenticeship framework. (Ryan 2002: 8)

Although, the NAAC was replaced by a Commonwealth and State Training Advisory Committee (COSTAC) in 1977 in yet another attempt to develop a national approach to apprenticeships (ACOTAFE & Kangan 1974), the structure of state-regulated apprenticeship training and the basic preferences among predominantly state-based union and employer bodies towards training regulation did not change until the 1980s (Ray 2001). This is a remarkable contrast to the developments that took place during the 1960s and 1970s in Ireland and the United Kingdom. Although the attempts to create a more standardized training system by including employers and unions more firmly into the framework of training governance largely failed in Ireland with the installation of AnCO in 1967, and the creation of the ITB system in 1964, complemented with the MSC in 1973 in the United Kingdom, those attempts were directed firmly at changing the national governance towards tripartite training structures. However, in Australia, a national training system was not on the horizon at the same time, with training being regulated at the state level and the inclusion of state craft unions and employer associations in tripartite training commissions.

While both Ireland and the United Kingdom moved towards training levies in order to increase firms' involvement in VET, Australia and its states refrained from training levies as mechanisms to increase employer commitment. As manufacturing was still effectively sheltered from competition and Australia relied on the system of domestic defence far into the 1970s, employers and trade unions were under less pressure to reform the training system. Moreover, as described above, employers had fewer incentives for job substitution than their European counterparts. There is little evidence that the differences in training standards and content between the states '[were] a major concern for employers' (Knight 2012: 15) as limited labour mobility also acted as a safeguard towards poaching skilled workers from competitors.

This resilience of the traditional system of apprenticeship in Australia has to be seen not only in the light of 'federal barriers to training reform' (AUS-14) but also in the context of the role that it played for skill formation in the context of Australian post-war economic development. The wage earners' welfare state coupled with the trade and immigration politics of the system of domestic defence had been sustained throughout a period of economic growth and prosperity for Australia in the 1950s and 1960s, which was characterized by full employment and steady rates of economic growth, averaging 5% throughout the respective period (OECD various). In this context of growth, the apprenticeship system helped to meet an increasing demand for skilled workers, which was occasionally complemented by selective immigration. With manufacturing effectively taken out of foreign competition by high tariffs on imports, the external pressure for upskilling the industrial workforce and updating occupational training standards was comparatively low under these conditions.

Within the system of industrial arbitration, skilled workers in manufacturing could gain large wage premiums over the basic wage set by arbitration, and, de facto, a lot of 'over award bargaining' took place (Archer 1992). While the basic wage was set on the basis of national productivity and cost-of-living adjustments since the 1960s, from 1954 onwards the national award for the metal trades had been set as the basic peg for skilled workers' wages, which was then used as a central referent for all other awards (Ewer et al. 1991).

The system of basic awards and margins for skilled work was brought under a single framework in the late 1960s ('single national wage case'), but powerful unions such as the metalworkers and public sector employees could rely on their organizational strength in order to achieve wage increases outside of the margins set in the national wage case. Thus, while arbitration acted as a proxy to multi-employer or centralized bargaining, it cannot be equated with bargained pay moderation between unions, employers and the state. Due to their pivotal position within the arbitration system, the wage settlements between metalworking employers and unions were central for driving wage development within the Australian economy (Schwartz 2000: 77). There had been several wage flow-ons from the metalworking trades throughout Australian history but the containment of negative economic effects rested crucially on the ability to generate economic growth via the exposed and competitive primary sector.

However, at the end of the 1960s, the solid institutional fundament of the Australian economy showed its first cracks, as over the long term the export sector could not engender 'enough foreign currency to fund imports of manufactured goods not locally produced, pay interest on foreign currency denominated debt, and repatriate profits for direct investors' (Schwartz 2000: 83). First, the terms of trade had already been falling since the mid-1950s, and as local consumption of imports developed on a steady level, Australia ran account deficits since the early 1960s. Second, with a steady reliance on import substitution as a 'politically easy' (Schwartz 2000: 85) solution, balance of payments deficits became a persistent problem for incumbent governments. Third, as arbitration kept sheltered sector wages over the productivity levels of domestic manufacturing and firms could shift the high wage costs onto consumers, inflation became another central problem.

Moreover, secular developments in the United Kingdom, a major trading partner for exports, and the effects of the first-oil-price shock and the collapse of the Bretton Woods system of fixed exchange rates confronted Australian governments with economic reform pressures. A first shock came, when the failure of arbitration rounds in the period from 1967 to 1969 to contain wage increases coincided with the deterioration of primary export prices, which was in part due to the United Kingdom's decision to join the EC in 1968, with the result that Australia lost its 'privileged position in [its] largest export market' (Ahlquist 2008: 22). However, the bigger shock occurred, when unions took advantage of rising commodity prices after the first oil crisis and embarked on a course of over-award wage bargaining in order to preserve between occupational wage relativities. Wage rises spilled over into imported goods consumption at the same time as the Australian dollar gained in worth due to the collapse of the Bretton Woods system. However, when the Australian dollar 'depreciated by [30 per cent] from 1974 to 1997, the current account deficit increased substantially' (Schwartz 2000: 87) afterwards.

Under these economically difficult conditions, a newly elected ALP government had to confront the effects of the oil-price shock and wage pressures as it had just set out to increase public spending for social policy development, which had lain dormant under the long rule of the Liberal-National coalition. The newly elected government under Prime Minster Whitlam had been elected on a programme of reform that was the 'high water mark of Australian post-war social democracy' (Bramble & Kuhn 2011: 88). The government introduced, *inter alia,* a sole parent pension, Medibank, as a central programme for public health insurance, paid maternity leave and abolished student fees for tertiary education with the effect that federal spending rose by 20% for public health and by 50% for education (Bramble & Kuhn 2011: 88).

Three political reforms enacted by the Whitlam government were of direct relevance for the trajectory of apprenticeship and VET more generally. Indirectly, the decision of the Whitlam government to reduce tariffs by 25% shortly after coming into office (Beilharz 1994, Bramble & Kuhn 2011, Schwartz 2000) increased the exposure of the sheltered manufacturing sector to foreign competition and revealed the sector's need to increase productivity in order to protect existing jobs and profits (AUS-3, AUS- 29, AUS-32). In turn, increased productivity via VET reform became a central cornerstone in the formation of a cross-class coalition between metalworking employers and unions in the next decade. This is remarkable as conflicts between powerful metalworking unions and their employer counterparts were historically frequent triggers of industrial strife (AUS-2), also due to the importance of the metal award as a central referent for wages in other sectors (Ewer et al. 1991).

More directly, the government enacted changes underpinning the financial dimension of training institutions. In contrast to Ireland and the United Kingdom, which had tried to balance the training costs between employers and the state more evenly in the 1960s and 1970s by installing training levies, the Whitlam government refrained from imposing additional costs for training on employers. Instead, the government created the National Apprenticeship Assistance Scheme (NAAS) in 1973.[49] This offered financial support to firms for taking on first-year apprentices on a large scale, which was about half the size of the budget allocated to federal programmes under active labour market policy (AUS-28, Ray 2001: 18). In addition, based on the recommendations of the Kangan report (ACOTAFE & Kangan 1974, AUS-27), the government started to infuse additional funding into expanding the TAFE system, which had formerly relied exclusively on state expenditure. This decision marked another watershed in the development of Australian VET, as it exposed the imbalance of spending and taxing capacities between states and federal government. While the states have most of the spending obligations, their taxation power is lower than their spending needs. This allows the federal government to exercise power via the purse when engaging in funding policies that are relevant to national competitiveness and economic affairs (Lundberg 1994). Thus, even with limited competencies in education policy making, the Commonwealth government can use co-funding of educational expenditures in order to entice the states to cooperate in its agenda of education policy making.

Taken together, these two decisions established a first bridgehead for the central government in VET policy, which had formerly been based on cooperation between employer associations, (craft) unions and the states (AUS-25, AUS-32, Ray 2001). These changes also foreshadowed basic aspects of VET policy making in the division of competences between the federal government and the states, which were to become salient in the area of 'high politics' during the late 1980s and especially in the reforms of establishing a national training system

49 The NAAS replaced the Country Apprenticeship Scheme, which offered employers and apprentices funding for travelling and off-the job training costs in areas remote from TAFE. Compared to the NAAS, it was on a tiny scale, however, which makes it adequate to view the introduction of the NAAS as a major starting point of federal VET funding in Australia.

which congealed in the formation of the Australian National Training Authority (ANTA) in 1992, as the first institutions that had statutory powers shared between the federal and state governments in the area of VET policy (Ryan 2002).

Yet, the education policy reform and spending increase for social policy of the Whitlam government took place under difficult economic conditions of the oil-shock aftermath and wage pressures due to the unions wage campaigns that aimed at settlements above award wages. As the government tried to push ahead with its expansionary spending agenda it became dependent on wage restraint from the union movement in order to contain inflationary pressures and rising government debt. Without offering further compensation apart from the envisaged investments, the Whitlam government proposed to return to partial wage indexation within the system of wage arbitration to foster an income policy, which implied reductions in real earnings for unionized workers (Ahlquist 2008, Schwartz 2000).

While some parts of the union movement were willing to consent to wage moderation (Schwartz 2000: 105), the main peak union ACTU was unable to unite workers to consent to wage moderation, especially as it did not yet include white-collar unions and failed to contain the militancy of many of its smaller blue-collar unions (Schwartz 2000: 107). Thus, ACTU president Bob Hawke, who later became responsible for the 'politics of the accord' under which the major training reforms towards collective skill formation occurred in the 1980s and 1990s, had to declare in 1984 that the unions would 'not indulge in a trade-off in wages for some conjectural reduction in inflation [...] our people will not be sacrificial lambs to the system's alter [sic]' (Singleton 1990: 33, cited in Ahlquist 2008: 23).

With this impasse between the union movement and the first federal ALP government for 23 years, the economic situation deteriorated rapidly. By 1975, unemployment had risen to an unprecedented post-war high of 4.5%; the current account balance in government outlays had developed from a surplus of 0.55% in 1973 to a deficit of almost 3% in 1975 (OECD various-a, various-b) and public spending continued to grow due to the expansion of social services. Relations between the union movement and the ALP had deteriorated steadily, and the government convinced the AIRC to introduce wage indexation that pegged wage increases to the level of inflation in May 1975, which forced unions on the defensive in the context of high unemployment (Bramble & Kuhn 2011: 96).

The expansionist course of the Whitlam government ended when it ultimately fell as a result of a *coup d'état* by the Liberal-National coalition, which had gained a majority in the Senate in 1975. The opposition announced that it would renounce the federal budget and the Governor-General, John Kerr, dismissed Whitlam and appointed the Liberal Malcom Fraser as Prime Minister, who emerged victorious from the ensuing election in late 1975 (cf. Bramble & Kuhn 2011: 94–100). However, more relevant for this study is the fact that the ALP and ACTU leadership were not able to manufacture consent in the context of an economic crisis, a situation that changed slowly during the following years of the Liberal Fraser governments (1975–1982) and ultimately formed the basis for the concerted policy reform between the ALP and ACTU from 1983 onwards. The new government continued the course of the ALP in the area of VET by keeping up federal funding for TAFE and extending funding to employers to compensate them for the off-the-job training productivity loss of their apprentices under the new Commonwealth Rebate for Full-Time Apprentice Training (CRAFT), which replaced the NAAC in 1977. Despite discussions on how to modernize the governance and training content of Australian VET in the late 1970s and early 1980s, which mostly took the form of reports by either COSTAC or the Departments of Labour Advisory Committee (DOLAC), little change ensued (Ray 2001, Ryan 2002).

In terms of general economic policy and industrial relations, the Fraser government tried to counter the economic crisis by exerting greater fiscal restraint based on monetarist underpinnings and expenditure cuts for Commonwealth-funded public services. On the industrial relations front, it tried to contain wage pressures through the arbitration system by partial indexation of wages, but ultimately failed to contain wage increases that were struck outside the system and culminated in another wage race between public white-collar and blue-collar unions in the context of a new commodity price shock triggered by the second oil crisis (Archer 1992, Schwartz 2000). Free wage bargaining followed again in early 1981, but the incoming recession brought an end to the short-lived commodity price boom. Public finances deteriorated once again with the public deficit reaching 3% and unemployment nearly reaching 10% in 1983.

In this economically difficult situation, an ALP government under former ACTU president Bob Hawke came to power in late 1983. In contrast with the situation under the earlier Whitlam government, the ACTU and the ALP now cooperated closely in finding a mutually advantageous solution to the imminent economic problems of the early 1980s. Although employers were never formally included into the Politics of the Accords (Ewer et al. 1991), the politics of policy concertation by the ALP enabled the formation of a cross-class coalition between metalworking employers and unions in training and microeconomic reform, which became a cornerstone of industrial relations reforms known as 'awards restructuring'. How the formation of these coalitions affected apprenticeships in Australia and how unions, employers and the government interacted in these processes is discussed next.

5.2 The critical juncture – awards restructuring and the training reform agenda (1983–1992)

The period from 1983, when the ALP replaced the National-Liberal coalition as the federal government, to 1992, when the decision was taken to create ANTA as a national statutory authority for coordination, regulation and standard-setting for training in Australia, was characterized by strong cross-class cooperation between unions and employers – most pronouncedly in the historically conflict-ridden metalworking sector – and the ALP governments and was a critical juncture for Australian training to become reformed towards collective skill formation. To reiterate, despite the decisions of the Whitlam government to support TAFE funding from the federal government's purse and to incentivize employers to take on apprentices, very little had changed in the parameters of apprenticeship training in Australia (AUS-2, AUS-15, AUS-25, AUS-30).

First, apprenticeship training was still concentrated on the classical trades with job roles and training content strongly determined by strict occupational demarcations, which shored up craft unions job-control politics. Second, despite the involvement of the Commonwealth since 1973, training was still essentially state based with varying training regulations and standards from state to state and little input from the organized interests of capital and labour beyond their respective state and/or sectoral boundaries. Third, training certification was still based on the time served as an apprentice and not by the formal competences acquired through a structured combination of workplace and off-the-job training. Thus, despite being entrenched more formally into wage arbitration and collective bargaining than under the voluntarist structures traditionally found in the UK and Ireland, the classical parameters of training of an Anglo-Saxon heritage were still clearly visible and comparable to the fundamental issues of training reform in Ireland and the United Kingdom.

The central questions were who would be responsible for the funding of training, how standard setting was to be controlled with a move away from indentured apprenticeships, and most importantly, who was to participate in the politics of training (AUS-2, AUS-3, AUS-4, AUS-14, AUS-27, AUS-29).

Yet, by the end of 1992, the NTRA was firmly in place, in which employers, unions and the government had agreed to reform training into a national policy with five central goals: to develop a nationally consistent system of competency-based training; national recognition of competencies, however attained; an open national training market in order to increase responsiveness to industry and individual training needs; fair access to vocational education and training; and an integrated system of entry-level training with clear educational pathways (Lundberg 1994). While these goals ran counter to the classical model of craft-union training, it is even more surprising that this policy agenda gained broad support not only by the industrial partners but also by the state governments, which gave up some of their long-held competences in vocational training policy making.

The NTRA emerged in the wake of coordinated reform of Australian industrial relations and economic institutions, which was, in the main part, carried by the cooperation between the ALP government and ACTU as the main federation of the trade union movement. The main aspect of reform was a form of generalized political exchange in the form of eight accords between ACTU and the ALP on economic policies, wage bargaining, industrial relations and social policy. Under the accord process, the union movement consented to a gradual liberalization of the Australian economy and to wage restraint to combat imminent economic crises in exchange for the expansion of the formal welfare state, the generation of more employment, a stable social wage and training reforms, which were intended to produce a national system of accredited skills to be remunerated under a new system of reformed industrial awards.

Employers were never formally part of this modernization coalition, the accords had the tacit consent of different groups of employers, which varied along with the direction taken by the policies developed under the accord process. Together with the unions, employers were central players in the NTRA and the process of awards restructuring akin to a cross-class coalition seldom found among liberal market economies. However, the processes of industrial relations and training reform, which had been closely connected from the mid-1980s to the mid-1990s, eventually became disjointed and gave way to a more liberal system of VET than the NTRA partners had originally envisaged, and the cross-class coalition ultimately vanished when a Liberal government took federal office in 1996.

Although this chapter is mainly concerned with the developments that led to the NTRA, it first describes the different stages and economic background conditions of the politics of the accords that had an impact on the development of training – either directly, or indirectly – by changing the incentives and motivations of the central collective actors of training reform.

Arguably, the beginning of 1983 marked a critical juncture in the development of the Australian political economy. Bob Hawke, the former president of the ACTU, had just won the challenge for the ALP's party leadership and, quite unexpectedly, emerged victorious from the federal election later that year. The previous Fraser government had failed to reign in high unemployment, inflation and public debt, and had been largely unsuccessful in moderating the wage claims of the union movement during the short commodity boom at the beginning of the 1980s. Wage indexation had failed, when the metal workers had shown their strength in the bargaining round of 1981 resulting in a reduction in working hours and an 18-month agreement with a secured wage increase of roughly 17% (Deery & Plowman 1991). In another wage race about parities between different occupations, the agreement spilled over into the rest of the economy, and the response of the Fraser government, which imposed a 12-month wage freeze, could not contain the negative effects on employment and inflation leading to a recession in 1982. In the 12 months up to the election of Hawke, employment in metalworking and engineering had fallen by 17% (Archer 1992: 391), which seriously damaged the powerful metalworkers' bargaining strength.

The incoming ALP government provided a new opportunity for the Australian union movement to be involved in policymaking, which was rare for the unions in the post-war years. To reiterate, despite having traditionally strong trade unions, Labour had only infrequently been in power and the Liberal government dominated post-war governments at the Federal level, with the exception of the short-lived Whitlam government. In the short period of this ALP government, the union movement had not been able to deliver wage moderation in the context of expansionary social policies, which coincided with the economic turmoil after the first-oil crisis. However, when the Hawke government came to power the willingness of the union movement to accept wage concessions had fundamentally changed, which enabled the emergence of the first accord between the newly elected ALP government and the ACTU.

First, being ACTU's former president, Hawke had strong ties to the labour movement (AUS-22, AUS-27, AUS-32) and was 'famous for resolving industrial disputes' (AUS-32). The basic foundations of the first accord had already been agreed prior to the federal elections with discussions about 'social contract drafts' dating back to 1982 (AUS-3). Second, while the Fraser government did not manage to dismantle the arbitration system as the traditional stronghold of the labour movement, organized unions had deliberately been excluded from policy making up to the election of Hawke. The change in government gave unions the option to have a stronger influence on governmental decisions, especially as the Hawke ALP signalled a willingness to steer a course of politics characterized by consensus and agreement (AUS-29, AUS-31, AUS-32). Third, during the 1970s and early 1980s, the union movement had become more centralized due to the inclusion of the major white-collar unions and amalgamations of smaller unions (Archer 1992, Schwartz 2000) and developed towards more industrial unionism (AUS-3, AUS-8,

AUS-22, AUS-23). The limited scope of VET and the need for more structured VET outside the traditional trades gained weight within the union movement (AUS-8, AUS-13), especially as many formal qualifications were not yet included in industrial awards (Ewer 2000, Ewer et al. 1991). Finally, after the recession had begun in 1982, unions – especially in the formerly sheltered manufacturing sectors – were hit hard by unemployment, while inflation reduced their members' incomes. Alongside the aforementioned factors, this acted as an additional incentive 'to seek negotiated change' (Schwartz 2000: 108).

After Hawke's election, the ALP and the unions entered the accord process and the accord was renegotiated seven times (referred to as Accord Mark I, II, etc.). The different accords were agreements on basic wages and pay-setting mechanisms within the system of industrial arbitration, and about the conditions under which wage increases above the agreed wage were possible. In terms of economic reform, the ALP government continued to liberalize the economy progressively by reducing protective tariffs and de-subsidizing product markets in order to increase economic competitiveness. The *accord* delivered a tool for wage moderation that helped to bring down wages in order to generate more employment but continued to provide a basic wage-floor agreed with the ACTU. Moreover, the government privatized public utilities and state-owned enterprises and introduced competitive tendering into the public sector in order to reduce public expenditures (Schwartz 1994a, 1994b). The later stages of the accord process ushered in industrial relations reform away from the traditional mode of arbitration and towards more wage flexibility and bargaining decentralization. These policies made wage increases contingent on increased productivity of the respective sectors, which pressured unions and firms alike to increase competitiveness.

From the perspective of the unions, these concessions were compensated by a gradual expansion of formal welfare policies, the sustenance of a social wage, employment generation, and – in the later stages of the accord process – skill investments, which the trade unions perceived as an important part of the 'social wage' (AUS-3, Ewer 2000, Ewer et al. 1991). After 1986, the decentralization of industrial relations, micro-economic reforms and training became a central component of this type of generalized political exchange.

Although employer organizations were never formal signatories to the ALP-ACTU accords (AUS-3, AUS-32), these always had the tacit support of one or more of the major bodies of organized business (Schwartz 2000, 2005). The training components of the accords were intended to compensate the union movement for wage restraint and the acceptance of broadly liberal economic policies that delivered business aims, thus '[b]usiness did not need to be an *Accord* partner, because the agreement delivered business aims, like increased profits and industrial peace' (Hampson 1997: 550). Yet, employers played a proactive role in the NTRA, in which they lobbied jointly with the unions for reforms towards more skill investment and more collective training governance (Ewer et al. 1991, Jenkins & Curry 2013). The formation of this cross-class coalition was assisted by the ALP and its decision for a continued gradual opening up of the economy and the incremental decentralization of wage-bargaining, which confronted workers and employers in formerly sheltered sectors with the question of how to increase international competitiveness. On a second front, the federal government, employers and unions moved jointly towards a national training system in order to overcome the impasse between the Commonwealth and the states regarding who should have the competencies to set training policies. This process was paralleled by policy discussion between the Commonwealth and the state governments about governance reforms towards a national training system with uniform training regulations among the states in exchange for more Commonwealth investment (Goozee 2001, Ryan 2002), which led to the creation of ANTA in 1992.

The emergence of the NTRA and the movement towards ANTA were preceded by reforms that were intended to counteract the mounting problem of stagflation that the Hawke government faced when coming into office. The first accord was explicitly designed to reduce inflation and shore up employment via wage moderation by the unions (ALP & ACTU 1983; Archer 1992: 392–393) which was to be balanced with expansionary governmental policies and thus did not follow Thatcher's monetarist recipe. Despite the publication of a 1984 report by the COSTAC committee, which had evaluated reform proposals to the training system, the reform of apprenticeships had to retreat behind political measures to provide immediate relief to high youth unemployment, which was a pressing issue in education and training policy for the ALP government (AUS-8, AUS-23, AUS-27, AUS-31, AUS-32). While expanding formal training opportunities in school-based VET would have been a viable option for parts of the union movement and employer organizations,[50] the government opted for a reform that would not endanger apprenticeships as a traditional stronghold of craft unions and followed the recommendations of the COSTAC report, which rejected the option of school-based training:

> full time institutional training, whereby trainees are required to full trade status without receiving actual work experience, cannot generally considered to be a viable option… [contrary to] good prospects for change [of the apprenticeship system] *provided that the social partners, particularly unions and employers, are consulted and involved in the planning process.* (COSTAC 1984: iv, italics added by author)

Due to the strong organizational position of craft unions within the apprenticeship system, the ALP government was challenged to devise solutions for the pressing problem of youth unemployment that would not erode the traditional apprenticeship system, which was treated as a 'sacred cow' (AUS-31) in negotiations on youth employment policy. In 1985, based on the recommendations of the Kirkby Report (Kirkby 1985), which had recommended a shift from passive to active unemployment policies and strongly emphasized the need for training, education and employment programs, the ALP government introduced the Australian Traineeship System (ATS), while leaving the traditional apprenticeship system untouched. Traineeships were directed at lower qualification levels than traditional apprenticeships and were only permissible for non-trade occupations.[51] Funding was shared between employers, the Commonwealth, which paid subsidies to firms providing traineeship places, and the states, which were to pay for the off-the-job component (AUS-25).

In essence, this was a compromise between craft unions within the ACTU and the ALP government (AUS-7, AUS-26) because they favoured reforms that would not endanger apprenticeships (AUS-12) and preserved occupational boundaries that were buttressed by the awards system (AUS-23). In effect, traineeships were the option to

50 Personal communication with interviewee AUS-2, 31 January 2013.

51 They were set at level 2 to of the Australian Qualifications Framework (AQF) and below the level of traditional apprenticeships set at level 3 or 4.

maintain clear demarcations between training provision admissible for trade (apprenticeships) and service (traineeships) occupations. The latter were usually not covered by traditional apprenticeship arrangements and thus represented an area where reform would not endanger trade union interests. As a double benefit for the union movement as a whole, traineeships offered their members structured training in sectors that were not formerly covered (AUS-8), and the strong occupational demarcation between traineeships and apprenticeships acted as a safeguard for skilled worker replacements. Compared to the United Kingdom, this consensual reform between unions and the ALP stands in marked contrast to YTS, which progressively replaced traditional apprenticeships and can be described as an instance of institutional layering compared to institutional displacement in the case of YTS.

After traineeships were introduced, they grew more slowly than had been envisaged by the government, and shortly after their inception most traineeships were still concentrated in the public sector (AUS-8). According to Robinson (2001, also: AUS-23), the real growth in traineeships started only 10 years later. At their peak in 1993, only 1 in 10 training contracts was for a traineeship, with apprentices representing the vast majority in training (NCVER 2000). Their impact on youth unemployment was at most modest and moving more or less on par with adult unemployment. After a modest reduction from 15% to 11% from 1985 to 1989, under new economic strains youth unemployment hit its historical peak of almost 20% in 1992, which was just at the time that the NTRA had become central in industrial relations reform.

In order to understand why the NTRA and a cross-class coalition between metalworking employers and unions emerged, it is useful to recapitulate the development of Australia away from its traditional model of domestic defence. Schwartz (2000: 83) summarized the vulnerability of this model as follows:

> First, arbitration plus protection led to diverging productivity levels between the stagnant sheltered sector and the more dynamic export sectors. Second, arbitration reduced the primary sector's long-term ability to export profitably. Third, European overproduction depressed global prices for food exports [...] As changes in the international economy removed the export sector's ability to extract rents by the late 1970s, the old redistributive model could not endure.

As described above, faced with changing world market conditions, the impact of commodity-market boom and bust caused by the two oil-price shocks and the breakdown of fixed exchange rates, Australian governments from Whitlam onwards had moved to progressively liberalize the economy and reduce trade barriers. The Hawke government broadly continued along these lines by further reducing tariffs, restructuring the public sector, privatizing state-owned businesses and liberalizing product markets. In sum, these changes were no less radical than the reforms that occurred under Thatcher in the United Kingdom. Yet, compared to her approach of *crash through or crash*, the Hawke government tried to manufacture macro- and micro-economic reform under the umbrella of *consensual cooperation* with the ACTU, underpinned by the accord process. While the first accords explicitly endorsed wage moderation as a central mechanism to cope with the economic crisis of the early 1980s, the original agreement between the ALP and ACTU had also stressed a second objective, which was

> to ensure that the living standards of wage and salary earners and non-income earning sectors of the population requiring protection are maintained and *through time increased with movements in national productivity*. (ALP & ACTU 1983: 4, italics by author)

This medium-term goal of increasing national productivity became central for socio-economic reform in the middle of the 1980s and was a focal point for the emergence of the cross-class coalition in metalworking, which, as a sector, stood at the centre of the arbitration system and emerged 'at the forefront of training reform in the period from 1988 to 1992' (Jenkins & Curry 2013: 75).

The early accords (Mark I and II) had been based on the goal of coping with stagflation via wage restraint. They were underpinned by a centralized wage-fixing system, where wages would only be increased in line with the development of living-costs based on unions making no extra wage claims. However, during 1986, a reduction of the balance-of payments deficit replaced stagflation as the centrepiece of governmental economic policy (Archer 1992: 394). However, commodity export prices had fallen significantly during the last decade before the Hawke government had come to power and continued to fall significantly after its inauguration. In parallel, import penetration and foreign indebtedness had risen sharply. Faced with an account deficit reaching almost −6% of GDP, treasurer and later Prime Minister Paul Keating asserted publicly that Australia was in danger of turning into a 'banana republic'. In a reaction to the crisis, Prime Minister Hawke made a National Economic Statement in June 1986 that called for cuts in real wages and public spending, the latter being cemented by the budget announced later that year. This put the reduction of unemployment and the maintenance of living standards into question as prime goals of the accord, but the ACTU decided to continue the accord process in order to keep an influence on policy making. The alternative to central-wage fixation was worked out in the negotiations preceding the accord Mark III, which proposed the introduction of a new, two-tier wage-fixing system. Under the first tier, workers could gain a flat-rate wage increase, while the second tier allowed wage increases that were conditional on enterprise-level agreements to increase productivity (Archer 1992).

As a reaction to the economic crisis of 1986 (AUS-31) the rearrangement of the accord's central wage-fixing mechanism, which established productivity-related wage increases alongside flat-rate increases for all workers, gave the notion of increased productivity a more prominent role in subsequent economic reform. Discussions about the effects of increased import penetration, reduced tariffs, and international competitiveness and their implications for the formerly sheltered manufacturing firms had already emerged within the peak associations of employers and unions since the 1970s, but now the question of how to reform production towards more competitiveness arrived at the top of the agenda (AUS-2), especially in the non-competitive domestic manufacturing sector.

The changes away from the model of domestic defence put pressure on employers and skilled workers in manufacturing alike to increase productivity (AUS-2, AUS-3, AUS-23, AUS-32): skilled unions were hit hard by unemployment and wage restraint and looked to preserve jobs and skilled wage premiums, while employers tried to preserve profits and market shares in the wake of increased competition. Although these pressures had already been on the way since the mid-1970s, the economic conditions of the mid-1980s augmented the need for reform. Under these circumstances, training emerged as a potential solution to the problems confronting industrial employers and workers alike (AUS-13, AUS-29) and thus as an area of policy reform that was 'cross-cutting to the class divide' (AUS-1) in the sense that employers and unions shared a 'common knowledge of the necessity' of skill formation reform (AUS-26).

In contrast to the new incentive to engage in training reform, unions and employers had previously not put joint emphasis on reforming apprenticeship training that had changed very little from its roots of craft-based apprenticeships (AUS-2, AUS-15, AUS-25, AUS-30): VET was still characterized by narrow and rigid job demarcations (AUS-1, AUS-2, AUS-3, AUS-8), specific skills training (AUS-1, AUS-7) and unstructured VET for many workers outside apprenticeships (AUS-30, Ewer et al. 1991). Thus, the central questions were how a new system could be designed, which role unions, employers and governments would play in a new system of vocational training, how standards should be set and who was responsible for the delivery and financing of training (AUS-27).

In contrast to the other two cases, the initiative for training reform appeared earlier among organized interests than in government circles and can be adequately described as social partner driven (AUS-2, AUS-7, AUS-14, AUS-26, AUS-29, AUS-31), although it must be seen in the context of changes in government policy away from tariff protection and a globalizing economy. That the initial impetus for training reform came from unions and employers in metalworking was pivotal for the development of the NTRA and the changes in the system of industrial relations that were to come in the following years.

First, the metal industry award was a centrepiece of the arbitration system that other awards were pegged against for the remuneration of skilled labour and had traditionally been the crucial case for over-award wage bargaining (AUS-2). Changes to the award and training conditions covered by it were highly relevant for the other sectors of the economy. Second, while employer organizations had grown since the 1970s, employers still had not developed a homogenous position on training and industrial relations reform more generally (AUS-2) as they were still split among several organizations (Bray & Neilson 1996: 81, Lansbury & Wailes 2011: 124–126). The Confederation of Australian Industry (CAI) had only been established in 1977 as the first single national employers body, but important large affiliates broke from it during the early years of training reform, most notably the Metal Trades Industry

Association (MTIA) in 1987 and the Australian Chamber of Manufacturers (ACM) in 1989.[52] Moreover, its ability to speak for employers as a whole and to affect policy making was reduced in 1983, when the largest enterprises joined together to form the Business Council of Australia (BCA), which, due to its membership, attained 'a high profile and significant authority' (Lansbury & Wailes 2011: 125) in terms of lobbying for policy. Finally, while the MTIA and its union counterpart in metalworking, the AMWU, had developed some common positions since the mid-1970s – shoring up the industry via mediation by arbitration, policies to increase productivity and competitiveness, support for the ALP-ACTU strategy of accorded politics (Culpepper 2005, Schwartz 2000: 105–114) – their relationship had been characterized by conflict until the emergence of the NTRA. This was exemplified by the AMWU's aggressive wage-bargaining strategy under the short commodities boom of the early 1980s and frequent clashes between their leaders Bert Evans (MTIA) and Laurie Carmichael (AMWU) (AUS-2), who later emerged as a central figure in the politics of training reform (AUS-2, AUS-8, AUS-15, AUS-32).

Due to the common challenge to increase productivity, the second half of the 1980s saw a shift from conflict to cooperation between MTIA and AMWU. Training became the central area of common interest and policy development as it provided a chance to change production patterns, work organization and the introduction of new technology, which were impeded by strong occupational demarcations and the rigid structures of state-based occupational apprenticeship training (Jenkins & Curry 2013). In comparison to other sectors, the MTIA and the AMWU were strongly centralized at the national level (AUS-2), which facilitated the emergence of political cooperation towards a national approach to training reform.

The agenda on training reform that finally emerged was strongly connected to ongoing debates about the restructuring of industrial relations in order to adapt them to the new economic challenges and

> motivated by joint union and employer interest in the link between skills and productivity, especially in manufacturing. This interest extended to pursuing new methods for the identification and use of skills by employees and was part of the broader industrial agenda known as award restructuring. (Jenkins & Curry 2013: 69)

52 In 1998, MTIA and ACM merged into the *Australian Industries Group* (AIG).

In 1986, the MTIA put forward a 'proposal for a compact with the Metal Unions' (MITA 1986), which centred on skill formation reforms as a central area of overlapping interest with the metal unions. The document called for training reform in order to '[develop] the skills and capacities of individual employees as well as increasing overall skill levels and capacities in the industries as a whole' (MTIA 1986: 3) and stressed the pressing 'need to effect a major change in the current approach to training and career development in the industry' (MTIA 1986: 3). It envisaged a broadening of skills and occupational tasks in order to enhance production and workforce flexibility, but also recognized that the need for 'proper training of unskilled on semi-skilled employees is necessary in order to improve their knowledge and broaden skills, to enable them to participate and contribute more effectively and productively' (MTIA 1986: 8). This perspective of broad skills as an asset for efficient production note only stood in marked contrast with the narrow traditional approach of craft apprenticeships but also wrote off strongly hierarchical and task-demarcated strategies akin to Taylorist production. Employers within the MTIA wanted flexible and re-deployable workers (AUS-3, AUS-7, AUS-26), in order to achieve productivity gains by following a 'high skills route' (AUS-1, AUS-9).

In parallel, reforms to the VET system had emerged as an important topic on the union agenda. While apprenticeships had been a traditional stronghold for craft unions, 'training reform promised to address the chronic equity problems of the apprenticeship system, by extending formal skill recognition into the many parts of the economy untouched by the craft tradition' (Ewer 2000: 37). Under difficult economic conditions, changes in the organization of training could remove occupational boundaries and extend skill recognition among workers not covered by the traditional system (AUS-14, AUS-26, Ewer et al. 1991, Hampson 2004). Training reform was seen as a promising way to link skill acquisition with wage progression (AUS-1, AUS-3, AUS-4, AUS-14), to make training an entitlement as an integral part of employment conditions that would facilitate clear career paths (AUS-2, AUS-8) and – given a changed economic environment – it could potentially preserve unions' influence over curriculum content and training delivery (AUS-8, AUS-27, Brown 2006, Ewer et al. 1991, Hampson 2004).

The state of discussion within the union movement is well captured in 'Australia Reconstructed' (ACTU & TDC 1987), which epitomizes the aspirations connected to training reform by the AMWU and ACTU (Brown 2006, Ewer 2000, Hampson 2004, Jenkins & Curry 2013, also: AUS-2, AUS-7, AUS-27, AUS-31). The report was based on a mission of ACTU and the Trade Development Council (TDC) members to several Western European countries (Sweden, Norway, Austria, West Germany and the United Kingdom) in order to find new ideas for tackling the structural economic problems and 'to gain insight into the processes and policies adopted in other countries which have proved successful and to adapt these to the Australian context' (ACTU & TDC 1987: xi). While the report addressed the industrial relations and economic policies found in these countries, it placed a special focus on the development of skills and different models of skill formation found across Europe based on the tenet that 'Australia's international competitiveness depend[ed] on the ability to develop the skills base of [its] workforce' (ACTU & TDC 1987: xiii). In comparison to the reference countries, the report found that 'Australia is not producing the right skills as well as not producing enough skilled people' (ACTU & TDC 1987: 118) and made several recommendations for reforms in order to address these perceived deficits. The report recommended, *inter alia,* the development of active labour market policies with strong training components, more efficient programmes in order to tackle youth unemployment and youth labour market transitions, and a two-tier strategy to adapt VET to changed economic circumstances.

The report also Pointed to the need to reduce labour market segmentation and changes in the awards system, but it connected these recommendations to the parallel requirement to invest in generic and occupationally specific skills (ACTU & TDC 1987: 124). Moreover, the report explicitly recommended stronger cooperation in skill formation between employers, unions and employees (ACTU & TDC 1987: 127) and the central role for skill investment was to be underpinned by the establishment of a National Employment and Training Fund, which was to be sponsored by (federal and state-level) governments and employers via a training levy. Thus, while the unions signalled a willingness to have the awards system reformed away from rigid occupational demarcations, they also stressed the financial responsibility of the state and employers for training provision and – more importantly – the connection between skill attainment and pay structures, which should be firmly institutionalized in a new system of wage bargaining (AUS-1, AUS-3, AUS-4, AUS-14).

With the possibility to cooperate with unions and employers, the federal government became more active in training reform, especially after Richard Dawkins became the Minster for Employment, Education and Industrial Relations (AUS-2, AUS-7, AUS-8, AUS-26, AUS-31). His new department, which was formed in 1987, set out to introduce greater coherence into the system of education in Australia, and created the National Board of Employment, Education and Training (NBEET) in mid-1988. The NBEET was established as a two-tier structure consisting of a main council and four specialist councils (Schools Council, Higher Education Council, Employment and Skill Formation Council (ESFC), and Australian Research Council) and was composed of business and industry representatives, trade unionists and further stakeholders from training, education and science and technology (Goozee 2001: 65). Within the new structures the ESFC – composed in line with tripartite 'quasi-corporatism' (AUS-31) – was responsible for advising the government in matters of industrial training provision, changes to the TAFE system and vocational skills-formation policies.

In its first major report the new department stressed that the 'education system should play an active role in responding to the major economic challenges now facing Australia' (Dawkins & Holding 1987: iii). While the report addressed the relevance of raising participation in education and increasing the quality of educational provision, it also pointed to the need to raise private sector investment in education and skill formation, for an improved recognition of uncertified skills and the development of broad and transferable skills, which were emphasized again one year later as central goals of VET reforms in 'A changing workforce' (Dawkins 1988). This latter report also emphasized the connectedness of training reform with the agenda of reviewing industrial relations and wage bargaining, where major changes were on the way.

Just when MTIA, ACTU, the AMWU and the government started to work towards a more collective training approach, a major change in industrial relations was on the way that came to have strong repercussions for the development of more collective skill formation. Workers already had to accept real wage reductions with the introduction of the two tier-wage system in 1986, but the partial decentralization of industrial relations was reinforced by the decisions of the AIRC on the national wage case in late 1988. Under the notion of a principle of 'structural efficiency', wage increases above the basic flat rate were made conditional on unions and employers agreeing to review their industrial awards in order to include measures aimed at increased competitiveness (AUS-26, Ewer et al. 1991). Under this process of awards restructuring, which was confirmed again by the AIRC in 1989, training finally became a central topic for the government, unions and employers (AUS-17, AUS-26, AUS-27, AUS-29, AUS-31) and was at this point a 'major component of the politics of agreement' (AUS-32, similarly: AUS-14).

The proposals of the MTIA, the AMWU, the ACTU, and the new Department for Employment, Education and Industrial Relations headed by Dawkins were now moving progressively into the same direction and became a 'baseline for training reform' (AUS-31): Despite having different incentives, all parties wanted to move training away from traditional apprenticeships with narrow job demarcations and specific training, towards an approach that would allow broader training and the development of re-deployable and flexible skilled employees. After the AIRC decision on the 'structural efficiency principle' that allowed for higher wages based on higher productivity, the ALP, ACTU, the metal unions and metal employers reached an agreement that skills were central to competitiveness and that VET reform had to be implemented in order to achieve a real change in industrial relations (Jenkins & Curry 2013). As the decision on awards restructuring placed a central emphasis on the role that skills play for increased productivity, cooperation between the industrial partners in VET reform was facilitated and they could more easily agree on the broadening of narrow occupational demarcations and skill formation.

At this point, the industrial partners agreed to a new system that was no longer based on 'time served' but was 'competency based', meaning that skilled worker status would be based on achieving specified standards of skill. Unions agreed to the process of awards restructuring, because they hoped that under a new system acquired and certified skills would be the central basis of pay scales of industrial awards (AUS-1, AUS-2, AUS-3, AUS-4, AUS-14, AUS-26, AUS-29, AUS-32), and that employers would be forced to pay wage rates depending on skill acquisition and not on the actual tasks performed at work (AUS-3, AUS-27, also: Brown 2006, Ewer 2000, Hampson 2004). Moreover, unions held high hopes that they would be able to entrench training entitlements such as paid training leave into the new industrial accords, which would have further increased the possibilities of skill acquisition and, concomitantly, wage level accession. In contrast to these aspects, during the negotiations under the 'politics of summits and consensus' (AUS-14) that characterized the training reform agenda, unions were still eager to protect the separation of apprenticeships and traineeships (AUS-14).

In what followed, the role of the MTIA and the AMWU remained central for the broader process of skill reforms, as the pay rate for a fitter of the metal industry award was traditionally the central peg that all other Australian wage awards were pitted against (Ewer et al. 1991, Hampson 1997). Overall, in the aftermath of the publications of 'Australia reconstructed' and the 'MTIA compact with the metal unions', it was agreed to change from approximately 360 award classifications, which were traditionally determined by the task the employee performed, to a 14-level skills-base classification structure, where pay would be based on skills held and not on tasks performed (Ewer et al. 1991, Jenkins & Curry 2013). The reforms that followed at the sectoral level were usually preceded by government-funded missions of key industry representatives to Western Europe, such as the mission of MTIA and EEF representatives (DIR 1988, MTIA & EEA 1988), on the basis of which the government collected recommendations for governance reforms in VET. Overall 31 recommendations were collected, which largely approved of the proposals given in 'Australia reconstructed' and the proposed MTIA-compact of 1986.

The proposed change that the ALP government envisaged was laid out in *Industry Training: The Need for Change* (Commonwealth Government 1988). The most important aspect was that training should be recognized on a national and industry basis, competency based instead of time served, accredited and certified on a national basis. It should integrate on- and off-the-job training and be available to all employees. Moreover, the industrial partners should be involved in curriculum design via *industrial training advisory bodies* (ITABs)[53] for the training at the state and at the Commonwealth level. However, despite the planned renegotiations of the metals award, at least two central questions were still open. First, the state, unions and employers still had to agree on who was responsible for financing a new training system and to what degree (AUS-2). Employers preferred low training wages and significant financial input of the government, whereas unions and the ALP were in favour of stronger employer contributions via a training levy (ACTU & TDC 1987, Dawkins 1988). While unions and employers had signalled the willingness to agree on a low training wage under the new awards (AUS-23), the amount to be contributed by each party was still not settled. Second, the question of the distribution of competences between the states and the Commonwealth was still an open question, as plans for a national training system necessitated a joint approach towards VET reform not only between the industrial partners but also between eight state-based training systems (Ryan 2002). Both issues were eventually resolved in 1990 after prolonged negotiations between the Commonwealth and the state governments.

Following the publication of the report *Improving Australia's Training System*, which portrayed reform pressures on the VET system as 'immediate and urgent' (Dawkins 1989: 2), a special conference of the responsible Commonwealth and state ministers agreed on the adoption of competency-based training (CBT) as a new standard for competence assessment and skill formation. A National Training Board (NTB) was established, with the aim of developing a national competence framework and bringing training and competence standards developed at the level of industry by ITABs in line with the new national framework (Goozee 2001: 67–69). The NTB membership was drawn in a 'corporatist orientation' (Ryan 2002: 75) from the industrial partners, with a chair from the business community and two representatives from employers and unions, which were joined by one official each from the federal and the state governments. Competency standards were to be devised according to a scale from the metal trades industry award in order to provide pay consistency across industries. This structure of competency-based training became the basis for establishing the

53 Redesignated as *Industry Skills Councils* in 2003.

National Framework for the Recognition of Training (NFROT) and the Australian Standard Framework (ASF).[54]

In terms of finance, the NTB became responsible for the administration of the *Training Guarantee Scheme* (TGS), as a levy that was introduced in July 1990. The idea of a training levy had been first raised in *Australia Reconstructed,* endorsed in the NBEET document *Industry Training: The Need for Change,* and had been 'vigorously opposed by business' (Ryan 2002: 67). After its introduction, employers with a payroll of over 200 000 Australian dollars, had to spend at least 1% (to rise to 1.5% in 1992) of their payroll for federally approved training or had to forfeit the amount to the tax office. The NTB also became responsible for 'registering, de-registering and supervising' (Goozee 2001: 68) newly created registered industrial training agents (RITAs), which were principally composed of unions and employers, and responsible for supervising employers' training expenditures. This represented a first friction between the ACTU and the ALP in terms of training policy under the NTRA, as:

> [i]n the ACTU scheme, employers would have to make a case to retrieve 'their' money and satisfy unions that it had been appropriately spent. In the government's scheme, employers had to satisfy RITAs, on which they had representation, that their training was *bona fide*. The onus of proof was thus favourable to business. (Hampson 2004: 78)

At this point, the NTRA had still been driven by 'changes in industrial relations associated with the structural efficiency principle and award restructuring' (Lundberg 1994: 2) and based on strong industry input and interest in training reform. To assess the likely near future costs of the NTRA and awards restructuring, COSTAC under chairman Ivan Deveson – then CEO of Nissan Australia – commissioned a report that proposed to develop nationally accredited standards and an expansion of government funding for TAFE (Training Costs Review Committee 1990). But it also endorsed the development of a more open training market, in which employers could purchase training products from external training providers other than TAFE in order to shore up industry expenditures for VET due to a better responsiveness of training

54 Reformed to *Australian Qualifications Framework* (AQF) in 1995, which brought together all post-secondary qualifications.

providers to firms' training needs.[55] While being still in the state of discussion in 1990, the expansion of a training market took place in the mid-1990s (AUS-28), which complicated the control of numbers of qualifications and the avoidance of different awarding bodies in a similar fashion to training in the UK (AUS-27).

Despite these deviations from the initial goals of the union movement, the early days of training reform avoided a 'British, deregulationist path' (AUS-27). The NTB opened up access to training politics for unions and employers alike, which complemented their role in the ITABs. Moreover, employers and unions were also included in the Vocational Education, Employment and Training Advisory Committee (VEETAC), which replaced COSTAC in late 1990. VEETAC was institutionalized to oversee and give recommendations to the process of moving to competency-based training and the national recognition of training. The new body, which, unlike COSTAC, had representatives from employer associations and ACTU, developed the NFROT, which included regulations pertaining to VET-course accreditation, registration of training providers as well as the Recognition of Prior Learning (RPL) and the assessment of competencies, which were progressively implemented from 1992 onwards.

The inclusion of the social partners also continued under the new structures of the Australian National Training Authority (ANTA), founded in 1992. It was enacted under the new Prime Minster, Paul Keating, who had won a contest against Hawke as ALP party leader in late 1991. The creation of ANTA had resulted from a compromise between states and the Commonwealth government (AUS-8, AUS-12, AUS-23, AUS-28, AUS-31). Shortly after coming to office, Keating had proposed a funding takeover of all state TAFE institutions with the concomitant influence, training provision and funding decisions, which met heavy resistance from the states. Bereft of the option to attain more direct control over training provision, ANTA represented the alternative option for the federal government to influence the structure of training provision besides TAFE co-funding. ANTA was made responsible for developing a strategic plan for national vocational training and could only set the parameters for state training profiles, which

55 This option had already been hinted at in the 1989 Dawkins report.

remained determined by state training agencies (STAs), answerable to their respective state ministers. ANTA was thus assigned the responsibility for devising an Australian Vocational Certificate Training System (AVCTS) based on competency-based training, with a possibility to the recognition of prior learning and the development of the Australian Qualifications Framework (AQF). The AQF was finally introduced in 1995 and brought all post-compulsory education and training qualifications into the one national system of qualification.

Quite paradoxically, the development towards ANTA, which took up work in 1994, marked an important point in the development of collective skill formation in Australia (AUS-32, Jenkins & Curry 2013, Ryan 2002). The cross-class coalition between MTIA, AMWU, ACTU and the ALP started to unravel when training and industrial relations reforms that the social partners in metalworking had envisaged became disjointed from the agenda of industrial relations reforms (AUS-26). As I detail in the next section, the emergence of a competitive training market, the uncoupling of training standards from industrial awards and the decentralization of industrial relations already gained traction during the ALP government of Keating (1991–1996), but provided an inroad for more extensive deregulatory reforms under the Howard coalition government that followed (1996–2007).

Yet, at the beginning of the 1990s, the Australian system of vocational training had evolved from its traditional configurations in significant aspects. First, in terms of occupational coverage and the development of *portable and certified qualifications*, training had been expanded beyond the traditional manufacturing and craft trades via the introduction of traineeships. Although their uptake was slow until the mid-1990s, they instituted a stream of formal training in occupation that had hitherto not been covered by training regulations. In contrast to the United Kingdom, when traineeships were first introduced in 1985 due to the union movement's influence, they were strictly separated from the areas of traditional apprenticeship, thus blocking off the options for employers to displace apprentices with trainees.

Second, the introduction of the training guarantee was intended to shore up *firm involvement* in training and was introduced despite the protests of employers, especially the BCA, as the organization representing Australia's largest firms (Baker 1994, Ewer 2000, Ewer et al. 1991; ESFC submissions by the BCA and CAI in Ryan 2002: 67). Third, the *involvement of intermediary associations* was strengthened as employers and unions, especially in the metalworking sector, had been closely involved in training reform under the process of *award restructuring*. Expanding their role in ITABs and training governance institutions, such as VEETAC and ANTA, to the national level, also shored up their cross-class cooperation and involvement in training politics. Moreover, union presence in the workplace had a positive effect on in-company training, at least during the phase of the NTRA (Kennedy et al. 1994). Finally, the decision to reform the old, time-served system of apprenticeships towards a system of competency-based training that was envisaged to produce occupationally specific *and* general skills in a reformed model of *dual training* was a further move in the direction of collective skill formation.

The next section shows how the movement towards collective skill formation was stalled after the heyday of the NTRA in the late 1980s and early 1990s but that the marketization of training that occurred from the mid-1990s onwards did not move as far as in the British case, especially as the unions remained entrenched into training institutions and the public sector retained a much stronger role in the provision of off-the-job training.

5.3 The end of the corporatist experiment and gradual displacement? The rise of market mechanisms and traineeships (1993–2008)

> To improve the implementation of [training] reform and achieve its fundamental objectives, a central recommendation is that *implementation of reforms should be refocused on the demand side.* This is conceived as developing a training market centred around *direct* client relationships between training providers on the one hand and enterprises and individuals on the other [...] A major element of 'User Buys' – and thus user choice – should be introduced to shift the focus to the demand side. We recommend that government funding for structured entry level

training in apprenticeships and traineeships progressively pass to the employers and trainees who would *jointly* decide on the purchase of recognised off the job training. (Allen Consulting Group 1994: iv)

> [T]he goals of meaningful reform, more jobs and higher wages, cannot be achieved unless the union monopoly over the bargaining process in our industrial relations system is dismantled. (John Howard before winning office in 1996, cited in van Barneveld & Nassif 2003: 27)

> The reforms being introduced through New Apprenticeships will deliver better training arrangements for employers and individuals. [...] The development of an effective and efficient training market will help ensure this happens. Indeed, the acceleration of market reforms will be one of the major influences for change in vocational training arrangements. (Minister for Schools, Vocational Education and Training: David Kemp 1998: 3)

When the cross-class coalition between metalworking employers and unions was still engaged in training reform, two developments in the early 1990s signalled the advent of a changed climate for training and industrial relations reform, which were to become dominant aspects of training and industrial relations politics under the governments of Keating (ALP) and Howard (Liberal Party). First, the decentralization of industrial relations proceeded further than the original partners of *awards restructuring* had envisaged, and effectively removed training as an industrial relations issue from the majority of industrial awards. Second, the topic of training marketization became a dominant aspect in training reform, which saw the large-scale introduction of market mechanisms in the provision of off-the-job training under the principle of user choice in 1998. These aspects will be described in turn.

Awards restructuring had still moved forward under the accord-framework that ACTU and the ALP had agreed upon, although the accords had moved away from the initial goal of fighting stagflation towards stabilizing inflation and foreign debt reduction. The gradual opening up of the economy had made the reorganization of domestic producers necessary in order to remain competitive compared to imported goods. Increasing productivity had been one of the bases for the AIRC to introduce the 'structural efficiency principle' in the late 1980s, which became a central impetus for award restructuring. Being at the forefront of award restructuring, the ACTU 'accepted, indeed championed, a form of "enterprise bargaining", which was eventually introduced by the [AIRC] in 1991' (Bray & Neilson 1996: 84). Under this system, maximum wage increases above the level set by the AIRC were supposed to be negotiated directly between unions and employers at the enterprise level and to be based on increases in productivity (Bray & Neilson 1996: 84). Similarly, the 1993 Industrial Relations Reform Act enhanced the option of negotiating wages outside of the arbitration system. However, the union movement had already lost some influence on this reform, which reflected the influence of the BCA and the Australian Chamber of Commerce and Industry (ACCI).[56] The BCA, in particular, had been lobbying since the late 1980s for a more flexible and decentralized system of industrial relations (Ewer 2000, Hampson 2004). The 1993 Act, for the first time, established a non-union bargaining stream, which allowed employers to negotiate wages with non-unionized employees outside of the arbitration system, but was initially used very little by employers (Cooper & Ellem 2008).

Why would the union movement champion the decentralization of the awards system if it were traditionally a stronghold for skilled workers? As described above, the wage agreements between ACTU and ALP from 1986 onwards had resulted in reduced take-home pay for workers as flat-rate wage increases did not match the development of living costs. Thus, wage increases became contingent on pacts between unions and employers to increase productivity, which was one of the central pillars the NTRA. The unions had hoped to use VET and the link between skills acquisition and productivity to shore up their bargaining power under a system of reformed industrial awards, and to broaden skill recognition within the whole working class.

However, the reformed metal award did not deliver to their expectations. While training was included as a central component into the award and occupational demarcations were replaced by a 14-level skill scale (AUS-2, AUS-3), the components of paid training leave and linking of VET to the national standards to be developed under NFROT were considerably weakened in the final award. While the union movement was still amidst the central players of the NTRA, already at this time it had lost considerable influence (AUS-3, AUS-7, AUS-26, AUS-29, also:

56 ACCI was formed in 1992 as the follow-up organisation to the CAI, which had merged with the *Australian Chamber of Commerce* (ACC).

Brown 2006). While unions and employer associations still cooperated strongly in devising VET standards via ITABs (AUS-4, AUS-12, AUS-25), the Commonwealth government and the BCA increasingly dominated the industrial relations reform agenda (Bramble & Kuhn 2011, Cooper & Ellem 2008, Hampson 1997, Hampson & Morgan 1998).[57]

Concerning VET provision, the MTIA, the AMWU and the ACTU had initially envisaged a training system characterized by national standards and high-quality training provision. However, during the 1990s and early 2000s, training provision became increasingly based on the provision of off the job training in a 'training market' that partly emulated developments in the United Kingdom (AUS-16, AUS-28). While the Deveson Report (Training Costs Review Committee 1990) and 'Improving Australia's Training System' (Dawkins 1989) had already pointed towards the possibility of more diverse training provision and the development of training providers outside the TAFE system, the idea of training marketization became pronouncedly stronger in policy circles in the early 1990s, where, however, it remained 'rare to find any discussion of what this market involves. Nor [were] there any explanations of the perceived gains or discussion of how disadvantages might be alleviated' (Fisher 1993: 27, in Goozee 2001: 90). The publication of the Hilmer Report on 'National Competition Policy' (Hilmer 1993), which recommended the introduction of competition into areas that had previously been government monopolies, spurred discussion about introducing competition into the TAFE system (Brown 2013). Similar, the BCA was moving into the direction of training provision diversification when it argued, in July 1993, 'that large employers themselves could become Registered Training Organisations (RTOs), accredit their own training programmes, and develop an "enterprise-stream" of training "within" the NTRA' (Hampson 2004: 81). This argument was endorsed in the following by ANTA and also by the NTB and MOVEET, despite objections of ACTU, which feared that partial privatisation would lead to huge differences in training delivery and quality (AUS-16).

These developments already signalled steps away from the path taken towards collective skill formation in the early days of the NTRA. That the ALP government also moved away from collective approaches

57 See BCA arguments for decentralized bargaining and VET geared towards the needs of individual firms (BCA 1989, 1993, in Ewer 2000).

after the failed TAFE takeover and the ANTA compromise in 1992 was already evident in 1994, when the government acted towards the direction of coupling employment and training policy. Since coming into office in 1991, the Keating government had been confronted with a high unemployment of around 10% and youth unemployment had constantly varied in between 15% and 20% from 1991 to 1994 (OECD various). Already in his 'One Nation' statement, Keating had announced that he would make the training system more relevant to employment in order to mitigate problems of high youth unemployment, and stated that he would make traineeships more attractive to employers (Keating 1992). He announced, *inter alia,* the expansion of funding for individual trainees, a new 2000 AUD subsidy for employers who hired trainees and the expansion of wage subsidies for second-year apprentices. The policy of encouraging traineeship growth was also a centrepiece in the large-scale strategy of reforming active labour market policy, which was introduced on the conceptual basis of two government White Papers that addressed the challenges for Australia as a 'Working Nation' (Keating 1994b, a). The two central pieces of a new employment policy strategy were Job Compact and the extension of the existing Jobstart programme. The former offered job placements in the private sector to the short-term unemployed, where the refusal of a placement offer could result in the loss of benefits in a similar fashion as under the ET programme that the Thatcher government had introduced in the United Kingdom in the late 1980s. The latter programme targeted long-term unemployed and provided subsidies to employers to take them on for a job with little training component.

Yet, bigger changes occurred in entry-level VET. In 1994, National Employment and Training Taskforce (NETTFORCE) traineeships were established to encourage employer take-up of training. Under the new programme, traineeships were expanded into the area so far only covered by apprenticeships and thereby exempted from long-standing regulations. This contributed to the growth of on-the-job-only traineeships (Ray 2001: 30) and broke the classical separation of admissible occupations for apprenticeships and traineeships, which unions had preserved when traineeships were first introduced under the Hawke government in 1985. Due to exemptions regarding training content, NETTFORCE traineeships can be seen as a labour market programme rather than real traineeships (AUS-12, AUS-21). Their introduction led to a 'distortion of apprenticeships' (AUS-5) and the problem that 'no clear equivalence of qualifications [had] been established in terms of training duration, difficulty or skill level' (Ray 2001: 29). The Keating government had also suspended the TGS and expanded funding for on-the-job only and adult training programmes.

Nevertheless, the process of devising a national training framework and overseeing the implementation of a move towards a new training system by ANTA continued with strong social partner involvement, despite the employment policies of Keating. Yet, following the centripetal movement in industrial relations away from coordinated wage-bargaining, the rising disappointment of unions about awards restructuring (Brown 2006) and the movement towards more training marketization, few of the strategic goals of the union movement with the NTRA remained after the accord process ended when a new coalition government took office in 1996.

The new partisan government was less favourable towards the unions, but could not dismantle the institutional legacy of union involvement in setting training standards and the role of the TAFE institutions as major providers. Nonetheless the Howard Coalition further diminished the differences between apprenticeships and traineeships. In 1998, it introduced a new apprenticeship system, which merged traditional (trades) apprenticeships and traineeships. The impetus for this reform came from stubbornly high levels of youth unemployment and shifts towards the service sector. It aimed to improve skill levels and it broke with the principle of declaring occupational demarcations and thereby contributed to the delineation of areas of workforce competence.[58] The reform included the inception of training packages and a training market, goals that had already been followed by the previous government. While the former specified the training agreement (in place of indentures), training plans, competencies to be attained and the method of assessment and assessment guidelines, the latter opened up the market for private off-the-job training providers under the Australian Recognition Framework (ARF),[59] which specified nationally agreed registration requirements for

58 The government of New South Wales continued to declare occupations.

59 In 2001 its regulations were reviewed and replaced by the Australian Quality Training Framework (AQTF).

training providers. Furthermore, the reform introduced *user choice principles* on a large scale; this meant that trainees and employers are free to choose the provider of the off-the-job training component, which is subsidized by central government grants.

This aimed at further liberalizing the training market, which had previously been dominated by TAFE, and has led to a multiplicity of training possibilities. Together with the abolition of ANTA in 2005, with its functions brought into the Department of Education, Science and Technology (DEST), and the introduction of the Work Choices Act in 2005, which has broken the link between training, pay and career progression, enabling employers to use piece rate, performance-based and flat-rate pay systems that do not include a training and skill progression element (Cooney & Long 2010), these changes have dismantled collectivism in skill formation quite significantly. Compared to the initial NTRA aims, the future of dual apprenticeships seems to be endangered in Australia as marketization and deregulation in industrial relations and VET have 'led to a deregulation of training curricula, training delivery and training providers and have created a [...] the development of an employer-led VET system' (Cooney & Long 2010: 28). Despite the argument that Australia has moved towards a more liberal model of skill formation in the late 1990s and 2000s, three qualifications should be made.

First, because of federalism and despite the Commonwealth's ability to incentivize state policies via co-funding, the states have retained control of their training systems. For example, liberalization went far in Victoria, which

> merge[d] the TAFE administration with elements of the State Department of labour and the Industry Training Commission. The new organization became the Office of the State Training Board, the board itself being a business-dominated body [...] [It] became the strongest advocate among State TAFE administrations of the use of market forces in vocational education. It was the first State agency to use public funding to encourage a training market in industry and the private training sector and to allocate funding to TAFE colleges on demonstrated industry responsiveness and lowest-cost criteria. (Ryan 2002: 52)

However, New South Wales retained a much stronger role not only for TAFE in the delivery of off-the-job training, but also a firm role for social partnership within its state training institutions (AUS-1). While the fragmentation made training reform towards a national system complicated, it can also act as an effective brake to deregulation.

Second, compared to the United Kingdom, where unions were effectively removed from training governance, Australian unions have retained a much stronger role in standard setting via ISCs and in controlling the use of apprenticeship by employers. For example, Cooney (2010) shows that training quality is higher and training standards are adhered to where unions have a stronger skills base. Moreover, despite attempts to displace the ITABs/ISCs in the mid-2000s, they still play a fair role in training policies, especially in the manufacturing sector.

Finally, despite the marketization of training and the increase of government funding for traineeships (partially in the form of labour market programmes), the states have retained a strong role in the public provision of VET. For Australia as a whole, TAFE and other government providers of vocational education make up almost two-thirds of all training places for off-the-job training (NCVER 2014). Moreover, while training under the apprenticeship frameworks of Advanced Apprenticeships and Apprenticeships in the United Kingdom is mostly situated at lower levels of qualifications the vast majority of training for Australian Apprenticeships is situated at certificate level 3 of the AQF (NCVER 2014), which is equivalent to skilled trades training.

5.4 Conclusion

The changes that have occurred in Australian apprenticeship reforms have to be understood in the broader context of the transformation of the Australian economy from a system of 'domestic defence' (Castles & Mitchell 1993) towards an internationally open economy and the corresponding reforms of 'awards restructuring' and retrenchment of wage arbitration. During the research period beneficial constraints such as arbitration-fixed wages and union workplace representation were progressively dismantled. Astonishingly, these developments were initiated under the Labor government of Paul Keating.

The changes in the international economy that have taken place after the impact of the two oil crises, the breakdown of fixed exchange rates and the liberalization of the international economy have triggered major changes in the Australian economy. In response to these changes the Hawke and Keating Labor governments negotiated an incomes accord with the unions while introducing markets into the service sector, liberalizing product markets and decentralizing wage bargaining. In what follows, the central characteristics of the subsequent accords between the governments and the unions are described and set into context with the development of training institutions.

The reform course steered by the Labor governments towards the problems of low international competitiveness and risen unemployment in the 1980s was based on coordination with the main Australian unions. The politics of *accords*, which were negotiated between 1983 and 1996, was based on the principle of keeping real wages high, while liberalizing the economy. The *accords* were used to disentangle horizontal wage parities by the progressive introduction of decentralized bargaining for competitive sectors. This spurred growth and competitiveness of skill-intensive sectors such as the metals sector, for training it proved a mixed blessing as it reduced wage parities between training in sectors of different productivity. However, the main problem was that unions hoped that training would be included in the process of awards restructuring, but the reforms towards firm-level bargaining and the introduction of the NETTFORCE traineeships did not deliver to their expectations. Various union representatives expressed this view in the interviews collected by Brown (2006). At the same time, the arbitration-wage coverage has reduced from 80% to less than 50% of the workforce, thus opening up possibilities for non-training firms to poach trainees from their training competitors.

6. Conclusion

This book has investigated the development of collective skill formation in Australia, Ireland and the United Kingdom, which represent least likely cases for the development of cooperative approaches to VET, at least if we adhere to the propositions set out by the initial VoC paradigm. This raises issues of path dependency, as all three countries shared a similar history of apprenticeship regulation, which was essentially based on contested relationships between employers and craft unions. If we abstract from the fact that in Australia these relationships were partly formalized via the arbitration system, state actors traditionally refrained from strongly interfering into what was basically a system of voluntarist regulation. Moreover, the finalization of apprenticeships was still based on the time served as an apprentice and not on the competences to be achieved during training or a strong standardization of this type of skill formation.

Yet, as I have shown for the three cases under study, the divergence of VET systems in the form of dual apprenticeships is greater in LMEs than expected. This pertains especially to *firm involvement* and *public commitment* in the VET system, which are highly developed among countries that belong to the regime of collective skill formation. To reiterate the main questions that motivated this study: to which degree have the cases developed in different directions regarding the parameters that are crucial components of collective skill formation? How can we explain reforms towards collective skill formation despite similar policy legacies and what were the main driving forces in terms of coalitions between employers, unions and governments? Finally, what are the implications for the study of skill-formation regimes and institutional change?

The case studies in Chapters 3 to 5 have treated the trajectories of training reforms in Australia, Ireland and England as typical examples of liberal market economies. All case studies have shown, that partisan governments did influence the development towards collective skill formation (Ireland, Australia until the mid-1990s) or towards a greater marketization of training in non-trivial ways. In the following, I will briefly summarize the main findings presented in the case studies above.

All three countries had largely similar policy legacies in the area of apprenticeships. These were traditionally heavily contested between craft unions, which tried to use their influence over apprenticeships to control the number of skilled crafts persons and drive up their members' wages, and employers who in turn tried to break the craft union influence over training. Where they did not succeed, they tried to minimize the use of skilled labour, but first and foremost they were reluctant to pay for the training of their workers beyond narrow skills. Thus, the preferences of craft unions and employers worked towards narrow skills training, and training remained rather loosely regulated, based on voluntarist principles and not finalized by the acquisition of certified competencies but rather by the time served as apprentices.

The basis of apprenticeships also remained contested between craft unions and employers, because governments of different party-political flavours traditionally refrained from strongly interfering in the voluntarist training arrangements between unions and employers. Where governments tried to intervene in training before the 1980s (as with the ITB and MSC reforms in the United Kingdom of the creation of AnCO in Ireland), these reforms were typically not successful, as they were still based on rather loose regulations and failed to fundamentally alter the preferences among employers and craft unions.

However, after the failed interventions of the post-war period, the three cases started to diverge quite heavily in the trajectories of their training reforms since the 1980s: Australia and Ireland moved towards collective skill formation and non-right-wing governments generally included employers and unions in the politics of apprenticeship reform and the design of the new programs. Conversely, the right-wing Thatcher government in the United Kingdom, used VET reforms to curtail the influence of unions in training by dismantling the weak but collective institutions for training governance (ITBs and the MSC) and replacing them by business-led TECs. Moreover, traditional apprentices were increasingly replaced by young trainees on government employment programmes as the YTS, which also contributed to freeing employers from their traditional obligations in VET.

Which patterns did this divergence result into? How did the central aspects of collective skill formation (Busemeyer and Trampusch 2012a), such as *firm involvement*, the *involvement of intermediary associations,* the provision of *highly standardized* and *portable, certified occupational skills,* and, the combination of *firm-based and off-the-job-training* develop in each case?

In the United Kingdom, *firm involvement* in apprenticeships is low. Here, a significant amount of the training costs is borne by individuals and the state, which sponsors training via 'quasi-markets' in which private and public providers compete for public funds and in turn offer off-the-job training and training modules to employers. Similarly, the *involvement of intermediary associations* is weakly developed in standard setting and policy making. The systematic exclusion of unions from training is probably the most telling example in this respect. Related to the former two aspects, training is *weakly standardized* and based on a loose regulatory framework (NVQs), which underpins the training market. Finally, apprenticeships especially at NVQ level two are better characterized as labour market programmes with training components than well-balanced systems of *dual training.*

In contrast, Ireland exhibits more features of collective skill formation. Here, *firm involvement* is higher and firms not only sponsor a proportion of off-the-job training via a levy, but firms are also strongly involved via their *intermediary associations* in training governance and policy making. They share a strong role in the development of occupational standards with unions, state representatives and educators under the institutional umbrella of FÁS and its National Apprenticeship Advisory Committee. Finally, training is *highly standardized* in terms of duration and training content, and structured as a *dual training system* with seven alternating phases, of which four take place with an employer.

Compared with the development of a training market in the United Kingdom and the reforms towards collective skill formation in Ireland, Australia occupies a middle ground between these two approaches to apprenticeships. *Firm involvement* was first shored up and then expanded under the National Training Reform Agenda, under which firms contributed to off-the-job training via a training levy. However, in the aftermath of the NTRA, firms became increasingly supported by financial incentives from the public purse, especially under labour-market programmes such as the NETTFORCE traineeships. However, the *involvement of intermediary associations* of capital and labour in standard setting and the development of occupational profiles remains more strongly developed than in the United Kingdom, as both sides' interests are included in industry skill councils, which remain an important 'collective' institution in Australian VET. Due to this aspect, training marketization in Australia, which became especially pronounced under the Coalition governments of John Howard, has not resulted into a strong fragmentation of *occupational training standards* and the role of the training market – and commercial training providers – has not expanded as much as in the United Kingdom. This has also helped to shore up *dual training*, which is typically provided by employers for firm-based training and TAFE for the off-the-job components. Finally, training is, to a large degree, provided at higher levels of the AQF and thus contrasts with the developments in the United Kingdom, where training is mostly situated at low qualification levels.

With regard to the driving forces of training reforms, the three case studies have also confirmed the expectation that industrial relations and training reforms were strongly interrelated in the three cases under study. However, and going beyond the initial expectations formulated in Chapter 2, the case studies have also shown that economic crises of the late 1980s and early 1990s constituted important windows of opportunity that partisan governments exploited to reform industrial relations and the apprenticeship system. However, *the course these reforms took was strongly influenced by the partisan composition of government*, and especially the presence or absence of secular-conservative, right governments.

In the United Kingdom, and to a lesser degree in Australia from the mid-1990s onwards, these partisan governments instituted reforms that largely freed employers from their traditional obligations in apprenticeships and strengthened their industrial-relations bargaining positions vis-à-vis unions. The dismantling of tripartite governance institutions for apprenticeships was not the only important tool for strengthening the position of individual employers: the use of youth employment programmes with training components (YTS in the UK and *traineeships* in Australia) could not only have been intended to encourage employer take-up of young trainees and to reduce youth unemployment; it also serves as a way for individual employers to circumvent stricter training regulations of traditional apprenticeships and encourage displacement. This strategy of freeing individual employers was, in both cases, complemented by the introduction of quasi-markets in training, where VET is, to a large degree, state sponsored in the form of labour market and training programs, which are delivered by public and private training providers that compete for money from the public purse.

However, the substantial weakening of the obligations of employers with regard to training in the United Kingdom in the course of three decades from 1980 onwards contrasts markedly with the Irish approach towards social partnership and the continuous involvement of capital and labour in industrial relations and apprenticeship reforms, and also with developments in Australia that occurred in the period of the National Training Reform Agenda. Both cases saw a movement towards more cooperative industrial relations and more collective approaches in skill formation via apprenticeship reforms.

As I showed in the case studies of Ireland and Australia (up to the mid-1990s), developments towards more cooperation and strategic coordination between employers and unions were strongly influenced by non-right-wing governments that used policy reforms in the areas of VET and industrial relations in order to secure the cooperation of business and unions in reforms that were intended to tackle a severe economic crisis that each country faced. In both cases these reforms altered the basic preferences among employers and craft unions towards VET and enabled tripartite approaches towards VET reform, which earlier attempts had failed to accomplish.

In Ireland, the process of reform was guided by a politics of social pacts among governments, unions and employers, which were based on tripartite proposals on macro-economic, industrial relations and VET reform. Within the politics of social pacts, craft unions agreed to a strategy of wage moderation and economic deregulation, for which the government compensated them with investments in education, infrastructure and welfare. Wage moderation and a course of stable monetary policy that were brought about by social partnership acted as important factors, which made it possible for the government to expand the training obligations of employers to release their apprentices for off-the-job training and contribute to the general training of their apprentices via a levy. Thus, a non-right-wing government significantly shaped the formation of a cross-class coalition between employers and unions and it was this coalition that formed an important basis for the introduction of a new system of Standards-Based Apprenticeships in 1993.

In Australia, labour governments also tried to use industrial relations and VET reforms to tackle an economic crisis. As in Ireland, the relationship between the ALP-government and the union movement played an important role in the political concertation of reforms that liberalized the Australian economy from the long-standing model of economic protectionism and domestic defence, which was no longer economically viable under the conditions of an increasingly open economy. The politics of the accords between ALP and ACTU, which had the tacit support of some parts of the business community, was also based on the logic of political exchange. The union movement agreed to the introduction of flexibility into wage bargaining, to wage moderation and to let go of rigid occupational demarcations. In turn, unions were compensated by an expansion of formal social policy and training reforms. The latter approached a model of more collective skill formation once the metalworking employers were convinced that more training investments were necessary in order to remain competitive under changed economic circumstances.

These developments saw the emergence of a national training reform agenda that was underpinned by a cross-class coalition between employers and unions in metalworking, which was supported by attempts of the federal government to reform VET towards a national training system. However, the cross-class coalition between unions and employers started to lose influence on the direction of the training reforms whereas the BCA became more influential. The BCA represented the training interests of Australia's largest companies and was geared towards more flexible training delivery for its member firms and, more generally, decentralized industrial relations.

However, some collective skill-formation institutions, such as the involvement of unions and employers in the politics of VET, as well as tripartite institutions in training governance have remained more robust when compared to the United Kingdom. The coalition government introduced market principles into training, which are quite similar to those in the United Kingdom, and tried to dismantle union influence in training but it did not have the political power to completely dismantle the collective institutions that were put in place during the era of the training reform agenda.

Given these findings, the concluding paragraphs of this chapter will outline the ways in which this study has contributed to the analysis of skill-formation regimes and institutional change.

First, it has contributed to a growing literature that analyses the difference of vocational training *within* ideal-types of training provision by showing that training arrangements differ within ideal-types *even in LMEs*. Thus, rather than basing analyses of vocational training on a functionalist logic of comparative advantage and path dependency, it is necessary to consider the interaction between governments of different political persuasions, employers and trade unions in order to obtain a more nuanced picture of the driving forces of institutional change in LMEs. Despite the common institutional origins of apprenticeships in Ireland, Australia and the United Kingdom, their systems of initial skill formation diverged substantively in the crucial period of the 1980s and 1990s. This underscores the need to complement historical institutionalist accounts that put a lot of explanatory weight on developments that took place at the end of the 19th century or during 1945–1975 with contemporary studies that exploit how historically supressed policy alternatives can re-enter the menu of political options under the conditions of an open economy.

Following this reasoning, I posit that it is necessary not only to look at the dimension of economic coordination but also to study the crucial element of *political coordination*. The three case studies suggest that more attention is required to the issue of how governments include organized interests in policy making during critical junctures of economic reforms, not only in training but also in industrial relations.

A possible reading of the book's findings is that non-right-wing governments can use VET to *secure union cooperation in economic adjustments* to bring about macroeconomic stability, which might be seen as a key prerequisite in order to attract capital investment. Conversely, as exemplified by the Thatcher government, *right-wing governments can use VET to weaken the role of unions in economic policy making and industrial relations* in order to strengthen the role of markets in economic coordination. These arguments would suggest that it is necessary to consider the interaction between the dimensions of economic coordination and political coordination, which are pivotal to the understanding of reform processes in contemporary political economies.

Finally, while all of the countries in this study departed from a low level of government involvement in apprenticeship training and more-less voluntarist systems, the growth in government funding and the regulation of apprenticeships did not have similar effects in the three countries. Thus, government involvement in the form of spending does not matter *per se* (Esping-Andersen 1990) but for the structure of spending between the state, apprentices and firms and the regulation of training content and provision it is crucial which economic actors and political parties cooperate in apprenticeship reforms.

References

Acemoglu, D., and J.-S. Pischke. 1998. 'Why Do Firms Train? Theory and Evidence.' *The Quarterly Journal of Economics* 113(1): 79–119.

Acemoglu, D., and J.-S. Pischke. 1999. 'Beyond Becker: Training in Imperfect Labour Markets.' *The Economic Journal* 109(453): F112–F42.

ACOTAFE, and M. Kangan. 1974. 'TAFE in Australia: Report on Needs in Technical and Further Education.' Canberra: Australian Government Publishing Service.

ACTU, and TDC. 1987. 'Australia Reconstructed: Mission to Western Europe. A Report by the Mission Members to the ACTU and TDC.' Canberra: Australian Government Publishing Service.

Adshead, M., and J. Tonge. 2009. *Politics in Ireland: Convergence and Divergence on a Two-Polity Island*. Basingstoke: Palgrave Macmillan.

Ahlquist, J. S. 2008. Policy by Contract: Social Pacts in Australia and New Zealand. University of Washington: Department of Political Science.

Ainley, P., and S. Vickerstaff. 1993. 'Transitions from Corporatism: The Privatisation of Policy Failure.' *Contemporary Record: The Journal of Contemporary British History* 7(3): 541–556.

Ainley, P., and M. Corney. 1990. *Training for the Future: The Rise and Fall of the Manpower Services Commission*. London: Cassell.

Allen Consulting Group. 1994. *Successful Reform: Competitive Skills for Australians and Australian Enterprises*. ACG: Melbourne.

Allen, M. 2004. 'The Varieties of Capitalism Paradigm: Not Enough Variety?' *Socio-Economic Review* 2(1): 87–108.

ALP, and ACTU. 1983. *Statement of Accord by the Australian Labor Party and the Australian Council of Trade Unions Regarding Economic Policy*. Melbourne: ACTU.

Amable, B. 2003. *The Diversity of Modern Capitalism*. Oxford: Oxford University Press.

AnCO. 1968. 'First Annual Report 1967–1968.' Dublin.
AnCO. 1973. *Apprenticeship: A New Approach.* Dublin.
Anderson, M., and J. Fairley. 1983. 'The Politics of Industrial Training in the United Kingdom.' *Journal of Public Policy* 3(2): 191–207.
Ansell, B. 2010. *From the Ballot to the Blackboard: The Redistributive Political Economy of Education.* Cambridge: Cambridge University Press.
Aoki, M. 1994. 'The Japanese Firm as a System of Attributes: A Survey and Research Agenda.' In *The Japanese Firm: Sources of Competitive Strenght*, eds. M. Aoki and R. Dore. Oxford: Clarendon Press. 11–40.
Archer, R. 1992. 'The Unexpected Emergence of Australian Corporatism.' In *Social Corporatism: A Superior Economic System?*, eds. J. Pekkarinen, M. Pohjola, and B. Rowthorn. Oxford: Clarendon Press. 377–417.
Aust, A. 1999. *The 'Celtic Tiger' and Its Beneficiaries: 'Competitive Corporatism' in Ireland.* Paper presented at the ECPR Joint Session of Workshops, Mannheim, March 1999.
Baccaro, L., and C. Howell. 2011. 'A Common Neoliberal Trajectory: The Transformation of Industrial Relations in Advanced Capitalism.' *Politics and Society* 39(4): 521–563.
Baccaro, L., and S.-H. Lim. 2007. 'Social Pacts as Coalitions of the Weak and Moderate: Ireland, Italy and South Korea in Comparative Perspective.' *European Journal of Industrial Relations* 13(1): 27–46.
Baker, M. 1994(5). 'Training Down Under: An Overview of the Australian Experience.' *International Journal of Manpower* 15(5): 70–88.
Baumgartner, F. R., B. D. Jones, and J. L. True. 2007. 'Punctuated-Equilibrium Theory: Explaining Stability and Change in Public Policymaking.' In *Theories of the Policy Process*, ed. P. A. Sabatier. Boulder, CO: Westview Press. 155–187.
Baumgartner, F. R., C. Breunig, C. Green-Pedersen, B. D. Jones, P. B. Mortensen, M. Nuytemans, and S. Walgrave. 2009. 'Punctuated Equilibrium in Comparative Perspective.' *American Journal of Political Science* 53(3): 603–620.

Becker, G. S. 1993. *Human Capital: A Theoretical and Empirical Analysis with Special Reference to Education*. Chicago: Chicago University Press.

Becker, U. 2007. 'Open Systemness and Contested Reference Frames and Change: A Reformulation of the Varieties of Capitalism Theory.' *Socio-Economic Review* 5(2): 261–286.

Beilharz, P. 1994. *Labour Tradition and the Labour Decade in Australia*. Cambridge: Cambridge University Press.

Blossfeld, H.-P. 1992. 'Is the German Dual System a Model for a Modern Vocational Training System? A Cross-National Comparison of How Different Systems of Vocational Training Deal with the Changing Occupational Structure.' *International Journal of Comparative Sociology* 33 (3–4): 168–181.

Blyth, M. 2003. 'Same as It Never Was: Temporality and Typology in the Varieties of Capitalism.' *Comparative European Politics* 1(2): 215–225.

Boix, C. 1998. *Political Parties, Growth and Equality*. Cambridge: Cambridge University Press.

Bonoli, G. 2012. 'Active Labour Market Policy and Social Investment: A Changing Relationship.' In *Towards a Social Investment Welfare State?* eds. N. Morel, B. Palier and J. Palme. Bristol: Policy Press. 181–204.

Bosch, G., and J. Charest. 2008. 'Vocational Training and the Labour Market in Liberal and Coordinated Economies.' *Industrial Relations Journal* 39(5): 428–447.

Boyle, N. 2005. *Fàs and Active Labour Market Policy: 1985–2004*. Dublin: The Policy Institute at Trinity College Dublin.

Bramble, T., and R. Kuhn. 2011. *Labor's Conflict: Big Business, Workers and the Politics of Class*. Port Melbourne: Cambridge University Press.

Bray, M., and D. Neilson. 1996. 'Industrial Relations Reform and the Relative Autonomy of the State.' In *The Great Experiment: Labour Parties and Public Policy Transformation in Australia and New Zealand*, eds. F. G. Castles, R. Gerritsen, and J. Vowles. St. Leonards: Allen & Unwin. 68–87.

Brown, K. 2013. 'How Do Providers Respond to Changes in Structures in a Period of Reform?' In *Structures in Tertiary Education and Training: A Kaleidoscope or Merely Fragments?*, eds. F. Beddie, L. O'Connor, and P. Curtin. Adelaide (SA): NCVER. 98–107.
Brown, P. 2001. 'Skill Formation in the Twenty-First Century.' In *High Skills: Globalization, Competitiveness and Skill Formation*, eds. Phillip Brown, Andy Green and Hugh Lauder. Oxford: Oxford University Press. 1–55.
Brown, T. 2006. 'From Union Inspired to Industry Led: How Australian Labour's Training Reform Experiment Turned Sour.' *Journal of Industrial Relations* 48(4): 491–505.
Busemeyer, M. R. 2007. 'Determinants of Public Education Spending in 21 OECD Democracies, 1980–2001.' *Journal of European Public Policy* 14(4): 582–610.
Busemeyer, M. R. 2009a. 'Asset Specificity, Institutional Complementarities and the Varieties of Skill Regimes in Coordinated Market Economies.' *Socio-Economic Review* 7(3): 375–406.
Busemeyer, M. R. 2009b. 'Social Democrats and the New Partisan Politics of Public Investment in Education.' *Journal of European Public Policy* 16(1): 107–126.
Busemeyer, M. R. 2009c. *Wandel trotz Reformstau: Die Politik der beruflichen Bildung seit 1970*. Frankfurt/New York: Campus.
Busemeyer, M. R. 2011. 'Varieties of Cross-Class Coalitions in the Politics of Dualization: Insights from the Case of Vocational Training in Germany.' *MPIfG Discussion Paper* 11/13.
Busemeyer, M. R. 2012. 'Business as a Pivotal Actor in the Politics of Training Reform: Insights From the Case of Germany.' *British Journal of Industrial Relations* 50(4): 690–713.
Busemeyer, M. R. 2015. *Skills and Inequality: Partisan Politics and the Political Economy of Education Reforms in Western Welfare States*. Cambridge: Cambridge University Press.
Busemeyer, M. R., and C. Trampusch. 2012a. 'Introduction: The Comparative Political Economy of Collective Skill Formation.' In *The Comparative Political Economy of Collective Skill Formation*, eds. M. R. Busemeyer and C. Trampusch. Oxford: Oxford University Press. 3–38.

Busemeyer, M. R., and C. Trampusch, eds. 2012b. *The Political Economy of Collective Skill Formation*. Oxford: Oxford University Press.
Busemeyer, M. R., and J. Vossiek. 2016. 'Global Convergence or Path Dependency? Skill Formation Regimes in the Globalized Economy.' In *The Handbook of Global Education,* eds. K. Mundy, A. Green, B. Lingard and A. Verger. Chichester: Wiley-Blackwell. 145–161.
Busemeyer, M. R., S. T. Franzmann, and J. L. Garritzmann. 2013. 'Who Owns Education? Cleavage Structures in the Partisan Competition over Educational Expansion.' *West European Politics* 36(3): 521–546.
Campbell, J. L., and O. K. Pedersen. 2007. 'The Varieties of Capitalism and Hybrid Success: Denmark in the Global Economy.' *Comparative Political Studies* 40(3): 307–332.
Capoccia, G. and R. D. Kelemen. 2007. 'The Study of Critical Junctures: Theory, Narrative, and Counterfactuals in Historical Institutionalism.' *World Politics* 59(3): 341–369.
Castles, F. G., ed. 1993. *Families of Nations: Patterns of Public Policy in Western Democracies*. Aldershot: Dartmouth.
Castles, F. G. 1985. *The Working Class and Welfare: Reflections on the Political Development of the Welfare State in Australia and New Zealand, 1890–1980*. Wellington et al.: Allen & Unwin/Port Nicholson Press.
Castles, F. G. 2010. 'The English-Speaking Countries.' In *The Oxford Handbook of the Welfare State*, eds. F. G. Castles, S. Leibfried, J. Lewis, H. Obinger and C. Pierson. Oxford: Oxford University Press. 630–642.
Castles, F. G., and D. Mitchell. 1993. 'Worlds of Welfare and Families of Nations.' In *Families of Nations: Patterns of Public Policy in Western Democracies*, ed. F. G. Castles. Aldershot: Dartmouth. 93–128.
Castles, F. G., and J. Uhr. 2005. 'Australia: Federal Constraints and Institutional Innovations.' In *Federalism and the Welfare State: New World and European Experiences*, eds. H. Obinger, S. Leibfried, and F. G. Castles. Cambridge/New York: Cambridge University Press. 51–88.

Coates, D. 2002. 'Book Review – Varieties of Capitalism: The Institutional Foundations of Comparative Advantage by Peter A. Hall; David Soskice.' *American Political Science Review* 96(3): 661–662.

Coates, D., ed. 2005. *Varieties of Capitalism: Varieties of Approaches*. Houndmills/New York: Palgrave Macmillan.

Commonwealth Government. 1988. *Industry Training: The Need for Change*. Canberra: Commonwealth Government.

Compston, H. 1994. 'Union Participation in Economic Policy: Making in Austria, Switzerland, the Netherlands, Belgium and Ireland, 1970–1992.' *West European Politics* 17(1): 123–145.

Compston, H. 2003. 'Beyond Corporatism: A Configurational Theory of Policy Concertation.' *European Journal of Political Research* 42(6): 787–809.

Cooney, R. and M. Long. 2010. 'Vocational Education and Training in Australia: The Evolution of a Segmented Training System.' In *Vocational Training: International Perspectives*, eds. G. Bosch and J. Charest. London: Routledge. 27–57.

Cooney, R. 2010. 'Australian Unions and Vocational Training: Theory and Cases.' *Labour and Industry: A Journal of the Social and Economic Relations of Work* 21(2): 529–544.

Cooper, R., and B. Ellem. 2008. 'The Neoliberal State, Trade Unions and Collective Bargaining in Australia.' *British Journal of Industrial Relations* 46(3): 532–44.

Corina, J. 1975. 'Planning and the British Labour Market: Incomes and Manpower Policy, 1965–1970.' In *Planning, Politics and Public Policy: The British, French and Italian Experience*, eds. J. E. S. Hayward and M. Watson. Cambridge: Cambridge University Press. 177–201.

COSAC. 1984. *Institutional Trade Training*. Department of Employment and Industrial Relations.

Costine, P., and T. N. Garavan. 1995. 'Trade Union Attitudes to Training and Development: The Road to a More Positive and Proactive Approach?' *Journal of European Industrial Training* 19(10): 38–44.

Crouch, C. 1992. 'The Dilemmas of Vocational Training Policy: Some Comparative Lessons.' *Policy Studies* 13(4): 33–48.

Crouch, C. 1993. *Industrial Relations and European State Traditions*. Oxford/New York: Clarendon Press.

Crouch, C. 1995. 'Organized Interests as Resources or as Constraint: Rival Logics of Vocational Training Policy.' In *Organized Industrial Relations in Europe: What Future?*, eds. Colin Crouch and Franz Traxler. Aldershot: Avebury. 287–308.

Crouch, C. 2009. 'Typologies of Capitalism.' In *Debating Varieties of Capitalism*, ed. Bob Hancké. Oxford/New York: Oxford University Press. 75–94.

Crouch, C., D. Finegold, and M. Sako. 2004 [1999]. *Are Skills the Answer? The Political Economy Of Skill Creation in Advanced Industrial Countries*. Reprinted edition. Oxford: Oxford University Press.

Crouch, C., M. Schröder, and H. Voelzkow. 2009. 'Regional and Sectoral Varieties of Capitalism.' *Economy and Society* 38(4): 654–678.

Culpepper, P. D. 1999a. 'Individual Choice, Collective Action, and the Problem of Training Reform: Insights from France and Eastern Germany.' In *The German Skills Machine: Sustaining Comparative Advantage in a Global Economy*, eds. P. D. Culpepper and D. Finegold. New York: Berghanh Books. 269–325.

Culpepper, P. D. 1999b. 'Introduction: Still a Model For the Industrialized Countries?' In *The German Skills Machine: Sustaining Comparative Advantage in a Global Economy*, eds. Pepper D. Culpepper and David Finegold. New York/Oxford: Berghahn Books. 1–34.

Culpepper, P. D. 2003. *Creating Cooperation: How States Develop Human Capital in Europe*. Ithaca/London: Cornell University Press.

Culpepper, Pepper D. 2005. 'Institutional Change in Industrial Relations: Coordination and Common Knowledge in Ireland, Italy and Australia.' *Center for European Studies Working Paper Series* 127.

Culpepper, P. D. 2008. 'The Politics of Common Knowledge: Ideas and Institutional Change in Wage Bargaining.' *International Organization* 62(1): 1–33.

Culpepper, P. D., and K. Thelen. 2008. 'Institutions and Collective Actors in the Provision of Training: Historical and Cross-National Comparisons.' In *Skill Formation: Interdisciplinary and Cross-National Perspectives*, eds. K. U. Meyer and H. Solga. New York: Cambridge University Press. 21–49.

Danaher, G., P. Frain, and J. Sexton. 1985. *Manpower Policy in Ireland.* Dublin: NESC.

Dawkins, J. S. 1988. *A Changing Workforce.* Canberra: Australian Government Publishing Service.

Dawkins, J. S. 1989. *Improving Australia's Training System.* Canberra: Australian Government Publishing Service.

Dawkins, J. S., and A. C. Holding. 1987. *Skills for Australia.* Canberra: Australian Government Publishing Service.

Deeg, R. 2007. 'Complementarity and Institutional Change in Capitalist Systems.' *Journal of European Public Policy* 14(4): 611–630.

Deeg, R., and G. Jackson. 2007. 'Towards a More Dynamic Theory of Capitalist Variety.' *Socio-Economic Review* 5(1): 149–179.

Deery, S. J., and D. H. Plowman. 1991. *Australian Industrial Relations.* Sydney: McGraw-Hill.

Deissinger, T. 1994. 'The Evolution of Modern Vocational Training Systems in England and Germany: A Comparative View.' *Compare: A Journal of Comparative and International Education* 24(1): 17–36.

Deissinger, T. 2008. 'Cultural Patterns Underlying Apprenticeship: Germany and the UK.' In *Divergence and Convergence in Education and Work*, eds. V. Aarkrog and C. Helms Jørgensen. Bern: Peter Lang.

Department of Labour. 1986. *White Paper on Manpower Policy.* Dublin: Stationery Office.

Dingeldey, I. 1996. 'Wandel Gewerkschaftlicher Strategien in der Britischen Berufsbildungspolitik der 1980er und 1990er Jahre.' *Politische Vierteljahresschrift* 37(4): 687–712.

DIR. 1988. 'Towards a New Metal and Industry Engineering Award.' Canberra: DIR.

Dore, R., and M. Sako. 1998. *How the Japanese Learn to Work.* 2nd ed. London/New York: Routledge.

Easton, B., and R. Gerritsen. 1996. 'Economic Reforms: Parallels and Divergences.' In *The Great Experiment: Labour Parties and Public Policy Transformation in Australia and New Zealand*, eds. F. G. Castles, R. Gerritsen and J. Vowles. St. Leonards: Allen & Unwin. 22–47.

Esping-Andersen, G. 1990. *The Three Worlds of Welfare Capitalism*. Cambridge: Polity Press.

Esping-Andersen, G. 1999. *Social Foundations of Postindustrial Economies*. Oxford: Oxford University Press.

Estévez-Abe, M., T. Iversen, and D. Soskice. 2001. 'Social Protection and the Formation of Skills: A Reinterpretation of the Welfare State.' In *Varieties of Capitalism: The Institutional Foundations of Comparative Advantage*, eds. P. Hall and D. Soskice. Oxford: Oxford University Press. 145–183.

European Commission. 1993. *Growth, Competitiveness and Employment: The Challenges and Ways Forward into the 21st Century*. Luxemburg: European Union.

Evans, B. 1992. *The Politics of the Training Market: From Manpower Service Commission to Training and Enterprise Councils*. London/New York: Routledge.

Ewer, P. 2000. 'Trade Unions and Vocational Education and Training: Questions of Strategy and Identity.' *Labour and Industry* 10(3): 37–56.

Ewer, P., I. Hampson, C. Lloyd, J. Rainford, S. Rix, and M. Smith. 1991. *Politics and the Accord*. Leichhardt: Pluto Press Australia.

FÀS. 1989. *Apprenticeship: A New Approach*. Dublin.

FÀS. 2012. *Apprenticeship Numbers and Apprenticeship Listings*. Dublin.

Field, J, and M. O Dubchair. 2001. 'Recreating Apprenticeship: Lessons from the Irish Standards-Based Model.' *Journal of Vocational Education and Training* 53(2): 247–261.

Finegold, D., and D. Soskice. 1988. 'The Failure of Training in Britain: Analysis and Prescription.' *Oxford Review of Economic Policy* 4(3): 21–53.

Fuller, A., and L. Unwin. 2009. 'Change and Continuity in Apprenticeship: The Resilience of a Model of Learning.' *Journal of Education and Work* 22(5): 405–416.

Fuller, A., and L. Unwin. 2011. 'Vocational Education and Training in the Spotlight: Back to the Future for the UK's Coalition Government.'. *London Review of Education* 9(2): 191–204.

Garrett, G. 1998. *Partisan Politics in the Global Economy*. Cambridge: Cambridge University Press.
Garritzmann, Julian L. 2016. *The Political Economy of Higher Education Finance: The Politics of Tuition Fees and Subsidies in OECD Countries, 1945–2015*. Basingstoke: Palgrave MacMillan.
Gerring, J. 2007. *Case Study Research: Principles and Practices*. Cambridge: Cambridge University Press.
Goozee, G. 2001. *The Development of Tafe in Australia*. Leabrook/SA: National Centre for Vocational Education Research Ltd.
Gospel, H. 1994. 'The Survival of Apprenticeship Training: A British, American, Australian Comparison.' *British Journal of Industrial Relations* 32(4): 505–522.
Gospel, H. 1995. 'The Decline of Apprenticeship Training in Britain.' *Industrial Relations Journal* 26(1): 32–44.
Gospel, H, and A. Fuller. 1998. 'The Modern Apprenticeship: New Wine in Old Bottles?' *Human Resource Management Journal* 8(1): 5–22.
Gospel, H., and J. Druker. 1998. 'The Survival of National Bargaining in the Electrical Contracting Industry.' *British Journal of Industrial Relations* 36(2): 249–267.
Government of Ireland. 1959. *The Apprenticeship Act 1959*. Dublin: Stationery Office.
Government of Ireland. 1987. *Programme for National Recovery*. Dublin: Stationery Office.
Government of Ireland. 1991. *Programme for Economic and Social Progress*. Dublin: Stationery Office.
Gray, A. 2004. *Unsocial Europe: Social Protection or Flexploitation?* London/Ann Arbor: Pluto Press.
Green, A. 2001. 'Models of High Skills in National Competition Strategies.' In *High Skills: Globalization, Competitiveness, and Skill Formation*, eds. P. Brown, A. Green and H. Lauder. Oxford/New York: Oxford University Press. 56–160.
Greinert, W.-D. 1993. *Das 'Deutsche System' der Berufsausbildung: Geschichte Organisation, Perspektiven*. Baden-Baden: Nomos.

Hacker, J. S., and P. Pierson. 2002. 'Business Power and Social Policy: Employers and the Formation of the American Welfare State.' *Politics and Society* 30(2): 277–325.
Hall, P. A. 1992. 'The Movement from Keynesianism to Monetarism: Institutional Analysis and British Economic Policy in the 1970s.' In *Structuring Politics: Hinstorical Institutionalism in Comparative Analysis*, eds. S. Steinmo, K. Thelen and F. Longstreth. Cambridge: Cambridge University Press. 90–113.
Hall, P. A. 2003. 'Aligning Ontology and Methodology in Comparative Research.' In *Comparative Historical Analysis in the Social Sciences*, eds. J. Mahoney and D. Rueschemeyer. Cambridge: Cambridge University Press. 373–404.
Hall, P. A. 2010. 'Historical Institutionalism in Rationalist and Sociological Perspective.' In *Explaining Institutional Change: Ambiguity, Agency, and Power*, eds. J. Mahoney and K. Thelen. Cambridge: Cambridge University Press. 204–224.
Hall, P. A., and R. C. R. Taylor. 1996. 'Political Science and the Three New Institutionalisms.' *Political Studies* 44(5): 936–957.
Hall, P. A., and D. Soskice. 2001a. 'An Introduction to Varieties of Capitalism.' In *Varieties of Capitalism: The Institutional Foundations of Comparative Advantage*, eds. Peter Hall and David Soskice. Oxford/New York: Oxford University Press. 1–68.
Hall, P. A., and D. Soskice, eds. 2001b. *Varities of Capitalism: The Institutional Foundations of Comparative Advantage.* Oxford/New York: Oxford University Press.
Hall, P. A., and D. W. Gingerich. 2004. '"Spielarten Des Kapitalismus" und Institutionelle Koplementaritäten in der Makroökonomie – Eine Empirische Analyse.' *Berliner Journal für Soziologie* (14) 1: 5–32.
Hall, P. A., and K. Thelen. 2009. 'Institutional Change in Varieties of Capitalism.' *Socio-Economic Review* 7(1): 7–34.
Hampson, I. 1997. 'The End of the Experiment: Corporatism Collapses in Australia.' *Economic and Industrial Democracy* 18(4): 539–566.
Hampson, I. 2004. 'Training Reform in a Weakened State: Australia 1987–2000.' In *The Skills That Matter*, eds. C. Warhurst, I. Grugulis and E. Keep. Basingstoke: Palgrave Macmillan. 72–90.

Hampson, I., and D. E. Morgan. 1998. 'Continuity and Change in Australian Industrial Relations. Recent Developments.' *Industrial Relations* 53(3): 564–591.

Hardiman, N. 1988. *Pay, Politics and Economic Performance in Ireland 1970–1987*. Oxford: Clarendon Press.

Hardiman, N.. 2000. 'Social Partnership, Wage Bargaining and Growth.' In *Bust to Boom? The Irish Experience of Growth and Inequality*, eds. B. Nolan, P. J. O'Connell and C. T. Whelan. Dublin: ESRI. 286–309.

Hardiman, N. 2002. 'From Conflict to Co-Ordination: Economic Governance and Political Innovation in Ireland.' *West European Politics* 25(4): 1–24.

Hardiman, N., P. Murphy, and O. Burke. 2008. 'The Politics of Economic Adjustment in a Liberal Market Economy: The Social Compensation Hypothesis Revisited.' *Irish Political Studies* 23(4): 599–626.

Hay, C. 2005. 'Two Can Play at That Game…Or Can They? Varieties of Capitalism, Varieties of Institutionalism.' In *Varieties of Capitalism, Varieties of Approaches*, ed. D. Coates. Basingstoke: Palgrave Macmillan. 106–121.

Heraty, N., M. J. Morley, and A. McCarthy. 2000. 'Vocational Education and Training in the Republic of Ireland: Institutional Reform and Policy Developments since the 1960s.' *Journal of Vocational Education and Training* 52(2): 177–199.

Hibbs, D. A. 1977. 'Political Parties and Macroeconomic Policy.' *American Political Science Review* 71(4): 1467–1487.

Hilmer, F. 1993. *National Competition Policy*. Canberra: Australian Government Publishing Service.

Honohan, P. 2009. 'Resolving Ireland's Banking Crisis.' *The Economic and Social Review* 40(2): 207–231.

Hoque, K., S. Taylor, and E. Bell. 2005. 'Investors in People: Market-Led Voluntarism in Vocational Education and Training.' *British Journal of Industrial Relations* 43(1): 135–153.

Howell, C.. 2005. *Trade Unions and the State: The Construction of Industrial Relations in Britain, 1890–2000*. Princeton/Oxford: Princeton University Press.

Huber, E., and J. D. Stephens. 2001. *Development and Crisis of the Welfare State: Parties and Policies in Global Markets*. Chicago: The University of Chicago Press.

Iversen, T., and D. Soskice. 2001. 'An Asset Theory of Social Policy Preferences.' *American Political Science Review* 95(4): 875–893.

Iversen, T., and D. Soskice. 2009. 'Distribution and Redistribution: The Shadow of the Nineteenth Century '. *World Politics* 61(3): 438–486.

Iversen, T., and J. D. Stephens. 2008. 'Partisan Politics, the Welfare State, and the Three World of Human Capital Formation.' *Comparative Political Studies* 41(4–5): 600–637.

Jenkins, R., and I. Curry. 2013. 'The Drivers of Industry Involvement in VET Reform.' In *Structures in Tertiary Education and Training: A Kaleidoscope or Merely Fragments?*, eds. F. Beddie, L. O'Connor, and P. Curtin. Adelaide: NCVER. 69–82.

Jessop, B. 1993. 'Towards a Schumpeterian Workfare State? Preliminary Remarks on Post-Fordist Political Economy.' *Studies in Political Economy* 40: 7–40.

Jones, S. 2008. 'Cooperative Federalism? The Case of the Ministerial Council on Education, Employment, Training and Youth Affairs.' *Australian Journal of Public Administration* 67(2): 161–172.

Keating, P. J. 1992. *One Nation.* Canberra: Australian Government Publishing Service.

Keating, P. J. 1994a. *Working Nation: Policies and Programs.* Canberra: Australian Government Publishing Service.

Keating, Paul J. 1994b. *Working Nation: The White Paper on Employment and Growth.* Canberra: Australian Government Publishing Service.

Keep, E. 2004. *The State and Power: An Elephant and a Snake in the Telephone Box of English VET Policy.* ESRC Centre on Skills, Knowledge and Organisational Performance. University of Warwick.

Keep, E. 2006. 'State Control of the English Education and Training System: Playing with the Biggest Train Set in the World.' *Journal of Vocational Education and Training* 58(1): 47–64.

Kelly, M. 2010. 'Whatever Happened to Ireland?' *CEPR Discussion Paper No. 7811*.

Kelly, P. 1994. *The End of Certainty: Power, Politics and Business in Australia*. St Leonards: Allen & Unwin.

Kemp, D. 1998. 'Keynote Adress: The VET Market.' Paper presented at Conference *The Market for Vocational Education and Training: Who Pays and Who Profits?*, Adelaide.

Kennedy, S., R. Drago, J. Sloan, and M. Wooden. 1994. 'The Effect of Trade Unions on the Provision of Training: Australian Evidence.' *British Journal of Industrial Relations* 32(4): 565–580.

Kenworthy, L. 2006. 'Institutional Coherence and Macroeconomic Performance.' *Socio-Economic Review* 4(1): 69–91.

Kern, F. G., and J. Vossiek. 2014. 'Get Organised: The 'Do's' Preceding Successful Field Research.' *European Political Science* 14(2): 137–148.

King, D. S. 1993. 'The Conservatives and Training Policy 1979–1992: From a Tripartite to a Neoliberal Regime.' *Political Studies* 41(2): 214–235.

King, D. S. 1995. *Actively Seeking Work? The Politics of Unemployment and Welfare Policy in the United States and Great Britain*. Chicago: The University of Chicago Press.

King, D. S. 1997. 'Employers, Training Policy and the Tenacity of Voluntarism in Britain.' *Twentieth Century British History* 8(3): 383–411.

King, D. S., and M. Wickham-Jones. 1998. 'Training without the State? New Labour and Labour Markets.' *Policy and Politics* 26(4): 439–455.

King, D. S., and D. Rueda. 2008. 'The New Politics of "Bread and Roses" in Industrial Democracies.' *Perspectives on Politics* 6(2): 279–297.

Kirkby, P. 1985. *Report of the Committee of Inquiry into Labour Market Programs.* Canberra: AGPS.

Knight, B. 2012. *Evolution of Apprenticeships and Traineeships in Australia: An Unfinished History*. Adelaide (SA): NCVER.

Knight, J. 1992. *Institutions and Social Conflict*. Cambridge: Cambridge University Press.

Korpi, W., and J. Palme. 1998. 'The Paradox of Redistribution and Strategies of Equality: Welfare State Institutions, Inequality and Poverty in the Western Countries.' *American Sociological Review* 63(5): 661–687.

Korpi, W.. 1983. *The Democratic Class Struggle*. London: Routledge and Kegan Paul.

Lane, C., and G. Wood. 2009. 'Capitalist Diversity and Diversity within Capitalism.' *Economy and Society* 38(4): 531–551.
Lansbury, R. D., and N. Wailes. 2011. 'Employment Relations in Australia.' In *International and Comparative Employment Relations: Globalisation and Change*, eds. G. J. Bamber, R. D. Lansbury, and N. Wailes. London et al.: SAGE. 117–137.
Lee, D. J. 1979. 'Craft Unions and the Force of Tradition: The Case of Apprenticeship.' *British Journal of Industrial Relations* 17(1): 34–49.
Lee, D. J. 1989. 'The Transformation of Training and the Transformation of Work in Britain.' In *The Transformation of Work? Skill, Flexibility and the Labour Process*. Ed. S. Wood. London: Unwin Hyman: 156–170.
Lundahl, L. 1997. 'A Common Denominator? Swedish Employers, Trade Unions and Vocational Training.' *International Journal of Training and Development* 1(2): 91–103.
Lundberg, D. 1994. *Where Are We? Reviewing the Training Reform Agenda*. Leabrook (SA): NCVER.
Lynch, L. M. 1994. *Training and the Private Sector: International Comparisons*. Chicago: University of Chicago Press.
Mahoney, J., and D. Rueschemeyer, eds. 2003. *Comparative Historical Analysis in the Social Sciences*. Cambridge: Cambridge University Press.
Mahoney, J., and K. Thelen. 2010. 'A Theory of Gradual Institutional Change.' In *Explaining Institutional Change: Ambiguity, Agency, and Power.*, eds. J. Mahoney and K. Thelen. Cambridge: Cambridge University Press. 1–37.
Mair, P. 1986. 'Locating Irish Political Parties on a Left-Right Dimension: An Empirical Enquiry.' *Political Studies* 34(3): 456–465.
Mair, P., and M. Marsh. 2004. 'Political Parties in Electoral Markets in Postwar Ireland.' In *Political Parties and Electoral Change: Party Responses to Electoral Markets*, eds. P. Mair, W. C. Müller and F. Plasser. London: Sage. 234–263.
Maloney, A. 2005. 'Labour Market Planning in Ireland.' In *Skill Formation and Globalization*, ed. M. Powell. Aldershot: Ashgate. 52–66.

Marsden, D., and P. Ryan. 1990. 'Institutional Aspects of Youth Employment and Training Policy in Britain.' *British Journal of Industrial Relations* 28(3): 351–369.
Marsden, D., and P. Ryan. 1991. 'Initial Training, Labour Market Structure and Public Policy: Intermediate Skills in British and German Industry.' In *International Comparisons of Education and Training for Intermediate Skills*, ed. Paul Ryan. London: The Falmer Press. 251–285.
Marsh, M., and P. Mitchell. 1999. 'Office, Votes, and Then Policy: Hard Choices for Political Parties in the Republic of Ireland, 1981–1992.' In *Policy, Office, or Votes? How Political Parties in Western Europe Make Hard Decisions*, eds. Wolfgang C. Müller and Kaare Strøm. Cambridge/New York: Cambridge University Press. 36–62.
Martin, C. J. 1999. *Stuck in Neutral: Business and the Politics of Human Capital Investment Policy*. Princeton: Princeton University Press.
Martin, C. J., and D. Swank. 2008. 'The Political Origins of Coordinated Capitalism: Business Organizations, Party Systems and State Structure in the Age of Innocence.' *American Political Science Review* 102(2): 181–198.
Martin, C. J., and D. Swank. 2012. *The Political Construction of Business Interests: Coordination, Growth and Equality*. Cambridge: Cambridge University Press.
McCann, D. 1993. 'Business Power and Collective Action: The State and the Confederation of Irish Industry 1970–1990.' *Irish Political Studies* 8: 37–53.
McCarthy, T. 1977. *Apprenticeships in Ireland*. Vol. 33, Social Policy Series. Brussels: Commission of the European Communities.
McCartney, J., and P. Teague. 2001. 'Private-Sector Training and the Organization of the Labour Market: Evidence from the Republic of Ireland in a Comparative Perspective.' *International Journal of Human Resource Management* 12(5): 772–799.
McIlroy, J.. 2008. 'Ten Years of New Labour: Workplace Learning, Social Partnership and Union Revitalization in Britain.' *British Journal of Industrial Relations* 46(2): 283–313.
Mill, J. S. 1973. 'A System of Logic ' In *On the Four Methods of Experimental Inquiry*, ed. J. M. Robson. Toronto: University of Toronto Press. 388–406.

Ministry of Labour. 1962. *Industrial Training: Government Proposals.* London: HMSO.
Minkin, L. 1991. *The Contentious Alliance: Trade Unions and the Labour Party*. Edinburgh: Edinburgh University Press.
MTIA. 1986. *MTIA Proposal for a Compact with the Metal Unions.* Canberra.
MTIA, and EEA. 1988. *Award Restructuring in the Meatal and Engineering Industry: The Way to Proceed.* Melbourne.
Mukherjee, S. 1970. 'Changing Manpower Needs: A Study of Industrial Training Boards.' *PEP Broadsheet* 523.
Murphy, G., and J. Hogan. 2008. 'Fianna Fáil, the Trade Union Movement and the Politics of Macroeconomic Crises, 1970–82.' *Irish Political Studies* 23(4): 577–598.
Murphy, T., and A. J. Coldrick. 1988. 'The Role of the Social Partners in Vocational Education, Including Continuing Education and Training, in Ireland.' Berlin: CEDEFOP.
National Joint Advisory Committee (NJAC). 1958. 'Training for Skill – Recruitment and Trainign of Young Workers in Industry (Carr Report).' London: HMSO.
NCVER. 2000. *Apprentices and Trainees in Australia 1985 to 1999: At a Glance.* Adelaide (SA): NCVER.
NCVER. 2014. *Historical Time Series of Vocational Education and Training in Australia, from 1981.* Adelaide (SA): NCVER.
NESC. 1985. 'Manpower Policy in Ireland.' Dublin: National Economic and Social Council.
NESC. 1986. *A Strategy for Development: 1986–1990.* Dublin: National Economic and Social Council.
NIEC. 1964. *Report on Manpower Policy.* Dublin: National Industrial Economic Council.
Nyhan, B. 2009. 'Creating the Social Foundations for Apprenticeship in Ireland.' *Journal of European Industrial Training* 33(5): 457–469.
Nyhan, B. 2010. 'Creating the Social Foundations for Apprenticeship in Ireland.' In *Rediscovering Apprenticeship*, eds. F. Rauner and E. Smith. Dordrecht: Springer. 45–57.
O'Connell, P. 1999. *Astonishing Success: Economic Growth and the Labour Market in Ireland.* Geneva: ILO.

O'Connor, E. 2002. 'Ireland in Historical Perspective: The Legacies of Colonialism – Edging Towards Policy Concertation.' In *Policy Concertation and Social Partnership in Western Europe: Lessons for the 21st Century*, eds. S. Berger and H. Compston. New York/Oxford: Berghahn Books. 155–166.

O'Connor, L. 2006. 'Meeting the Skills Needs of a Buoyant Economy: Apprenticeship – the Irish Experience.' *Journal of Vocational Education and Training* 58(1): 31–46.

O'Connor, L., and N. Harvey. 2001. 'Apprenticeship Training in Ireland: From Time-Served to Standards Based; Potential and Limitations for the Construction Industry.' *Journal of European Industrial Training* 26(6): 332–342.

O'Donnell, R., M. Adshead, and D. Thomas. 2011. 'Ireland: Two Trajectories of Institutionalization.' In *Social Pacts in Europe: Emergence, Evolution and Institutionalization*, eds. S. Avdagic, M. Rhodes and J. Visser. Oxford: Oxford University Press. 89–117.

O'Donnell, R., and .n Thomas. 2002. 'Ireland in the 1990s: Policy Concertation Triumphant.' In *Policy Concertation and Social Partnership in Western Europe: Lessons for the 21st Century*, eds. S. Berger and H. Compston. New York/Oxford: Berghahn Books. 167–189.

O'Leary, D. 2000. *Vocationalism and Social Catholicism in Twentieth Century Ireland: The Search for a Christian Social Order*. Dublin/Portland: Irish Academic Press.

O'Rourke, M. 1993. 'Speech before the Dáil. Industrial Training (Apprenticeship Levy) Bill, 1993: Second Stage. 2 December 1993.

OECD. 1994a. *The OECD Jobs Study: Evidence and Explanations. Part 1 Labour Market Trends and Underlying Forces of Change*. Paris: OECD.

OECD. 1994b. *The OECD Jobs Study: Facts, Analysis, Strategies*. Paris: OECD.

OECD. 1999. 'Economic Survey: Ireland.' In *Secondary Economic Survey: Ireland*. Paris: OECD.

OECD. 2004. 'Employment Protection Regulation and Labour Market Performance.' *Employment Outlook*.

OECD. various-a. *Economic Outlook*. Paris: OECD.

OECD. various-b. *Labour Force Statistics*. Paris: OECD.

Ornston, D. 2012. *When Small States Make Big Leaps: Institutional Innovation and High-Tech Competition in Western Europe*. Ithaca: Cornell University Press.

Payne, J., and E. Keep. 2011. One Step Forward, Two Steps Back? Skills Policy in England under the Coalition Government. SKOPE paper.

Pemberton, H. 2001. 'The 1964 Industrial Training Act: A Failed Revolution.' Paper, Economic History Society, Bristol, 30 March 2001.

Perry, P. J. Charles. 1976. *The Evolution of British Manpower Policy: From the Statute of Artificers 1563 to the Industrial Training Act 1964*. London: British Association for Commercial and Industrial Education.

Pierson, P. 1993. 'When Effect Becomes Cause: Policy Feedback and Political Change.' *World Politics* 45(4): 595–628.

Pierson, P. 1994. *Dismantling the Welfare State? Reagan, Thatcher, and the Politics of Retrenchment*. Cambridge: Cambridge University Press.

Pierson, P. 2000a. 'Increasing Returns, Path Dependence, and the Study of Politics.' *American Political Science Review* 94(2): 251–267.

Pierson, P. 2000b. 'Not Just What, but When: Timing and Sequence in Political Processes.' *American Political Development* 14(1): 72–92.

Pierson, P. 2000c. 'The Limits of Design: Explaining Institutional Origins and Change.' *Governance* 13(4): 475–499.

Pierson, P. 2004. *Politics in Time: History, Institutions, and Political Analysis*. Princeton, NJ: Princeton University Press.

Pontusson, J. 2005. 'Varieties and Commonalities of Capitalism.' In *Varieties of Capitalism: Varieties of Approaches*, ed. D. Coates. Houndmills et al.: Palgrave Macmillan. 163–187.

Power, C. 2009. *Metamorphosis: Lessons from the Formative Years of the Celtic Tiger, 1979–1993*. Cork: Oak Tree Press.

President of Board of Trade, Chancellor of the Exchequer, Secretaries for Transport, Environment and Trade, Chancellor of the Duchy of Lancaster, Secretaries of State for Education of Scotland, Northern Ireland and Wales, 1994. *Command Paper 2563: Helping Business to Win*. London: HMSO.

Raggatt, P., and S. Williams. 1999. *Governments, Markets and Vocational Qualifications*. London: Falmer Press.

Rainbird, H. 2010. 'Vocational Education and Training in the United Kingdom.' In *Vocational Training: International Perspectives*, ed. G. Bosch and J. Charest. New York/Oxon: Routledge. 242–270.
Ray, J. 2001. 'Apprenticeship in Australia: A Historical Snapshot.' Kensington Park: NCVER.
Rhodes, M. 1998. 'Globalisation, Labour Markets and Welfare States. A Future of Competitive Corporatism?' In *The Future of European Welfare: A New Social Contract?*, eds. M. Rhodes and Y. Mény. London: Macmillan. 178–203.
Rhodes, M. 2000. 'Restructuring the British Welfare State: Between Domestic Constraints and Global Imperatives.' In *Welfare and Work in the Open Economy: Diverse Responses to Common Challenges*, ed. Fritz W. and Vivien A. Schmidt. Vol. II. Oxford/New York: Oxford University Press. 19–68.
Rhodes, M. 2001. 'The Political Economy of Social Pacts: 'Competitive Corporatism' and European Welfare Reform.' In *The New Politics of the Welfare State*, ed. P. Pierson. Oxford: Oxford University Press. 165–194.
Robinson, C. 2001. *Australian Apprenticeships: Facts, Fiction and Future*. Leabrook (SA): NCVER.
Roche, W. K. 1994. 'Pay Determination, the State, and the Politics of Industrial Relations.' In *Irish Industrial Relations in Practice*, eds. T. V. Murphy and W. K. Roche. Dublin: Oak Tree Press. 126–205.
Roche, W. K. 2007. 'Social Partnership in Ireland and New Social Pacts.' *Industrial Relations* 46(3): 395–425.
Roche, W. K. 2009. 'Social Partnership: From Lemass to Cowen.' *The Economic and Social Review* 40(2): 183–205.
Rose, R., and P. L. Davies. 1994. *Inheritance in Public Policy: Change without Choice in Britain*. New Haven: Yale University Press.
Ruggie, J. G. 1982. 'International Regimes, Transactions, and Change: Embedded Liberalism in the Postwar Economic Order.' *International Organization* 36(2): 379–415.
Ryan, P. 2000. 'The Institutional Requirements of Apprenticeship: Evidence from Smaller EU Countries.' *International Journal of Training and Development* 4(1): 42–65.

Ryan, P. 2005. 'The Institutional Requirements of Apprenticeship Training in the Context of the British Isles.' In *Apprenticeship as a Paradigm of Learning*, eds. Len O'Connor and Tom Mullins. Cork: Cork Institute of Technology. 15–34.

Ryan, P., H. Gospel, and P. Lewis. 2007. 'Large Employers and Apprenticeship Training in Britain.' *British Journal of Industrial Relations* 45(1): 127–153.

Ryan, P., and L. Unwin. 2001. 'Apprenticeship in the British 'Training Market'.' *National Institute Economic Review* 178(1): 99–124.

Ryan, R. 2002. *Building a National Vocational Education and Training System*. Adelaide: Flinders University Institute of International Education.

Ryan, R. 2011. 'How VET Responds: A Historical Policy Perspective.' Adelaide: NCVER.

Sako, M.. 1991. 'Institutional Aspects of Youth Employment and Training Policy: A Comment on Marsden and Ryan.' *British Journal of Industrial Relations* 29(3): 485–490.

Scharpf, F. W. 2000a. 'The Viability of Advanced Welfare States in the International Economy: Vulnerabilities and Options.' *Journal of European Public Policy* 7(2): 190–228.

Scharpf, F. W. 2000b. 'Economic Changes, Vulnerabilities, and Institutional Capabilities.' In *Welfare and Work in the Open Economy: Volume I: From Vulnerability to Competitiveness*, ed. F. W. Scharpf and V. A. Schmidt . Oxford: Oxford University Press.

Scharpf, F. W. 2000c. 'Institutions in Comparative Policy Research.' *Comparative Political Studies* 33(6–7): 762–790.

Scharpf, F. W. 2000d. *Interaktionsformen*. Wiesbaden: VS Verlag für Sozialwissenschaften.

Schmidt, M. G. 1982. *Wohlfahrtsstaatliche Politik unter Bürgerlichen und Sozialdemokratischen Regierungen: Ein internationaler Vergleich*. Frankfurt a. M./New York: Campus.

Schmidt, M. G. 1996. 'When Parties Matter: A Review of the Possibilities and Limits of Partisan Influence on Public Policy.' *European Journal of Political Research* 30(2): 155–183.

Schwartz, H. M. 1994a. 'Public Choice Theory and Public Choices: Bureaucrats and State Reorganization in Australia, Denmark, New Zealand, and Sweden in the 1980s.' *Administration and Society* 26(1): 48–77.

Schwartz, H. M. 1994b. 'Small States in Big Trouble: State Reorganization in Australia, Denmark, New Zealand, and Sweden in the 1980s.' *World Politics* 46(4): 527–555.

Schwartz, H. M. 2000. 'Internationalization and Two Liberal Welfare States: Australia and New Zealand.' In *Welfare and Work in the Open Economy: Diverse Responses to Common Challenges*, eds. F. W. Scharpf, and V. A. Schmidt. Oxford: Oxford University Press. 69–130.

Schwartz, H. M. 2005. 'The Australian Miracle: Luck, Pluck or Being Stuck Down Under?' In *Employment Miracles: A Critical Comparison of the Dutch, Scandinavian, Swiss, Australian and Irish Cases Versus Germany and the US*, eds. U. Becker, and H. Schwartz. Amsterdam: Amsterdam University Press. 157–182.

Secretary of State for Employment, ed. 1988. *Employment for the 1990s*. London: House of Commons Parliamentary Papers Online.

Senker, P.. 1992. *Industrial Training in a Cold Climate: An Assessment of Britains Training Policies*. Aldershot: Avebury.

Senker, P. 1998. 'The Development and Implementation of National Vocational Qualifications: An Engineering Case Study.' *New Technology, Work and Employment* 11(2): 83–95.

Sheldrake, J. and S. Vickerstaff. 1987. *The History of Industrial Training in Britain*. Aldershot: Avebury.

Singleton, G. 1990. *The Accord and the Australian Labour Movement*. Melbourne: Melbourne University Press.

Sinn, H.-W. 2002. 'EU Enlargement and the Future of the Welfare State.' *Scottish Journal of Political Economy* 49(1): 104–115.

Smith, E. 2010. 'We're Here to Help: Agencies Dealing with Apprenticeships in Australia.' In *Rediscovering Apprenticeship*, eds. F. Rauner and E. Smith. Dordrecht et al.: Springer. 113–123.

Soskice, D. 1994. 'Reconciling Markets and Institutions: The German Apprenticeship System.' In *Training and the Private Sector: International Comparisons*, ed. L. M. Lynch. Chicago: University of Chicago Press. 25–60.

Steedman, H. 2010. *The State of Apprenticeship in 2010. International Comparisons*. Centre for Economic Performance. London School of Economics.

Steedman, H. 2011. 'Apprenticeship Policy in England: Increasing Skills Versus Boosting Young People's Job Prospects.' *CEP Policy Analysis*. London School of Economics.

Steinmo, S., K. Thelen, and F. Longstreth, eds. 1992. *Structuring Politics: Hinstorical Institutionalism in Comparative Analysis*. Cambridge: Cambridge University Press.

Stephens, J. D. 1979. *The Transition from Capitalism to Socialism*. London: Macmillan.

Stevens, M. 1999. 'Human Capital Theory and Uk Vocational Training Policy.' *Oxford Review of Economic Policy* 15(1): 16–32.

Streeck, W. 1989. 'Skills and the Limits of Neo-Liberalism: The Enterprise of the Future as a Place of Learning.' *Work, Employment and Society* 3(1): 89–104.

Streeck, W. 1991. 'On the Institutional Conditions of Diversified Quality Production.' In *Beyond Keynesianism: The Socio-Economics of Production and Full Employment*, eds. E. Matzner and W. Streeck. Aldershot: Edward Elgar. 12–61.

Streeck, W. 1992. 'Training and the New Industrial Relations: A Strategic Role for Unions?' In *The Future of Labour Movements*, ed. M. Regini. London: SAGE. 250–269.

Streeck, W. 1998. 'Beneficial Constraints: On the Economic Limits of Rational Voluntarism.' In *Contemporary Capitalism: The Embeddedness of Institutions*, eds. J. Roberts Hollingsworth and Robert Boyer. Cambridge: Cambridge University Press. 197–219.

Streeck, W. 2009. *Re-Forming Capitalism: Institutional Change in the German Political Economy*. Oxford: Oxford University Press.

Streeck, W. 2010. 'E Pluribus Unum? Varieties and Commonalities of Capitalism.' *MPIfG Discussion Paper*.

Streeck, W. 2012. 'Skills and Politics: General and Specific.' In *The Political Economy of Collective Skill Formation*, eds. M. R. Busemeyer and C. Trampusch. Oxford: Oxford University Press. 317–352.

Streeck, W., and P. C. Schmitter. 1985. *Private Interest Governments: Beyond Market and State*. London: Sage.

Streeck, W. and K. Thelen. 2005. 'Introduction: Institutional Change in Advanced Political Economies.' In *Beyond Continuity: Institutional Change in Advanced Political Economies*, eds. W. Streeck and K. Thelen. Oxford: Oxford University Press. 1–39.

Swank, D. 2002. *Global Capital, Political Institutions, and Policy Change in Developed Welfare States*. Cambridge: Cambridge University Press.

Swank, D. 2005. 'Globalization, Domestic Politics, and Welfare State Retrenchment in Capitalist Democracies.' *Social Policy and Society* 4(2): 183–195.

Swenson, P. 1991. 'Labor and the Limits of the Welfare State: The Politics of Intraclass Conflict and Cross-Class Alliances in Sweden and West Germany.' *Comparative Politics* 34(4): 379–399.

Swenson, P. 2002. *Capitalists against Markets: The Making of Labor Markets and Welfare States in the United States and Sweden*. Oxford: Oxford University Press.

Tanzi, V. 2002. 'Globalization and the Future of Social Protection.' *Scottish Journal of Political Economy* 49(1): 116–127.

Teague, P. 1995. 'Pay Determination in the Republic of Ireland: Towards Social Corporatism?' *British Journal of Industrial Relations* 33(2): 253–273.

Teague, P. and J. Donaghey. 2009a. 'Social Partnership and Democratic Legitimacy in Ireland.' *New Political Economy* 14(1): 49–69.

Teague, P. and J. Donaghey. 2009b. 'Why Has Irish Social Partnership Survived?'. *British Journal of Industrial Relations* 47(1): 55–78.

The Economist. 2014. 'Keeping up with the Schmidts.', (26. April). 29–30.

Thelen, K. 2004. *How Institutions Evolve: The Political Economy of Skills in Germany, Britain, the United States, and Japan*. Cambridge: Cambridge University Press.

Thelen, K. 2009. 'Institutional Change in Advanced Political Economies.' *British Journal of Industrial Relations* 47(3): 471–498.

Thelen, K. 2012. 'Foreword.' In *The Political Economy of Collective Skill Formation*, eds. M. R. Busemeyer and C. Trampusch. Oxford: Oxford University Press. v–xii.

Thelen, K. 2014. *Varieties of Liberalization and the New Politics of Social Solidarity*. Cambridge: Cambridge University Press.
Thelen, K, and M. R. Busemeyer. 2012. 'Institutional Change in German Vocational Training.' In *The Political Economy of Collective Skill Formation*, eds. M. R. Busemeyer and C. Trampusch. Oxford: Oxford University Press. 68–100.
Thelen, K., and I. Kume. 2003. 'The Future of Nationally Embedded Capitalism: Industrial Relations in Germany and Japan.' In *The End of Diversity? Prospects for German and Japanese Capitalism*, eds. W. Streeck and K. Yamamura. Ithaca: Cornell University Press. 183–211.
Toner, P. 2008. 'Survival and Decline of the Apprenticeship System in the Australian and UK Construction Industries.' *British Journal of Industrial Relations* 46(3): 413–438.
Training Costs Review Committee. 1990. *Training Costs of Award Restructuring*. Canberra: Australian Government Publishing Service.
Training Services Agency. 1975. *Vocational Preparation for Young People. A Discussion Paper*. London: HMSO.
Trampusch, C. 2010. 'Employers, the State and the Politics of Institutional Change: Vocational Education and Training in Austria, Germany and Switzerland.' *European Journal of Political Research* 49(4): 545–573.
Traxler, F., S. Blaschke, and B. Kittel. 2001. *National Labour Relations in Internationalized Markets: A Comparative Study of Institutions, Change, and Performance*. Oxford: Oxford University Press.
Unwin, L. 2010. 'Learning and Working from the MSCc to New Labour: Young People, Skills and Employment.' *National Institute Economic Review* 212(1): R49–R60.
Van Barneveld, Kristin, and Ross Nassif. 2003. 'Motivations for the Introduction of Australian Workplace Agreements.' *Labour and Industry: A Journal of the Social and Economic Relations of Work* 14(2): 21–37.
van Kersbergen, K. 1995. *Social Capitalism: A Study of Christian Democracy and the Welfare State*. London/New York: Routledge.

Visser, J. (ed.). 2009. *The ICTWSS Database: Database on Institutional Chracteristics of Trade Unions, Wage Setting, State Intervention and Social Pacts in 34 Countries between 1960 and 2007.* Amsterdam: Amsterdam Insitute for Advanced Labour Studies (AIAS).

Vossiek, J. 2017. 'Wandel von Policies oder Institutionen? Politische Prozesse und die Rolle von Kammern in der Berufsbildung.' In *Wirtschaftskammern im europäischen Vergleich*, ed. Sack, D. Wiesbaden: Springer Fachmedien. 337–360.

Weaver, R. K.. 1986. 'The Politics of Blame Avoidance.' *Journal of Public Policy* 6(4): 371–98.

Weeks, L. 2010. 'Parties and the Party System.' In *Politics in the Republic of Ireland*, eds. John Coakley and Michael Gallagher. Abingdon/New York: PSAI Press/Routledge. 137–67.

Weishaupt, J. T. 2011. *From the Manpower Revolution to the Activation Paradigm: Explaining Institutional Change and Continuity in an Integrating Europe.* Amsterdam: Amsterdam University Press.

Wilensky, H. L. 1975. *The Welfare State and Equality: Structural and Ideological Roots of Public Expenditures*. Berkeley: University of California Press.

Williams, G. 1963. *Apprenticeship in Europe: The Lesson for Britain.* London: Chapman & Hall.

Wood, S. 1999. 'Building a Governance Structure for Training? Employers, Government and the Tec Experiment in Britain.' In *The German Skills Machine: Sustaining Comparative Advantage in a Global Economy,* eds. P. D. Culpepper and D. Finegold. Oxford: Berghahn Books. 363–402.

Wrigley, C. 2002. *British Trade Unions since 1933*. Cambridge: Cambridge University Press.

Zeitlin, J. 2005. 'The Internal Politics of Employer Organization: The Engineering Employers' Federation, 1896–1939.' In *The Power to Manage: Employers and Industrial Relations in Comparative Historical Perspective*, eds. S. Tolliday and J. Zeitlin. London: Routledge. 46–70.

Zeitlin, J. 2008. 'Re-Forming Skills in British Engineering, 1900–40: A Contingent Failure.' *Historical Studies in Industrial Relations*: 19–77.

Appendix A: List of interviews by code and date

Code	Role (Organization)	Date
UK-1	Researcher (King's College London)	2. 10. 2012
UK-2	Researcher (London School of Economics)	10. 11. 2012
UK-3	Researcher (London School of Economics)	13. 11. 2012
UK-4	Coordinator (Skills CFA – Standard and Framework Setting Body)	13. 11. 2012
UK-5	Policy Advisor (Sector Skills Council/Awarding Body for NVQs)	15. 11. 2012
UK-6	Researcher (NIESR – National Institute of Economic and Social Research)	19. 11. 2012
UK-7	Policy Advisor (CBI)	22. 11. 2012
UK-8	Manager (NAS – National Apprenticeship Service)	22. 11. 2012
UK-9	Senior civil servant (Department of Education)	23. 11. 2012
UK-10	Deputy Director, Policy Advisor (Department for Business, Innovation and Skills) (2 Interviewees)	26. 11. 2012
UK-11	Management (UKCES – UK Commission for Employment and Skills)	27. 11. 2012
UK-12	Management (CITB –Construction Skills Council)	27. 11. 2012
UK-13	Management (Retailing company) (4 interviewees)	28. 11. 2012
UK-14	Senior Civil Servant (Department for Business, Innovation and Skills)	29. 11. 2012
IRE-1	Member (ITAC – Institutes of Technology Apprenticeship Committee)	16. 10. 2012
IRE-2	Committee Member (Higher Education Authority)	16. 10. 2012
IRE-3	Manager (CIF – Construction Industry Federation)	23. 10. 2012
IRE-4	Member (ITAC)	24. 10. 2012
IRE-5	Management (FÀS)	24. 10. 2012
IRE-6	Management (FÀS)	25. 10. 2012
IRE-7	Policy Advisor Apprenticeship (NAAC)	25. 10. 2012
IRE-8	Union leader (ITUC)	26. 10. 2012
IRE-9	Researcher (Trinity College Dublin)	26. 10. 2012

Code	Role (Organization)	Date
IRE-10	Senior Policy Advisor (CII – Confederation of Irish Industry)	30. 10. 2012
IRE-11	Researchers (ESRI) (2 Interviewees)	31. 10. 2012
IRE-12	Researcher (CEDEFOP)	31. 10. 2012
IRE-13	Management (FÀS)	19. 11. 2012
AUS-1	Researcher (Sydney University)	14. 02. 2013
AUS-2	Policy Advisor (Metal Trades Industry Association)	15. 02. 2013
AUS-3	Research Officer (AMWU)	15. 02. 2013
AUS-4	Research Officer (ACTU)	18. 02. 2013
AUS-5	Management (Group Training Australia) (2 Interviewees)	18. 02. 2013
AUS-6	Management (ASQA –Australian Skills Quality Authority)	19. 02. 2013
AUS-7	Management (Industry Skills Council)	21. 02. 2013
AUS-8	Researchers (NCVER/University of Victoria, Melbourne) (2 Interviewees)	26. 02. 2103
AUS-9	Researcher (University of Ballarat)	27. 02. 2013
AUS-10	Management Education and Training (AIG – Australian Industry Group) (2 Interviewees)	27. 02. 2013
AUS-11	Management (Industry Skills Council)	04. 03. 2013
AUS-12	Management (CEPU – Communications, Electrical and Plumbing Union)	04. 03. 2013
AUS-13	Senior Civil Servant (DIISRTE – Department of Industry, Innovation, Science, Research and Tertiary Education)	05. 03. 2013
AUS-14	Management (ACCI – Australian Chamber of Commerce and Industry)	05. 03. 2013
AUS-15	Senior civil servant (DIISRTE)	05. 03. 2013
AUS-16	Senior civil servant (DIISRTE)	05. 03. 2013
AUS-17	Management (Industry Skills Council)	06. 03. 2013
AUS-18	Civil Servant (DIISRTE)	06. 03. 2013
AUS-19	Senior civil servant (DIISRTE)	06. 03. 2013
AUS-20	Civil Servant (DIISRTE)	06. 03. 2013
AUS-21	Senior civil servant (DIISRTE)	06. 03. 2013
AUS-22	Researcher (Australian National University)	07. 03. 2013
AUS-23	Management (NCVER) (2 Interviewees)	18. 03. 2013
AUS-24	Researcher (NCVER)	20. 03. 2013
AUS-25	Senior civil servant (State South Australia)	25. 03. 2013

Code	Role (Organization)	Date
AUS-26	Research officer (AMWU)	25. 03. 2013
AUS-27	Researcher (University of South Australia)	26. 03. 2013
AUS-28	Senior civil servant (State South Australia)	26. 03. 2013
AUS-29	Management (AQFC – Australian Qualifications Framework Council) (2 Interviewees)	27. 03. 2013
AUS-30	Senior civil servant (State South Australia)	27. 03. 2013
AUS-31	Researcher (Flinders University)	21. 03. 2013
AUS-32	Researcher (NCVER)	28. 03. 2013

Appendix B: List of abbreviations

A/AA	Apprenticeship/Advanced Apprenticeship
AAAC	Australian Apprenticeship Advisory Committee
AACs	Apprenticeship Advisory Committees (Ireland)
ACC	Australian Chamber of Commerce
ACC	Apprenticeship Board (Ireland)
ACCI	Australian Chamber of Commerce and Industry
ACM	Australian Chamber of Manufacturers
ACTU	Australian Council of Trade Unions
AEC	Australian Education Council
AGTWU	Amalgamated Transport and General Workers Union
AIRC	Australian Industrial Relations Commission
ALMP	Active Labour Market Policies
ALP	Australian Labor Party
AMWU	Australian Metal Workers' Union
AnCO	Training Council (Ireland)
ANTA	Australian National Training Authority
AQF	Australian Qualifications Framework
AQTF	Australian Quality Training Framework
ARF	Australian Recognition Framework
ASF	Australian Standard Framework
ATS	Australian Traineeship System
ATTITB	Air Transport and Travel Industry Training Board
AVCTS	Australian Vocational Certificate Training System
BCA	Business Council of Australia
CAI	Confederation of Australian Industry
CBI	Confederation of British Industry
CBT	Competency-Based Training
CE	Community Employment (Ireland)
CEDP	Community Employment Development Programme
CIF	Construction Industry Federation (Ireland)
CII	Confederation of Irish Industry
CME	Coordinated Market Economy

COAG	Council of Australian Governments
COSTAC	Commonwealth and State Training Advisory Committee
CRAFT	Commonwealth Rebate for Full-Time Apprentice Training
CRC	Central Review Committee (Ireland)
CTC	Central Training Council (United Kingdom)
DES	Department of Education and Science (Ireland)
DEST	Department of Education, Science and Technology
DITB	Distribution Industry Training Board (United Kingdom)
DOLAC	Department of Labor Advisory Committee (Australia)
EEC	European Economic Community
EITB	Engineering Industrial Training Board (United Kingdom)
EMU	European Monetary Union
ESA	Employment and Services Agency (United Kingdom)
ESF	European Social Fund
ESFC	Employment and Skill Formation Council (Australia)
ET	Employment Training (United Kingdom)
FA	Foundation Apprenticeships (United Kingdom)
FÁS	Irish National Training and Employment Authority
FF	Fianna Faíl (Ireland)
FG	Fine Gael (Ireland)
FIE	Federation of Irish Employers
FMA	Foundation Modern Apprenticeships (United Kingdom)
IBEC	Irish Business and Employers Confederation
ICOS	Irish Co-operative Society
ICTU	Irish Congress of Trade Unions
IFA	Irish Farming Association
ILA	Individual Learning Accounts (United Kingdom)
ILP	Irish Labour Party
ITAB	Industrial Training Advisory Body (Australia)
ITB	Industrial Training Board (United Kingdom)
ITCs	Institutes of Technology (Ireland)
ITO	Industrial Training Organization (United Kingdom)
LLSC	Local Learning and Skills Council (United Kingdom)
LME	Liberal Market Economy
LSC	Learning and Skills Council (United Kingdom)
MA	Modern Apprenticeships (United Kingdom)

MOVEET	Council of Ministers of Vocational Education, Employment and Training (Australia)
MSC	Manpower Service Commission (United Kingdom)
MTIA	Metal Trades Industry Association (Australia)
NAAC	National Apprenticeship Advisory Committee (Ireland)
NAAS	National Apprenticeship Assistance Scheme (Australia)
NAS	National Apprenticeship Service (United Kingdom)
NBEET	National Board of Employment, Education and Training
NCVER	National Centre for Vocational Education and Training
NESC	National Economic and Social Council (Ireland)
NETTFORCE	National Employment and Training Taskforce (Australia)
NFQ	National Framework of Qualifications (Ireland)
NFROT	National Framework for the Recognition of Training
NIEC	National Industrial and Economic Council (Ireland)
NMS	National Manpower Service (Ireland)
NQAI	National Qualifications Authority of Ireland (Ireland)
NTB	National Training Board (Australia)
NTRA	National Training Reform Agenda (Australia)
NVC	National Vocational Qualification (United Kingdom)
NVQC	National Council for Vocational Qualifications
PD	Progressive Democrats (Ireland)
PNR	Programme for National Recovery (Ireland)
RITA	Registered Industrial Training Agent (Australia)
RPL	Recognition of Prior Learning (Australia)
RTC	Regional Technical College (Ireland)
RTO	Registered Training Organizations (Australia)
SBA	Standards-based Apprenticeship (Ireland)
SES	Social Employment Scheme (Ireland)
SIPTU	Services Industrial Professional and Technical Union
SMEs	Small and Medium Enterprises
SSC	Sector Skills Council (United Kingdom)
SSO	Standard Setting Organisations (United Kingdom)
STA	State Training Agency (Australia)
TAFE	Technical and Further Education Colleges (Australia)
TC	Training Commission (United Kingdom)
TDC	Trade Development Council (Australia)
TEC	Training and Enterprise Council (United Kingdom)

TGS	Training Guarantee Scheme (Australia)
TOPS	Training Opportunities Scheme (United Kingdom)
TSA	Training Services Agency (United Kingdom)
TUC	Trade Union Congress (United Kingdom)
ULR	Union Learning Representatives (United Kingdom)
VEC	Vocational Education Committee (Ireland)
VEETAC	Vocational Education, Employment and Training Advisory Committee (Australia)
VET	Vocational Education and Training
VoC	Varieties of Capitalism
YEA	Youth Employment Authority (Ireland)
YMC	Youth Ministers Council (Australia)
YOP	Youth Opportunities Programme (United Kingdom)
YT/YTS	Youth Training/Youth Training Scheme

studies in vocational and continuing education

edited by
philipp gonon & anja heikkinen

The aim of this series is to present critical, historical and comparative research in the field of vocational and continuing education and human research development, seen from a pedagogical, organisational, economic and societal perspective. It discusses the implications of latest research to contemporary reform policies and practices. One central issue reflected in all publications is gender. A basic feature of all volumes is their cross-cultural approach.

The series has a firm basis in the international research network "VET and Culture" (Vocational Education and Training and Culture; www.peda.net/veraja/uta/vetculture) and the editors invite distinguished researchers from Europe and other continents to contribute to the series. Studies in vocational and continuing education include monographs, collected papers editions, and proceedings.

Vol. 1 Antony Lindgren & Anja Heikkinen (eds)
Social Competences in Vocational and Continuing Education
2004. 256 S. ISBN 3-03910-345-8 / US-ISBN 0-8204-7013-9

Vol. 2 Liv Mjelde
The Magical Properties of Workshop Learning
2006. 230 S. ISBN 3-03910-348-2 / US-ISBN 0-8204-7014-7

Vol. 3 Liv Mjelde & Richard Daly (eds)
Working Knowledge in a Globalizing World
From Work to Learning, from Learning to Work
2006. 406 S. ISBN 3-03910-974-X / 0-8204-8364-8

Vol. 4 Philipp Gonon, Katrin Kraus, Jürgen Oelkers & Stefanie Stolz (eds)
Work, Education and Employability
2008. 324 S. ISBN 978-3-03911-294-4

Vol. 5 Olav Eikeland
The Ways of Aristotle
Aristotelian Phrónêsis, Aristotelian Philosophy of Dialogue, and Action Research
2008. 560 S. ISBN 978-3-03911-471-9

Vol. 6 Vibe Aarkrog & Christian Helms Jørgensen (eds)
Divergence and Convergence in Education and Work
2008. 441 S. ISBN 978-3-03911-505-1

Vol. 7 Anja Heikkinen & Katrin Kraus (eds)
Reworking Vocational Education. Policies, Practices and Concepts
2009. 230 S. ISBN 978-3-03911-603-4

Vol. 8 Markus Weil, Leena Koski & Liv Mjelde (eds)
Knowing Work. The Social Relations of Working and Knowing
2009. 252 S. ISBN 978-3-03911-642-3

Vol. 9 Philipp Gonon
The Quest for Modern Vocational Education – Georg Kerschensteiner between Dewey, Weber and Simmel
2009. 278 S. ISBN 978-3-0343-0026-1

Vol. 10 Thomas Deissinger, Josef Aff, Alison Fuller & Christian Helms Jørgensen (eds)
Hybrid Qualifications: Structures and Problems in the Context of European VET Policy
2013. 280 S. ISBN 978-3-0343-1059-8

Vol. 11 Stefanie Stolz & Philipp Gonon (eds)
Challenges and Reforms in Vocational Education. Aspects of Inclusion and Exclusion
2012. 260 S. ISBN 978-3-0343-1068-0

Vol. 12 Markus Maurer & Philipp Gonon (eds.)
The Challenges of Policy Transfer in Vocational Skills Development.
National Qualifications Frameworks and the Dual Model of Vocational Training in International Cooperation
2014. 363 S. ISBN 978-3-0343-1536-4

Vol. 13 Gabriele Molzberger & Manfred Wahle (eds.)
Shaping the Futures of (Vocational) Education and Work.
Commitment of VET and VET Research
2015. 240 S. ISBN 978-3-0343-1617-0

Vol. 14 Esther Berner & Philipp Gonon (eds.)
History of Vocational Education and Training in Europe.
Cases, Concepts and Challenges
2016. 599 S. ISBN 978-3-0343-2120-4

Vol. 15 Fernando Marhuenda-Fluixá (ed.)
Vocational Education beyond Skill Formation.
VET between Civic, Industrial and Market Tensions
2017. 439 S. ISBN 978-3-0343-2806-7

Vol. 16 Janis Vossiek
Collective Skill Formation in Liberal Market Economies?
The Politics of Training Reforms in Australia, Ireland and the United Kingdom
2018. 228 S. ISBN 978-3-0343-2969-9

www.ingramcontent.com/pod-product-compliance
Ingram Content Group UK Ltd.
Pitfield, Milton Keynes, MK11 3LW, UK
UKHW021012120926
8556IPUK00039B/1042

9 783034 329699